Praise for *Building Trust*

"I was stunned by the simple practical power of Stickel's ideas. He cuts through the confusing morass of leadership challenges in today's world to clarify how trust may be *the* master skill for dynamic leaders at every level. In the fluid, disrupted world in which we now operate, this book illuminates how a new generation of leaders must cultivate benevolence and integrity to generate the trust on which high-performing organizations now depend. I hope that all of us engaged in working with and learning from a diverse workforce read this book and apply its wisdom in our day-to-day practices."

—JOHN SEELY BROWN, former Chief Scientist, Xerox Corporation and Director of Xerox's Palo Alto Research Center

"I knew from my first conversation with Darryl that he and his work are extraordinary. Over the last several years, I've had the opportunity to partner with, learn from, and laugh with Darryl, and the concepts he outlines in *Building Trust* have influenced how I lead. It's incredibly powerful to witness what happens when individuals and teams have a common language and understanding of what builds trust, and I have experienced this firsthand with my global team. Trust creates an environment where people can thrive. *Building Trust* can help. With generosity and a fine balance of deep intellect and empathy, Darryl Stickel takes us on a journey filled with thought provoking questions and real-life examples. My unsolicited advice is: read *Building Trust*, share it with a friend, and then find a way to have a connection or conversation with Darryl Stickel. His work will make our world a better place."

—KELSY TRIGG, Global Head, HR Advisors, SAP

"Chock-full of stories, insights, and very helpful techniques, *Building Trust* by Darryl Stickel is precisely the type of field guide you need to become a leader who builds and demonstrates trust in all your interactions and relationships. Trust me on this one! It's a book that will help."

—DAN PONTEFRACT, Leadership Strategist and Best-selling Author of *Lead. Care. Win.* and *Open to Think*

"The world today seems defined by division and anger as we grapple with real crisis. Sometimes it feels hopeless. Darryl Stickel shows us that rebuilding trust is not only the way forward but that it is both practical and possible."
—**NAHEED NENSHI,** former Mayor of Calgary

"Darryl Stickel has spent decades working with highly capable clients to build trust into their portfolios of critical organizational and interpersonal skills. In this book, he reveals how he thinks about trust, how he helps leaders effectively foster trust, and how he helps organizations and their employees learn not only to build trusting relationships, but—equally important—to actually merit being trusted by becoming more trustworthy. As you would want from a promoter of trust, Stickel shares his secrets—he explains his underlying model, provides practical advice on how to implement it, and makes clear how he came to these insights and has used them successfully in the past. For those who are confronting an uncertain and challenging world of change—in other words, all of us—this book provides an accessible guide for trust-focused action."
—**SIM B. SITKIN,** Michael W. Krzyzewski
University Professor of Leadership, Professor
of Management and Public Policy, and Faculty
Director of the Center on Leadership and
Ethics, Duke University and President, Delta
Leadership, Inc.

"As a social capital scholar, I've known about the importance of trust since Fukuyama's groundbreaking work in the nineties but have never seen something remotely practical about what to *do* about our tragic loss of trust in today's society. Stickel navigates the literature, clarifies the challenge, and walks leaders and professionals through practical how-to steps. Probably the single-most important book a high-level or aspiring executive could read for the next several years."
—**DAVID OBSTFELD,** Professor of Management
Cal State Fullerton and Founder of the Social
Capital Academy

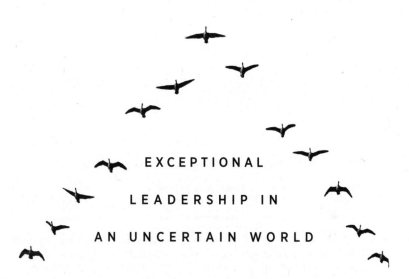

EXCEPTIONAL

LEADERSHIP IN

AN UNCERTAIN WORLD

BUILDING
TRUST

DARRYL STICKEL

Forefront
BOOKS

Building Trust: Exceptional Leadership in an Uncertain World

© 2022 Darryl Stickel

All rights reserved.

Published by Forefront Books.

Cover Design by Bruce Gore, Gore Studio, Inc.
Interior Design by Bill Kersey, KerseyGraphics

ISBN: 978-1-63763-079-2 print
ISBN: 978-1-63763-090-7 e-book

Dedication

To my sons Thomas and Alex, who instill in me the desire to be a better person. You give me hope and make me want to contribute to making the world a better place. You are why I strive every day to overcome my ongoing health challenges. You are my reasons for being.

To Drake, my guide dog and best friend. Drake opens doors to a previously inaccessible, shadowy, and lonely world. He not only helps people recognize I am visually impaired but, through his warm and welcoming nature, invites them to interact with us.

Contents

Introduction 9

CHAPTER 1: Origins of the TU Trust Model. 13

CHAPTER 2: Trust Is Everywhere (Except When It Isn't) 35

CHAPTER 3: The Trust Challenge for Leaders. 67

CHAPTER 4: The Benefits of Trust 93

CHAPTER 5: Introducing the TU Trust Model 125

CHAPTER 6: Fifty Ways to Love Your Lever:
            Using the Trust Model. 155

CHAPTER 7: Repairing a Trust Deficit:
            A Future Needs Case Study 193

CHAPTER 8: Building Trust with the Locals in Afghanistan:
            A Diagnostic Case Study. 209

CHAPTER 9: Organizations of the Future. 223

CHAPTER 10: There Are Many Miles to Go Before We Sleep. . . .237

Notes. 251

Acknowledgments 255

Introduction

WE LIVE IN TURBULENT TIMES. THIS STATEMENT ALMOST FEELS AS IF IT needs a caveat since I don't know who will be reading this or when, but I'm comfortable leaving it out there to stand alone, uncontested. Why am I so confident? I started writing this book in 2020, and as I carry out the final edits a year later, I still firmly believe that for the foreseeable future we will continue to live in tempestuous and often perplexing times.

It is during periods such as these that our awareness of the importance of trust becomes heightened and our need for trust increases; however, we simultaneously witness a decrease in the amount of trust in the world. Leaders in the political sphere, the private sector, and academia have come forward to make the case that society is facing significant trust issues. Measures of trust such as the Edelman Trust Barometer suggest that trust levels are at some of their lowest levels ever. Yet rather than seeing suggestions on how we might build or rebuild trust, we are witnessing an alarming pattern of public and private behaviors that are exacerbating the problem.

It's not surprising that leaders are seeing lack of trust as a fundamental problem because their success as leaders depends on their ability to build trust. In reality, people who hold senior positions have less direct control over outcomes and greater dependency on those they lead. Their goals, dreams, and success all depend on the energy and determination of others—effort that is often contingent on the level of trust those people have in their leaders. Therefore, the ability to build trust becomes one of the primary differentiators between leaders who are merely good and those who are exceptional. This is especially true in today's world in which we are experiencing a rapid pace of technological, social, and societal change (as I will discuss later in this book).

Given the growing consensus that trust is incredibly valuable, why don't we have more of it? The answer is, at least in part, a profound lack of awareness. We often fail to properly identify trust (or the lack thereof) as the underlying cause of problems, and this leads to a host of symptoms that may not be obviously connected to trust. Even when we properly identify trust problems, we usually don't know what to do about solving them.

There are some fundamental challenges when it comes to trustworthiness. It's not a stretch to say that most of us would classify ourselves as trustworthy, and because of this we assume that other people trust us—why wouldn't they? The trouble with this assumption is simply that it is not always the case; maybe we are not as trustworthy as we think, or perhaps we are not communicating our trustworthiness effectively to others. This is compounded by the difficulty we face in knowing whether people trust us at all—how do we tell? And it doesn't stop there because it goes both ways: we are constantly wishing we could place greater trust in the people with whom we interact. Unfortunately, most of us see issues surrounding trust as someone else's concern, not our own. At this point you may be wishing your boss/partner/coworker were more benevolent, more competent, and acted with greater integrity (or perhaps that they would just read this book). However, we need to accept the role we play, and a level of responsibility, in any trust problems we face—be they global, corporate, or within our circle of family and friends. Sadly, our default position is often that it's somebody else's problem to fix.

This speaks to a general lack of awareness about what trust is, how it works, and how to build it. On a positive note, trust can be learned and honed as a skill. I've spent much of my career conducting workshops and coaching senior executives to do exactly this.

The purpose of this book is to raise awareness about what trust is, how it works, and how to actually build it. The model used here has helped thousands of people get a better understanding of trust and take action to build it in their workplaces, their relationships, and their lives. It has been tested across a wide range of industries, relationships, and even nations, and it's now ready to be presented to a global audience. This book is an attempt to share my trust model beyond my company's immediate clientele and hopefully reach and help a wider audience. It is an attempt to scale up the impact of my insights into trust; break through today's social media, publishing, and broadcasting "chatter"; and make a real difference in turning back the tide on the all-too-real global decline in trust levels.

If I have convinced you that trust is important and that the ability to build it is indeed a skill that can be nurtured and sharpened, your next question might be, "Should I buy this book? Can I trust this guy?" This is a trust decision. By purchasing this book, you are deciding to invest your money, time, and energy against an uncertain future payoff. Will reading this book, trying some of its suggestions, and using the model provided make a positive difference in the relationships that matter to you? Will it make you a better leader? As the author, I believe the answer is yes, of course, but how do I help you come to that conclusion? How can I earn your trust?

To begin, I'll make the case that I have a perspective and skills few others have. I have a PhD in business from Duke University and wrote my doctoral thesis on building trust in hostile environments. I have spent the last twenty years as a consultant and coach helping individuals and organizations understand trust and how to build it, from spouses and parents to financial advisors and military personnel serving in Afghanistan. Dip into chapter 1 and you'll find more information about my background as I describe how my trust model evolved. You will see testimonials from people who have worked with me, hired me, or who read the book in manuscript form prior to publication. You can visit the Trust Unlimited website (www.trustunlimited.com) to see sample applications of my trust model.

Of course, the academic knowledge and credentials of an author should be only contributory factors in your decision to invest your hard-earned cash. You could justifiably be suspicious that the writing and presentation of my principles and philosophies surrounding trust might be turgid or, worse, unfathomable. Or that I might be miserly or cautious with details so that you will need to make additional purchases to get the full story. All these things might play a part in your willingness to trust me and this book. You see, trust can be difficult to pin down.

Let me try to demonstrate a level of integrity and benevolence that will further strengthen my case. Understanding trust and helping people are passions for me that are surpassed only by my love for my sons Thomas and Alexander. I don't want you just to buy this book; I want you to understand it and apply it. I care deeply that leaders like you start using this model to make the world a better place. To that end, I've tried to write a book, with the help of others, that is readable, accessible, and practical. This book is heavy on real-world suggestions and approaches to actually building trust. Finally, this is a comprehensive explanation of my trust model. There are no secrets to be revealed in future books—you have it all. I urge you to use it in good faith.

CHAPTER 1

Origins of the TU Trust Model

How does a guy from Fort St. John, Canada, end up developing a new model for understanding trust? And why is this model different from those that have come before it? To fully understand my Trust Unlimited (TU) trust model, which I'll lay out later in this book, it may be helpful for you to understand how I got here—from my childhood and upbringing, multiple concussions, and being beaten to an inch of my life during a hockey game, through my groundbreaking doctoral thesis on trust, to teaching at the Luxembourg School of Business, losing my sight, and, yes, writing this book.

When a layperson looks at my trust model, they often comment that it's obvious that this is how trust works; however, leading experts who study trust react very differently. They tell me that my model is years ahead of current trust research and that they learn more about trust from conversations with me than they have from years of study. This has nothing to do with intelligence or being superior in any way, but it has everything to do with the fact that my perspectives on life and resulting insights into trust have been shaped by a particular set of experiences. In this opening chapter, I'll walk you through a small set of those experiences and share with you how they shaped my view of trust. What I've lived through certainly isn't the only way to gain insight about trust and how it works; it's simply the path I ended up following.

My Story: The Early Years

I was born and raised in Fort St. John in northeastern British Columbia, Canada. When I was a kid it was still a relatively small town. At that time it was quite isolated, almost an hour's drive from the closest neighboring small community. Looking back, I can see how growing up there significantly affected my worldview. The climate was often harsh, and the relative isolation forced people to rely on one another more than they would elsewhere. My perception was, and still is, that this created a sense of community that doesn't always exist in places where life is a little easier. Most of the people I was exposed to displayed a distinctive degree of honesty and humility. This is not to say that everyone was an angel—far from it. It was a rough-and-tumble place, but there was a strong sense that if you needed help, others would arrive to lend a hand. It was from living there that I came to believe it is the responsibility of the strong to protect the weak. I also came to believe that if I could help someone, I should.

I was fortunate to have a protective older brother who had a strong group of close friends. Richard and his friends allowed me the opportunity to stand up for what I believed in. I was able to speak up when I saw something I thought wasn't fair. I was able to have the confidence to be a bit mouthy, to express my opinions, and to think independently. Today these traits sometimes get me into trouble, but far more often they free me to think about things differently.

When I was seven years old, my father was in an automobile accident. He lost his left leg, crushed vertebrae in his back, broke his hip, and cracked his pelvis. In retrospect, his process of rehabilitation from his injuries was an incredible example of resilience, perseverance, and toughness. Although I didn't know it at the time, of course, this role modeling would serve me well later in life.

As a pipeline welder with an eighth-grade education, my father saw few other options to support his family other than returning to work.

Providing for his family was a key part of my father's identity. The amount of money he brought into the household was, in part, how he measured himself as a man. Always a hard worker, he approached his rehabilitation with a relentless determination—not just to return to work as soon as possible but to return his gait to normal so that most people would not realize he'd lost a leg. I remember watching him practice walking for hours on end. I saw him return from work with his stump rubbed raw and bleeding. He was entitled to a full pension and benefits, so at any point he could've chosen to give up, to surrender to the pain and discomfort. Instead, he continued to work, determined to earn a living and provide for his family. Heavyweight boxing legend Jack Dempsey once said a champion is someone who gets up when he can't. Jack likely would have called my dad a champion.

For most of my life, I remember my father being in almost constant pain. Unfortunately, he wouldn't take prescribed pain medication; instead, he self-medicated with alcohol. I wish I could say my father and I had a wonderful relationship and that he was a happy drunk, but that would be untrue. In reality, my father and I would likely have struggled to get along regardless of the circumstances. We were so similar yet so very different. We saw the world differently and valued different things. He valued hard physical labor and manual skills, like those he understood as a pipeline welder.

Imagine his difficulty, later in life, accepting a son with a profound visual impairment who had chosen to train his brain to a point where he could think for a living. It was simply something he could not understand. Of course, I never made it easy for him; as I mentioned earlier, I was a little mouthy.

My father struggled with his temper and didn't quite know how to handle me when I was young. Many years later, I learned from his friends and colleagues that he had seen potential in me. Unfortunately, he tried to get me to reach that potential by being extremely critical of me, almost never offering praise. This approach led to a great deal of resistance and conflict between us. However, I am happy to say that my relationship with my father ended well. Near the end of his life, my father told me that he was afraid he was going to hell for the way he had treated me. At that time, I was in my early forties and had matured enough to recognize the role I had played in our relationship and what I had gained from it. I told him that if I got a vote, that would not be the case. I told him about the successes I'd had and the role he had played in helping me get to where I was in life. I said if it were up to me, he would go to heaven and hopefully keep a spot warm for me. I forgave my father. It lifted a great weight off me; it was one of the kindest things I've ever done for myself.

My mother, Moyra, also came from humble beginnings. She grew up on a small farm in a small town in Saskatchewan, Canada. She graduated from high school but had little other formal training or education. She worked, at various times, as a clerk at a clothing store and as a waitress. She managed the family home and provided stability and everything we needed to survive and thrive growing up, during a time when my father was often away for work.

Growing up in Fort St. John, I played a lot of hockey. At the age of seventeen, I was playing for the Elks, a team of seventeen- and eighteen-year-olds competing in a Junior B league with players two to three years older. This meant we were usually playing against teams whose members were bigger and often stronger than us. On one particular night, we were playing in a tournament in Fort Nelson, a town north of Fort St. John. During one game, we were winning against the hometown team when things started to get rough and tensions started to mount. I found myself standing a couple of feet from an opening in the glass at the gate that led to the dressing rooms. A man standing on the other side of the boards asked me if I wanted a shot in the head. I looked at the player next to me and said, "This is crazy," and turned to skate away. The man lunged forward, grabbed me by the collar, and pulled me back halfway over the boards into the crowd. He had a wooden club that he used to shatter my helmet and beat me repeatedly over the head. A brawl ensued. One of my teammates pulled me from the crowd and lunged at my attacker, while a player from the opposing team grabbed me and proceeded to beat me. I tried to play turtle, covering my head with my hands and pulling my knees to my chest. The opposition player grabbed me by the hair, slammed my head into the ice, then proceeded to kick me with his skates. I know all of this only because the game was televised and I got to see the tape during the court proceedings.

I regained consciousness in the team dressing room. The police, fire department, and paramedics were all in the room along with the referees and my teammates. I was rushed to the hospital by ambulance; on the way, according to a teammate who rode with me, I stopped breathing three times. Due to concerns that my attacker or his friends might come looking for me, I spent the night in intensive care under police guard. I was eventually flown back to Fort St. John, but my ordeal was far from over.

It was 1984, and little was known about concussions or head injuries. I was to learn a great deal about the topic over the following months and years. I went from being on the honor roll at school to not being able to remember a thing; I had the attention span of a fruit fly. My plan had been to attend university, but my grades were so poor during my last semester of high school that it was hard to believe any university would accept me. Instead, I attended community college in Grande Prairie, Alberta. I continued to play hockey and experienced a series of concussions. One of the side effects I experienced was profound fatigue, which seemed to mystify my doctors and led to a series of tests looking for serious diseases that had fatigue as a component. It seemed that every week I was tested for something new and terrible. Leukemia, chronic Epstein-Barr virus, multiple sclerosis, and AIDS were all thought to be possibilities.

College and University

Not surprisingly, it was a challenging time in my life. I was failing at school—one of the things at which I'd always excelled. My sense of self was profoundly challenged. My ambition had always been to live based on my ability to think, but I was no longer able to do that effectively. My two years at college proved a brutal failure academically. I applied to transfer to the University of Victoria (UVic) and was initially denied because my track record in college was so poor. I subsequently appealed on compassionate grounds because of my injuries and was accepted in the summer of 1986. During my first year at UVic I failed every class I took.

I experienced a couple of additional concussions in my early years playing hockey at UVic. I've lost count of how many concussions I have sustained in my life, but I'm fairly confident it's at least ten. People ask me why I kept playing. There is no one simple answer, but back in those days doctors didn't understand the seriousness of concussions, especially the damage that multiple hits to the head did to the brain. I recall only one doctor ever suggesting I quit hockey, and that was only after I had landed in the hospital for the umpteenth time. I also loved the game and was a good player. It stoked my self-esteem—playing felt good. I never once seriously considered quitting the game. As I say to my sons, the last guy you should ask how he's doing is the guy with the head injury.

Each injury has been a test of my resilience—and a reminder of human fragility. Growing up in Fort St. John taught me a measure of humility. Recovering from multiple concussions, experiencing vulnerability, being weak, and knowing that a simple bump or fall could shatter me only served to deepen that humility. It also increased the amount of empathy I feel for others.

In retrospect, it's unclear how long it took me to recover from the original concussion I received at the Fort Nelson hockey rink. The several concussions in the years immediately following that incident likely compounded and delayed my recovery. Slowly, however, the world came back into focus. In part, this was a matter of my body naturally recovering, and in part it was taking a break from hockey for a few years so my brain could return to something close to normal. As a result, I started taking an increased load at UVic and started doing better in my classes. I would eventually earn my undergraduate degree in psychology with honors.

I'm sharing these early experiences because they helped me understand human behavior and gave me a strong empathy for others. I found people sensed this and tended to open up around me; oftentimes complete strangers would tell me about their struggles—people just seemed to feel safe with me. On more than one occasion a person would say something like, "I don't know why I'm telling you this, but you somehow seem both strong and gentle." It was these experiences that led me to consider becoming a clinical psychologist.

I switched my undergraduate major to psychology and started working with children who were in the care of the state at group homes. I learned a lot from working with teenagers and from my colleagues at the homes in which I worked, especially about connecting with people who had developed an early cynicism about the world, people with whom it was not easy to connect. Through this work I began to build experience and strengthen my skills; I wanted to make myself a strong candidate for graduate programs.

I also volunteered for a crisis line and eventually began working with troubled teens and families in crisis. While working with these groups, I came to realize what challenging work it is being a mental health professional. Usually I could quickly see both the issues my clients were facing and a relatively easy path for them toward a better life. Unfortunately, most of them were already doing the best they could and failed to make the necessary changes to their lives that would improve their situations; what seemed so easy and obvious to me was difficult or even impossible for them.

I came to realize that working in this field would drive me crazy if I stayed in it for too long. Watching people struggle and be in pain, knowing there was a potential path forward but witnessing their inability to move in the right direction, was heartbreaking. When I thought about this being the sole focus of my career, I realized I needed to take a different path.

Studying Trust with Leading Experts

Upon completing my undergraduate degree in psychology, I switched direction and entered a master's in public administration program at UVic. As part of my training, I had work terms that provided practical experience in government. During one of those work terms, I was employed by the Federal Treaty Negotiations Office of the Canadian government. This resulted in me being retained as a contractor and subsequently a research analyst.

British Columbia was, and still is, one of the last places on the planet to resolve land claims with its indigenous populations. As a research analyst, I was asked deep, philosophical questions: What is self-government? What will the province look like fifty years after a settlement is reached? How do we convince a group of people we've mistreated for the last one hundred years to trust us? The last question intrigued me. It provoked thoughts about long-standing disputes and why we never seem to fully resolve them. With these in mind, I decided to pursue a PhD at the Fuqua School of Business at Duke University, where I wrote my thesis on building trust in hostile environments.

I began by studying a variety of topics related to conflict resolution, negotiation, procedural and distributive justice, ethics, power and dependence, and, of course, trust. Exposure to academic writings on these topics, along with a heavy dose of decision-making theory, began to hone my thinking and tailor my perspective; it informed my previous experiences. I was fortunate that several truly remarkable academics were present during my doctoral program.

Sim Sitkin arrived at Duke the same year I did and eventually became cochair of my doctoral committee. Sim is considered one of the world's leading academic experts on trust and leadership. He helped challenge my thinking and remains a good friend.

Karen Cook arrived at Duke the year after me and was the other cochair of my doctoral committee. She now teaches in the sociology department at Stanford, having left Duke the year before I completed my PhD. She is also considered one of the world's leading experts on trust and is one of the most impressive people I've ever met. Karen is remarkably well regarded within her field, has tremendous influence, and is incredibly smart and capable. I can't say enough positive things about Karen's brilliance, yet she remains personable, friendly, and approachable. Karen played a significant role in my academic development, and I can't believe how fortunate I was that she was at Duke for three years during my doctoral program.

Fritz Mayer was at the School of Public Policy at Duke while I was working on my PhD. He is one of the smartest and kindest people I've

ever met. He has since left Duke to become dean of the Josef Korbel
School of International Studies at the University of Denver. Fritz carries
out compelling research on narrative that still influences my thinking
about trust. He was a student of Howard Raiffa, the author of *The Art
and Science of Negotiation*, one of the earliest and most influential books
on negotiation. Fritz acted as my mentor and thought partner, and he
was a close friend. It would be understandable if he and Karen Cook
thought they were better than the rest of us. (They would both be right,
but neither ever acted that way, which make them exceptional people
and role models.)

A Mental Model for Interactions

Through my studies and research I was acquiring an overwhelming
amount of information. To help me make sense of it all and see where
possible gaps existed in my knowledge, I created my own mental model.
It was a simple way to help me understand the perspectives being taken by
different authors in different academic disciplines. The model consisted
of a large square with two circles inside it and an arrow pointing in oppo-
site directions between the two circles.

The two circles in the diagram represent the people engaged in an
interaction (psychology). The double-headed arrow represents the inter-
actions between them (social psychology, sociology). The space inside the
square represents the context they are working in (economics, political
science). This simple model helped me identify different levels of anal-
ysis and better understand the research I was compiling to explain how
people were making decisions to trust.

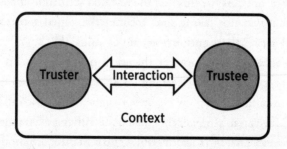

Business schools aim to help future business leaders excel through the application of research findings in the social sciences. Unfortunately, faculty members often become focused on perspectives that are consistent with only a single discipline or level of analysis. However, the problems being examined are often too complex to be explained completely by any one discipline. Often a more elaborate, multidisciplinary approach is required. This is certainly true when considering the topic of trust.

Once I had built my framework for classifying research findings from different disciplines, I was able to use it to look for gaps. I noticed that most of the trust research focused on either the person doing the trusting or the person trying to be trusted. This made sense, given that trust is a psychological state. It seemed reasonable that we would start by thinking about how humans come to trust someone, or something else, by looking at the individuals involved. However, I could see that something was missing.

Existing Research and Its Limitations

I spent a massive amount of time reading all the articles I could find on trust. What eventually struck me was that virtually all the material seemed to be talking about some form of uncertainty. Most of the work was greatly insightful, yet on the whole it felt scattered and disorganized. I returned to the definition I had adapted from the work of Roger Mayer and his colleagues: trust is the willingness to make ourselves vulnerable to another party when we can't completely predict how that other party will act.[1] This definition includes three components: uncertainty (about how the other party will act), vulnerability, and choice (to make ourselves vulnerable or not). At the time, all the research seemed to focus on uncertainty, but it was not taking into account the varied sources of uncertainty, and very little attention was paid to vulnerability.

My realization that most of the work on trust was limited came about in part through my learning about the concepts of moderators and mediators in statistics. A *moderator* is a variable that influences the impact of one variable on another, like a magnifying glass increasing the impact of sunbeams on a leaf. Feelings, for instance, are moderators, as

I will discuss in more detail later. A *mediator* is a variable that explains the relationship between two different variables; for example, the rate of snow melting on a spring day and the proportion of people wearing light clothing may be related, with the air temperature serving as the mediator between them.

I realized that uncertainty was a mediator for all the factors people were pointing to that would promote or deter trust. Essentially, this meant that one variable (such as transparency) was influencing another (in this case, uncertainty), which was in turn having an impact on a third variable (trust). The correlation between transparency and trust was being driven by the mediator, uncertainty. This realization allowed me to make sense of research that had previously felt like it was all over the place; uncertainty was the common thread tying seemingly unrelated findings together. It may seem obvious in retrospect, but this was actually a big step in the development of the model I now use.

These revelations also allowed me to think about sources of uncertainty that hadn't yet been studied. I believe that when it comes to trust, uncertainty derives from the characteristics of the individuals trying to build trust with others and from the situations in which these individuals are entrenched. This latter aspect, not considered in previous research, is what I refer to as context or "the rules of the game." Clearly, some element of context is required in any trust model.

Once I included context as a source of uncertainty, it allowed me to understand why we trust, or distrust, certain people without knowing anything about them as individuals. This also helped me discern why we would trust someone in one setting and potentially not trust the same person in a different setting. It was at this point that I thought economics and political science research could be relevant to the study of trust. After all, these were the disciplines that tended to focus on elements of the external, or situational, context and how they impact our behavior, more so than research in psychology.

In analyzing trust, I also included a vulnerability component that wasn't present in any of the models or research I had been reading about. There clearly needed to be something at stake; otherwise, trust wasn't an issue. If there was no vulnerability, a more appropriate term would be indifference.

This failure to include vulnerability as part of the equation has made it difficult to talk effectively about different levels of trust. The overwhelming majority of the research, or popular literature, on the topic treats trust like a binary variable: it's either present or absent, yes or no, on or off. If trust is binary, then we either trust someone or we don't. But in real life, trust is clearly a continuous variable: we trust some people more than we trust others, or our level of trust in someone can increase or decrease as we get to know them. We also trust the same person more in some situations and less in others, depending on what we think is at stake. These insights led me to the realization that an element of vulnerability was essential in any model aimed at truly understanding what trust is and how it works.

Much of the available research treated the trust decision in terms of inputs and outputs. Inputs included such things as transparency or following through on commitments. If there were sufficient inputs, trust was the output. I found this unsatisfying and ultimately unhelpful. Instead of focusing on trust as an output, I decided to center my model on a trust *decision* that incorporated levels of uncertainty and vulnerability along with people's propensity to trust. Duke's strong focus on decision-making theory likely influenced me on this point.

Most of our meaningful trust decisions, however, are not isolated incidents; they are made in the context of some sort of ongoing relationship with multiple points of interaction between the parties involved. This meant I needed to have a sense of how past interactions would influence future ones. A factor that most profoundly impacts one's expectations for future interactions is how well or poorly one thinks previous exchanges have played out.

There was already a fair amount of research on how we perceive outcomes (i.e., whether things went well or poorly) and how we attribute outcomes (i.e., who gets the credit or the blame). We often believe that the outcome we experience is a result of our own actions, the actions of others, the environment, or some combination of the three. While there has been a great deal of research into how we interpret outcomes, it hasn't really been applied to how we make future trust decisions.

In my model, therefore, I added an element pertaining to perception and attribution of the outcome of the trust decision. Our perceptions of how an interaction plays out with an individual, group, or an organization—potentially including a trust decision—influence our expectations regarding the next interaction with that party. This means that perceived outcomes should be included in a model for trust, and they need to feed back into our expectations for the next time we face another trust decision. I discovered a small number of models in existing literature (primarily in the extensive work on game theory that included repeated plays[2]) that included a feedback loop, but they were definitely in the minority.

Finally, since my thesis was focused on building trust in hostile environments, I needed a way to explain why some disputes seemed to last so long and are so hard to resolve. I realized that our emotions and feelings were playing a significant role in our decision to trust others, and I was among the first to study the role of emotions in trust. Virtually all the existing research at that time treated people as though they were rational actors. Well, have you ever *met* people? If you've ever dated someone, or had children, or waited in line at customer service anywhere, then you know that people aren't always rational. There was no doubt in my mind that feelings had to be included in any comprehensive trust model that would help us understand how to build trust in hostile environments.

What I've described in these past few paragraphs often seems simple and obvious, but it took me years of thinking, studying, and effort to figure out. Maybe I'm just a bit slow. As I said earlier, when laypeople see the full model, which will be described fully in chapter 5, they say, "Duh! That's obvious!" However, academics who study trust usually have a different response when they see the model, and I lead them through it. They feel, because of the TU model's inclusion of things such as vulnerability, context, and emotions, that it provides insights into trust problems that they would have never reached through their own approaches to thinking about trust.

The Learning Curve Increases

Upon completing my PhD, I had a couple of options to stay within academia. However, I had also interviewed and been offered a position at McKinsey & Company, one of the world's leading management consulting firms. While I seriously considered the academic opportunities, the offer from McKinsey, which included a signing bonus and a generous salary, ended up being too tempting to resist for a long-impoverished graduate student. Since my approach had always been more practical and applied than many of my academic colleagues, consulting seemed like a good fit. In retrospect, I think it was the right decision. I learned a lot and met some of the most amazing people I've ever encountered, several of whom I still count among my best friends.

Life at McKinsey was both fascinating and overwhelming. The learning curve was incredibly steep. I learned how to be a consultant and gained industry expertise on a variety of assignments. Early on, I was identified as someone with "good client hands," which meant I was able to make clients, colleagues, and potential new recruits comfortable. This meant I spent a fair amount of time at recruiting events and dealing with challenging client service situations, where the clients weren't happy or didn't want to share information. Working with people and organizations that were resistant to change—not to mention uncomfortable sharing information with strangers—was an incredible learning experience, especially as I got to see how well my theories about trust could be applied in the real world.

A Case Study

McKinsey called its client engagements "studies," and it was on one of these studies that I got to learn and explore a great deal about building trust. On one occasion, my team was working for a heavy industry client that wanted to improve the profitability of its plants. It was a global project, with several teams involved around the world. The team I was on consisted of an "engagement manager" (team leader), two associates, and a business analyst working directly with the client at one of its plants. In this situation, the engagement manager was in charge of the team on the ground at the client site and interacted with senior client management, the McKinsey partner, and the other team members. Associates were usually relatively junior consultants who had, on average, one to three years of experience. Business analysts were even more junior, usually didn't have a graduate degree, and were typically on two-year contracts. I was one of the two associates on the team.

The goal of our study was to evaluate all aspects of the production cycle, work with experienced client employees, and come up with solutions that would increase efficiency. We were tasked both with finding solutions and training a client team to continue the work at other plants. After a few weeks at the client site, we had a progress review with the client's senior management. The review went reasonably well, but the client's team members weren't happy because they felt we hadn't been doing enough in terms of training them to take over when we pulled out. Unfortunately, our engagement manager had scheduled his vacation to start the day after the progress review, leaving him unavailable to follow up on their concerns.

I received a call from the McKinsey partner overseeing the study telling me the client wasn't happy, although I was apparently the sole exception to their discontent. "They are mad at all of us except for you," the partner told me. Naturally, this meant it was my job to fix things. Monday morning arrived, and the three remaining members of the team, including me, headed to the client site, determined to get a fresh start. Before we got there, the other associate received a phone call; his father had had a heart attack and he needed to leave immediately for Boston. Now we were down to two: me and a business analyst, a young Russian with a deeply entrenched command-and-control style. Unfortunately, men with thirty-plus years of experience don't respond well to being ordered around by a kid in his early twenties who doesn't really understand their industry. It was obvious that I had to keep the analyst away from the client team as much as possible.

I had a meeting with the client team and summarized the situation; we agreed that now was a good time for them to start stepping up. One of the main complaints from the client team had been that we weren't giving them enough responsibility. There were concerns that they wouldn't be ready to move on to the second phase of the project if our team continued doing so much of the heavy lifting. They wanted to learn and start doing more of the work themselves, and this was the perfect opportunity. The client team was happy with the new plan, and productivity on the study surged. When the other McKinsey team members returned, their roles and responsibilities had already been taken over by client team members. As a result, the first phase of the study was remarkably successful.

The second phase of the project was to take place at three different plants. The engagement manager and each of the associates was assigned to a plant along with two members of the (now fully trained) client team. Plant 1 and Plant 2 appeared to be already in good working order. They were stable and well run, and personnel were open to the idea of working together to make things even better. Plant 3, however, was a different story. It had the lowest production levels of our client's plants worldwide. There had recently been aggressive strike action, including gunfire, and the plant manager had been killed when his vehicle was run over by a five-hundred-ton dump truck. The company had fired all its employees to break the union and then hired them all back when the strike ended. A new union had formed, but morale was poor.

The McKinsey partner, my boss, was very pleased with the outcome of the first study and my role in it. As a reward I was promised I wouldn't have to go to the "difficult" plant. The client, however, had a different plan, and their VP of operations for North America was quick to say, "The only way this project goes to phase 2 is if Darryl goes to Plant 3." The partner looked at me and said, "Done." They then haggled over how long I would stay. So much for the promised reward.

After one month, we had a progress review with the client. At the start of the meeting, the head of the new union stood up and said, "Before this begins, I want to acknowledge that costs are a problem and that labor is committed to doing whatever we have to do for this to work." The McKinsey partner and the vp for the client both looked at me with barely concealed astonishment. Later they took me aside and asked how on earth I had managed what had just happened. The truth was that I simply had an honest conversation with the union leader. The company was in the midst of a potential hostile takeover. The plant's performance was so poor that if it didn't see improvements, it was likely to close whether the takeover was successful or not. If the plant closed, everyone would be out of work. The union leader believed me, he trusted me, and because of that we were able to move forward.

Fate Intervenes

I could have spent many years at McKinsey. I really enjoyed the people I worked with, and I was well paid and well treated. Unfortunately, on January 9, 2001, fate intervened. I was on my way to a client site when my taxicab rear-ended another vehicle. I was thrown forward and side-ways, striking my head on the right rear passenger window. I suffered a mild to moderate traumatic brain injury, which, compounded by the TBIs I sustained from my earlier concussions, mean I have struggled with post-concussion syndrome ever since. This ended my career with McKinsey as I simply couldn't work the eighty-plus-hour weeks expected of their consulting staff.

Early on my symptoms included profound fatigue, relentless head-aches, and problems with memory, concentration, and executive func-tion. Twenty years later I still struggle with some of these, but fatigue remains the most prevalent. During the first year after the accident, I would get lost if I was more than a couple of blocks from my home. I was back where I had been as a seventeen-year-old recovering from the significant concussion from that hockey game. It would have been easy to curl into a ball and just give up.

My rehabilitation was made far more stressful by having to deal with the numerous insurance companies involved. They refused to pay for treatment for years and forced me to undergo what seemed like a nearly endless series of tests and evaluations. The evaluations always came back the same: "Dr. Stickel is struggling and needs treat-ment." Unfortunately, the insurers repeatedly refused to follow those recommendations. Court proceedings related to the accident lasted

nearly twenty years. During that period, my lawyers would period-
ically forward photos or videos showing that the insurers (which
were legally obliged to inform my lawyers of the surveillance) had
hired detectives to follow me, looking for evidence I was malingering
or otherwise faking my symptoms. They provided zero compelling
evidence, or any rational reason, why I would give up making a job
with significant salary and benefits to sit at home for $400 a week. It
was almost twenty years before a settlement was reached, and the sum
I eventually received was exceptionally modest in relation to what I
had lost.

It was at this point that Fritz Mayer, one of my mentors at Duke,
reached out and asked me to join him teaching a two-day negotiation
workshop. Fritz is an expert on negotiation, among many other things,
and certainly didn't need my help. His offer was more about helping me
get back on my feet by giving me an opportunity to do something at
which I was experienced. He was there to support and guide me if need
be. Negotiation was a familiar topic that I had taught a few times. The
session went well and helped start my path to recovery. If the insurance
companies weren't going to provide any support, perhaps this could be
my path toward a meaningful life and making a real impact on other
people's lives.

Building My Life Back and Launching Trust Unlimited

The next step occurred when a friend and former colleague reached out
to me. We had worked together at McKinsey, and he was now the head
of strategy for a mutual fund company. Andrew asked me to talk to
his company about sustainable competitive advantage. I found myself
standing in front of a large group of people that included fund managers,
frontline sales staff, and senior executives, saying, "Sustainable competi-
tive advantage means you do something better than any of your compet-
itors, something they can't copy. Right now, you don't do anything I can't
copy. I could buy one share of each of your funds, and I'd know exactly
how they were all built. I could now sell exactly what you sell, but I could
do it at a discount because I don't have to pay the fund advisors. The only

way for you to have a sustainable competitive advantage is to build deep, long-term relationships with your customers."

This resulted in the mutual fund company deciding that building relationships with its clients was a strategy it would adopt moving forward. My company, Trust Unlimited, was founded on this first contract. The company asked that I develop a workshop to train their people. (I will discuss the mutual fund company in more detail in chapter 7 because it forms the basis of a case study used to illustrate how to identify and act on trust gaps.)

I subsequently developed a two-day workshop on trust, which is the precursor of the one I still use today. Fritz Mayer was instrumental in the development of the workshop, and he, along with other colleagues, helped me deliver it in the early days. The workshop continued to grow and develop over time, along with my understanding and experience. My dear friend Hannah Carbone spent a year with me, helping me refine and strengthen the material along with my delivery. Several former McKinsey colleagues pitched in and made the content stronger.

As the years passed, a series of experiences helped me hone the workshop and improve the learning experiences for those involved. I, too, experienced an incredible learning curve as I worked in different settings to help people understand trust. At every step along the way, I made the material simpler and easier to understand and developed exercises to help bring home key points to participants.

I began applying my model to a broad range of industries and situations. After my success in financial services, I began applying the model to nonprofit, public sector, heavy industry, and tech organizations. The model seemed to work across the board, and the positive experiences and responses continued to grow. I was then asked by my good friend John Leahy to help the Canadian military rebuild trust with the locals in Afghanistan. John, then a major and now a lieutenant colonel, worked with me to help promote his understanding of how trust works so he could apply it. (This experience will also serve as a case study in chapter 8.)

I started volunteering and occasionally speaking for programs on parenting delivered by Dr. Allison Rees. Allison is, in my opinion, one of the world's leading experts on parenting. This opportunity allowed me to combine the things that matter most to me: trust and being a father. I was able to share my perspectives on building trust with my kids. I had years of practice building the strong relationships I'm thrilled to have with my sons Thomas and Alexander. They are the center of my world and mean more to me than anything. A significant number of my stories revolve around them and the incredible relationships we have. Helping other parents figure this out and, by extension, making the lives of their kids better, are truly fulfilling.

I took a course in executive coaching at Royal Roads University and began applying my work to onc-on-one coaching sessions with senior executives. Once again, this accelerated my learning as I helped people solve existing trust problems and build their skills. I was working directly with people on problems they were struggling with and helping them apply the model, not just telling them some theory about how things might work.

In 2018 I was hired by the Luxembourg School of Business and began teaching in the heart of the European Union. I traveled there for two or three weeks at a time, taught a couple of workshops, and then returned home to my sons. Teaching at this illustrious business school exposed me to a remarkable array of students and organizations that, in turn, led to more connections with companies all over the world. It was an opportunity to see if my TU model held up in places other than North America. The results were phenomenal, and I continued to grow and learn.

Much like seeing images of the divine in one's grilled cheese sandwich, if you squint just right, much of my journey can seem as though it were intentional or at least destiny. This may just be an example of Karl Wieck's "retrospective sense-making" in action.[3] I certainly didn't have a lifelong master plan in place to become someone with a novel perspective on trust. However, I am here now, and I feel it's my responsibility to help others who haven't had my training and experiences to better understand trust. I firmly believe trust is an essential component to leading a happier, more fulfilled, and productive life.

For some time now, I've been immensely frustrated that I have knowledge and insights that could help others yet have struggled to get these out to a wider, more diverse audience where they can be used, particularly on a large scale. *Building Trust* is an attempt to find my voice and spread those thoughts and perspectives more broadly. I have often felt as though I'm dropping pebbles in the water and creating small ripples. I can only train a limited number of people every year, and they go forth in the world and, hopefully, have a positive impact on those around them. My hope is that this book is a big rock capable of creating much larger ripples—maybe even a splash.

CHAPTER 2

Trust Is Everywhere (Except When It Isn't)

TRUST. IT'S A SIMPLE WORD, ONE WE ALL THINK WE UNDERSTAND. IT underpins all human connection, from our impersonal daily interactions with strangers to our most intimate and long-lasting personal relationships. It is a priceless commodity that is becoming rarer by the day. Take a moment and think about someone you trust unreservedly: perhaps your mother or father, spouse, sibling, child, family doctor, pastor, or mentor. Now think about how much you really trust them. Is that trust absolute or is it conditional? As in, "I trust them with my life, but I wouldn't trust them to pay me back if they borrowed $5,000."

Now think about how much you trust politicians, the police, the people who are managing the COVID-19 pandemic, climate change advocates and naysayers, or the anchors on CBC, BBC, CNN, Fox News, or other media sources. Trust can be complicated, and a lot depends on your personal perspective. For instance, if you are a Black person in the United States, on a scale of one to ten how comfortable would you be if you are pulled over late at night by white police officers?

On a broader scale, trust, or its absence, is an underlying critical factor in how society deals with its biggest and hairiest challenges. The problem is that most of us have a *feeling* about trust but lack a deep *understanding*. We don't know whom to trust, who trusts us, or what it really means to trust or be trusted, nor do we know how to decide whom to trust (or not).

While there is a growing understanding that in today's world there is a lack of trust, few people understand the role it plays in the function or dysfunction of personal relationships or larger societal issues. This absence, and its impact, is highlighted when multiple police officers are accused and charged with murder close to where you live. Or when a virus roams the earth indiscriminately infecting people and your chances of contracting the disease, or dying, is dependent on where you live—or more to the point, who is governing you.

In this chapter I look at the global trust crisis, but we need to be aware that historically low levels of trust in society also challenge the corporate environment. There is a trickle-down effect that will affect your business at every level. Like most challenges, this trust crisis also presents an incredible opportunity for those who are able to get it right. Those who are able to effectively build trust will be seen as offering a safe harbor, an environment that provides reduced levels of uncertainty and where vulnerabilities don't feel as significant. The result is a place where customers want to do business and will share and recommend to their friends, an organization that both attracts and retains the best people, an institution that is seen as a thought leader whose opinions have weight.

Big, hairy problems are knocking at the door, and we all need to become aware of trust and the role it plays in our ability to address these problems—or not.

The Global Trust Crisis

In 2020 the secretary-general for the United Nations (UN), António Guterres,[4] stated that trust is at a breaking point and could have profound implications for international cooperation. Mr. Guterres stated that world peace was the primary goal of the UN; without it, humanity could not thrive. Rising turmoil, division, and hatred were cited as primary threats to the UN's charter, and the secretary noted a decline in trust within and between nations. This has led to profound discontent and frustration among everyday people around the world who feel their governments are out of touch, incapable, or indifferent. His comments appear prophetic given that they were made before the death of George Floyd in the United States and the rise of often violent protests worldwide triggered by that event.

Clearly the underlying concern here is that peace cannot be maintained without some level of trust within and between nations. The bottom line is that low trust levels can and will lead to unnecessary conflict. Given the interdependence of nations around the globe, as tensions rise and conflict becomes increasingly prevalent, worldwide suffering could ensue.

The Edelman Trust Barometer has, for the past two decades, been the world's most comprehensive study of trust levels in government, nongovernmental organizations (NGOs), the business world, and the media. Over the past few years, it has consistently shown some of the lowest trust levels ever measured. Its 2020 report stated, "This year's Trust Barometer reveals that none of the four institutions is seen as both competent and ethical. Business ranks highest in competence, holding a massive 54-point edge over government as an institution that is good at what it does (64 percent vs. 10 percent). NGOs lead on ethical behavior over government (a 31-point gap) and business (a 25-point gap). Government and media are perceived as both incompetent and unethical."[5] As we'll see when we get into the details of the TU trust model in chapter 5, competence (ability) and ethical behavior (integrity) are key elements of trustworthiness.

This global lack of trust has the potential to be particularly troubling since it can lead to unnecessary, and potentially disastrous, conflict or misunderstandings. We're already seeing nation-states' inability to work collaboratively on significant problems such as climate change, terrorism, world hunger, policing, and the COVID-19 pandemic. Later in this chapter I'll look more closely at some of these examples and the part an endemic lack of trust is playing in how they are being managed (or mismanaged).

Why Trust Matters

Trust has incredible value. This is not a new insight or revelation. People have been studying the topic of trust for decades. Its importance and value have been clearly articulated by academics and leaders throughout the world. Research has shown us that higher levels of trust lead to better performance, higher levels of creativity and innovation, higher returns to shareholders, higher levels of employee engagement, and better customer retention. In chapters 7–9, I'll take you through case studies illustrating how organizations have shown improvements in all these dimensions by addressing underlying trust issues.

We consistently see that organizations, communities, and nations with higher trust levels are more resilient and capable of overcoming crises when times are bad. When times are good, research shows that they consistently outperform peer groups with lower trust levels.

Of particular concern are the positive and negative feedback loops that evolve when traumatic events occur. Communities that have high trust levels tend to band together when crises occur. They share resources, work collaboratively to face shared challenges, and engage in group problem-solving. High levels of trust create a "virtuous cycle" leading to more trust; low levels of trust create a vicious cycle leading to less trust when disasters occur, exacerbating the situation.

For example, in the fall of 2013 a ship loaded with more than 2,700 tons of ammonium nitrate arrived in the port of Beirut after experiencing technical difficulties. The owners attempted but failed to take on new cargo to enable them to pay port fees, and the ship was subsequently impounded due to unpaid fines. In 2014, the chemical-filled sacks were unloaded and stored in a nearby warehouse for fear they might leak into the water. Over the following six years, efforts were made by customs officials to get advice from local authorities how best to dispose of the dangerous cargo. Multiple reports were filed concerning the dangers of continuing to store the ammonium nitrate unsafely. This led to various government agencies arguing about who was responsible. Finally, in August 2020, the warehouse exploded, killing more than 135 people, injuring around 5,000, and causing widespread devastation.

What happened can be interpreted in multiple ways: the responsibility can be laid at the feet of individuals, government departments, or the entire system. At this point, however, assigning blame and getting even would do little to help those suffering from the short- and long-term effects of the blast. In a high-trust environment (which Beirut is not), people would be distraught but would pull together to clean up the mess and problem-solve the impending food shortage resulting from lack of storage and other logistical issues. In a low-trust environment, however, people take to the streets shouting for revolution and looking for people to punish. Had Beirut been a high-trust environment, government departments would have collaborated more effectively and resolved the dangerous situation before it was too late.

Similarly, during the COVID-19 pandemic, close-knit, high-trust communities pulled together and gained control of the situation quickly through collaborative action. People decided to buy local and become even more connected than they were before the pandemic. Low-trust communities argued about the best approach to take, blamed one another for the spread of the virus, and became increasingly divided.

The shared sense of purpose felt by any group faced with a challenge can promote higher levels of trust. However, in communities where there are low levels of trust, we witness hoarding of resources and a tendency toward self-interest and isolation. This puts pressure on the overall fabric of an institution and exposes and exacerbates preexisting weaknesses.

Understanding Trust

Given the incredible value of trust and the severe consequences we face in environments and situations where there is an absence of trust, why do we have so little of it? We are all aware of the value and importance of trust; however, trust levels continue to drop worldwide.

My extensive experience working with individuals and organizations suggests that part of the problem is a deep lack of awareness about whom we trust and how much we trust them. We often proceed through life not thinking about trust in our relationships or interactions; it happens more at a subconscious level. When we do try to think about trust, we often treat it like a light switch—it's either on or it's off; we trust someone or we don't. In reality, we trust some people more than others and may trust someone in one situation but not another. This lack of nuance also shows up in a great deal of the research and writing on the topic of trust.

All too often, people fail to connect the challenges they are experiencing to an issue of trust. Even when correctly identifying an issue as one that relates to trust, people often have little idea of how to resolve the problem.

During seminars and coaching sessions, I regularly ask leaders, "Whom do you trust?" The most common answers include parents, siblings, spouses, and best friends. This is a natural default reply because when we think about trust we think about close, deep, personal relationships. In reality, however, we trust people all the time: we simply trust some people more than others or we trust them in different ways.

Organizations, communities, even economies can't function without some level of underlying trust. On a personal level we have to trust people all the time: doctors, pharmacists, law enforcement officials, cab drivers, servers and chefs in restaurants, even people in the street. Trust acts as a social lubricant. It allows us to go about our lives without having to constantly monitor and inspect everything and everyone. Ronald Reagan's well-known saying "trust, but verify" may be a prudent approach to certain situations (such as nuclear disarmament) but is an impractical approach to everyday life.

When I flip the question and ask leaders, "Who trusts you?" I often get a long pause, eventually broken by a person naming the same group of people they trust: their intimate, personal relationships. Others ask, "How would I know?" Of course, that's a loaded question. To identify the people who trust us, we first need to understand what trust is. At times, it seems there are as many definitions as there are people talking about trust. My definition—and the basis of my Trust Unlimited (TU) model—is the following:

Trust is a willingness to make yourself vulnerable in the face of uncertainty when you can't completely predict what will happen.

The challenge with this is that to identify those who trust us, we first have to understand how they can demonstrate their vulnerability. I will often ask leaders, "How can those you lead make themselves vulnerable to you, and do they do so?" People can make themselves vulnerable to leaders in many ways: by giving clear and direct feedback, pushing back against ideas they don't think will work, taking risks, sharing real development needs, and delivering bad news in a timely manner. As a leader, if you're seeing these behaviors, it is more likely that your followers trust you.

Even when we know someone trusts us, we often don't know to what degree. This can be particularly challenging. People don't know the level of trust they have until they reach a point of discomfort.

Several years ago, my good friend Kevin attended one of my workshops and I asked him point-blank if he trusted me. First, I should give you a little background. Kevin and I have worked together for several years, and I can safely say we are good friends. I have stayed at his home and spent time with his family. We've had extremely personal conversations and have an excellent, deep relationship.

His response to my question was that, yes, of course he trusted me. Pushing it a little, I said, "That's fantastic, can I borrow your car?" Now, Kevin has a very nice car—a bright red, shiny Porsche. You may think that my request was fairly modest, but I should give you a little more context. It was the middle of winter, driving conditions were awful, and I'm legally blind. I can't see through a car windshield to save my life. Literally.

All of this Kevin knew but, channeling Dustin Hoffman in *Rain Man*, I assured him, "I really am an excellent driver." Predictably, Kevin was uncomfortable with the prospect of lending me his car; I had put him into an almost untenable position. However, a little later he approached me and said, "I've been giving this some thought, and I have an idea. I'm more concerned about your safety than I am about the car. Why don't we go out to the salt flats and you can drive my car there? That way you get to drive the car and you're not in any danger." Now, I already knew that Kevin trusted me; the thing is, it wasn't until we came to a situation where he felt too vulnerable, too exposed, that he realized his trust in me had limitations. The ridiculously difficult position I had put him in forced him to rethink the level of trust he had in me, and that made him feel bad about refusing my request. To his credit, he came up with a way to reduce his level of vulnerability and agree to my request.

Assessing Trust Levels

You can see from my story that trust can be complex and messy. It can be difficult to navigate. We often lack awareness about whom we trust and how much we trust them. At the same time, we are often reluctant to tell others we don't actually trust them because we are concerned about the damage it might do to the relationship. This lack of self-awareness—combined with the social stigma around admitting we don't trust others—can make measuring trust extremely tricky. Clearly, we can't simply ask individuals whom they do or do not trust. Sophisticated surveys and measurement tools exist that can overcome these challenges, but applying them to every relationship and organization is a nearly impossible task.

Instead, academics often observe behaviors to ascertain if trust is present. For instance, when cooperation, information sharing, and the free exchange of thoughts and ideas are present, it is safe to assume that some level of trust exists. Conversely, in the corporate world, a lack of trust can manifest in the following observable symptoms:

- Lack of feedback—between employees, customers, suppliers
- Massive bureaucracy (lots of inefficiency)
- Lack of risk-taking
- Fear of change
- Passive management group
- High employee turnover rates
- Unstable customer base
- Volatile (or depressed) stock price

The presence of several of these symptoms is usually sufficient to suggest hidden trust issues.

Overcoming Barriers to Building Trust

Earlier in this chapter, one of the questions I asked was that if trust is so valuable, why don't we have more of it? As discussed, a lack of awareness and understanding are significant barriers in and of themselves, but there are several additional barriers to building trust.

I regularly speak with senior management in organizations that struggle to get a mandate to deal with the trust issue, despite their company's understanding that trust is an important issue for its organization. The reason for this is that, in part at least, building trust requires resources. These include time, money, and the efforts of those involved. My colleagues and I often run into numerous barriers that prevent organizations from truly working toward resolving trust issues or even improving the trust-building skills within their organization.

My company has identified four primary barriers to building trust:
- Overestimation of one's own trustworthiness
- A feeling that trust is too complicated to do anything about it
- Being "too busy" for trust-building
- The assumption that trust takes too long to build

The first barrier, and arguably the most powerful, is the false belief that we are intrinsically trustworthy. Research suggests that 95 percent of people believe they are more trustworthy than the average person; you don't need to be a mathematician to realize that this cannot be accurate. When leaders are interviewed and surveyed, we discover a large gap between the level of trust they believe they enjoy and the true level of trust people have in them. The knock-on effect of this is that even when people recognize trust problems exist, they don't work toward fixing them because they believe they are someone else's problem. This myopic viewpoint, along with an inability to see the other person's perspective, is common because we are all absorbed by our own story, our own narrative (the one that is constantly chattering in our head). It prevents us from being able to see things from the other person's perspective. When my colleagues and I begin to systematically outline steps that people can take to build trust with others, we frequently hear the comment, "I already do that." The challenge lies in the fact that what *we* think we are doing has little bearing on another person's decision to trust us. What matters is what *they* think we are doing.

The second barrier to building trust is the belief that it is simply too complex and fuzzy for us to control effectively or too complicated to remedy. This is untrue. Someone in one of my workshops even said, "It's simply what it is, and for me to try to influence the situation is manipulative and morally questionable." When dealing with an issue of trust, people often appear defeated before they even try to do anything. Trust levels are fluid; they can become better or worse, but we all have the power to do something about trust in any environment. Failing to take action, however, is not an option when so much is at stake.

The third barrier to building trust is the "I'm too busy" argument. It's common to hear, "I have all of these fires to fight; I don't have time to invest in people skills." I know both from research and personal experience that higher trust levels lead to greater productivity, efficiency, and improved employee engagement. Building stronger relations within a team helps that team function more efficiently and increases productivity. Make no mistake: get this trust thing right and you won't have to work quite as hard or be as frenetic. It is an investment that will pay off in better leadership and team performance. Remember, any fires you are fighting are more than likely symptomatic of underlying trust problems.

The fourth barrier that hinders building trust is the belief that it is a long-term investment. This makes leaders apprehensive because they are assessed and evaluated based on short-term criteria. This is a valid concern, but it's a mistake to assume building trust takes years. I have witnessed remarkable turnarounds in very short periods. Parents have reported almost immediate improvements in their relationships with their children, leaders have observed dramatic changes in behavior on the part of their subordinates, and organizations have experienced transformations within weeks or months of adopting the techniques explained in this book.

Big, Hairy Problems

Every generation thinks it is facing a set of cataclysmic challenges that far exceed those faced by earlier generations. But as I put the final touches to this book toward the end of 2021, the last two years seem to have been unprecedented in the size and scope of societal upheaval.

We are facing not only the COVID-19 pandemic but also a crisis in relations between police and those they serve and protect; growing concerns about possibly irreversible environmental damage due to climate change; disruptive populist political movements in the United States, United Kingdom, and Europe; geopolitical tensions in the Middle East, between China and the United States, and elsewhere; and accelerating, dramatic technological changes. Each of these problems has global reach and will have significant impact. I like to call problems like these "big, hairy problems." These are the problems that put serious strain on the relationships that allow our societies to function.

There is a story about a cohort of undergraduate students at Duke University taking an introductory business course in which they're learning the concepts of internal and external locus of control. They are told that an internal locus of control means that you are the master of your own destiny and are an actor in the world—that you make things happen. An external locus of control, they learn, means that things happen to you, that you are buffeted by the winds of fate and that external forces are too powerful for you to alter outcomes. They are then asked to raise their hands if they feel they have an internal locus of control. Not surprisingly, all of them raise their hands. The professor smiles and says, "This is great news! It means that if you don't do well in this course, it's not because I didn't teach you properly, that the test was too hard, or that something was unfair. It's all on you." The students were suddenly less sure of their response.

The reality is, we often exhibit an internal locus of control when we are successful and an external locus of control when times are tough or we fail at something. This can be a powerful defense mechanism for our ego and sense of self. It allows us to continue striving when we might otherwise falter. If taken to extremes, however, it can be debilitating. If we are unaware, or unwilling, to accept the role that we played when we failed, then we are unable to learn, grow, and develop. Similarly, if we are unable to identify the role the environment played in our successes, then we forgo the opportunity to identify environments that increase our probability of success in the future, and we may give too much credit to the actions we took, only to be surprised if those actions are later unsuccessful under different circumstances.

In the face of these big, hairy problems, it's natural to wonder what we, as individuals, can possibly do about them. And what does trust have to do with any of them? As it turns out, quite a lot. Big, hairy problems can rarely be solved by any one individual. Rather, they require collective, collaborative action involving many individuals. Such collaboration is very difficult, perhaps impossible, in the absence of trust-based relationships among those individuals. However, building such relationships is truly within an individual's control.

Big, hairy problems can feel like they are outside our control (external locus). But if everyone thinks that way, no one will act. What we need to understand is that building collaborative networks or groups is within our control and is a step toward addressing problems like the ones I outline in the following case studies. Let's look at three big, hairy problems through a trust lens and see how this is playing out today.

Case Study #1: The COVID-19 Pandemic

The COVID-19 pandemic swept across the globe in 2020 and 2021, with different geographical and political regions experiencing profoundly different infection and mortality rates. Some areas demonstrated extremely effective responses to the pandemic. Unfortunately, others struggled with overwhelming numbers of cases and an inability to contain the spread of the virus. This crisis checks all the boxes of a big, hairy problem requiring high levels of trust to solve.

On July 9, 2020, the director-general of the World Health Organization, Dr. Tedros Adhanom Ghebreyesus, stated that a lack of leadership in pandemic response, not the virus itself, posed the greatest threat to the world. He argued that the virus thrives on division and could be thwarted by global solidarity. He was reminding us that collective, collaborative action is a powerful approach to dealing with issues like a pandemic. The challenge is that such solidarity or collaboration will actually occur only in the presence of high levels of trust in leaders and organizations—levels of trust that, in many jurisdictions, are sadly lacking.

Earlier in the year, an article by Charles Duhigg in the *New Yorker* described how Seattle had done a much better job of coping with the coronavirus than New York, thanks to its superior execution of the Centers for Disease Control (CDC) playbook, or field manual, for dealing with outbreaks.[6] Reading the CDC playbook or watching their publicly available training videos makes it clear that the CDC understands that building trust between health-care providers and the communities they serve is vital to successfully dealing with any type of outbreak. Seattle authorities understood this and followed the CDC playbook; New York authorities—where the strained relationship between the mayor of New York City and the Office of Public Health may have played a contributory role in the flawed response—not so much.

A significant element of the CDC playbook involves having politicians step back and allow public health officials to take the lead in pandemic response. This is a good idea, given that around 50 percent of the population already mistrusts the politicians in charge, depending on the jurisdiction. The CDC believes that public health officials will have greater credibility than politicians and come across as more trustworthy because of their expertise. The CDC further recommends having a single person act as the spokesperson to create familiarity, comfort, and trust. That spokesperson should have a single overriding health communication objective (SOHCO) for every briefing. They should state the SOHCO at the start and end of each communication, along with an empathetic statement about the struggles being faced by all concerned. These are all very clear steps aimed at reducing uncertainty (by demonstrating ability and benevolence, as we'll explore in more detail in chapter 5) and building trust.

Duhigg's article follows the story of Dr. Francis Riedo, a graduate of the CDC's Epidemic Intelligence Service, which is described as America's "shock troops" for battling disease outbreaks. Riedo argues that dealing with a pandemic is as much a communications emergency as a medical crisis. Once again we see trust play a role; for instance, patients need to believe that the cure won't be worse than the disease. If they don't, they won't make the trip to the hospital. Patients also need to be comfortable sharing information about whom they have been in contact so steps can be taken to reduce the spread of the disease. It's easy to see that where there is a lack of trust in local authorities, these voluntary actions are less likely to occur.

There are documented examples of people who contracted COVID-19 and failed to seek medical help for a variety of reasons, including the fact that they were illegal immigrants, they lacked trust in the medical system, or they could not afford treatment. Others continued to work, even though they were showing symptoms, because they would not receive sick pay if they stayed home and isolated. Some of these people took to the streets (in order to self-isolate), and mixed with the homeless population in an attempt to protect their family. But at what cost?

While it seems that the CDC had a clear understanding of the role trust plays in managing disease outbreaks, they may nevertheless still have underestimated the importance of building trust with civic leaders prior to the outbreaks. The organization misunderstood the fact that the vulnerability experienced by all parties extended beyond the virus itself. On one side, individuals were concerned about finances, social isolation, mental health, and other issues, whereas politicians were more concerned about the economy and their political futures.

There are some amazing examples where jurisdictions appear to have followed the CDC guidelines and have, as a result, seen remarkable success in dealing with the pandemic. It is frustrating that these regions appear to be the exception rather than the rule. A deeper understanding of trust, along with a commitment to strengthening relationships with key stakeholders, may well have prevented a lot of suffering.

One incredible display of trust came out of Washington State in late February 2020. At the time, the United States had only nineteen confirmed cases. But the King County executive was advised by the state's medical experts that they should begin advising people not to frequent bars and clubs and for residents to stay at home and work from home as much as possible. He realized that it would be tough to get people to buy in to this message with so few COVID cases at that point. Closing schools was the first thing he could do to raise peoples' perceptions of the danger of the situation, but the logistics of making that happen would take several days. He decided to call Brad Smith, the president and vice chair of Microsoft, which is headquartered in Redmond in King County, and ask him to advise his employees to work from home if they could. Smith respected and trusted the reputation of King County's medical team and obliged the request. Amazon followed suit, and residents of the county saw approximately one hundred thousand fewer vehicles on the road daily. The message was clear: something serious was happening.

The CDC also should have been building strong relationships with other key stakeholders to prepare the path for an outbreak. This would have included other medical services groups and large employers.

Let's look at a country and a region that each stand out as examples of successful coronavirus responses and then examine a country that was markedly less successful. The first two followed the CDC playbook, but the final example used a different approach.

New Zealand did particularly well flattening the curve, reducing the number of cases, and limiting the duration of the pandemic in that country. Much of its success has been attributed to the leadership of Prime Minister Jacinda Ardern, who acted quickly to close New Zealand's borders and announced stay-at-home orders at the recommendation of experts on public health. New Zealand was one of the most successful regions in the world at coping with the COVID-19 crisis, and Ardern continues to have high popularity ratings and the respect of those she leads.

What truly set New Zealand apart was the collective, collaborative action of its citizens. Advice and encouragement regarding social distancing, frequent handwashing, wearing masks, and the elimination of public gatherings were all heeded by the majority of the population. The prime minister made the matter less political by stepping aside and allowing medical experts to take the lead. On June 8, 2020, the country removed all restrictions after a seventeen-day period with no new cases. This is a remarkably rapid recovery after restrictions were initially placed in late March. It should be noted that there were further small outbreaks sometime later; however, that was to be expected. There will always be bumps in the road, but victories provide knowledge and experience and breed confidence that in turn leads to long-term success.

Part of the reason for this country's success was early action taken at the first sign of the virus. The citizens of New Zealand were willing to endure short-term discomfort even before it had become obvious there was a serious problem. This acceptance required a high degree of trust in their leadership.

The province of British Columbia, Canada, showed a similar pattern of response and success in dealing with the pandemic. The citizens of British Columbia (where I am lucky to live) were blessed to have Dr. Bonnie Henry as their head of public health. Dr. Henry reacted quickly and decisively at the first signs of the outbreak. She was remarkably calm and eloquent when informing the public about what was happening and what might happen in the future. She was consistent with her messaging and showed care and compassion for the citizens she served. She regularly acknowledged the suffering of those afflicted, their families and loved ones, and those being impacted by the restrictions required to cope with the pandemic.

The politicians leading the province of British Columbia also played their roles remarkably well. They made it clear that Dr. Henry was in charge with regard to issues related to the pandemic and that she had their full and unwavering support. There appeared to be no issues of ego or self-serving political grandstanding getting in the way of what needed to be done. It was as if they had read the CDC playbook. There was a consistency of response and messaging with the clear understanding that Dr. Henry would be given whatever resources were needed to help care for the citizens of the province. These displays of ability, benevolence, and integrity went a long way toward reducing the population's uncertainty and building (or reinforcing) their trust in authority.

Both New Zealand's and British Columbia's leaders were able to act quickly and convince their citizens that the danger was real and action needed to be taken, even before the situation seemed dire. By doing so, they took a risk with their credibility because little was known about the virus at that time. As a result, they have emerged from this crisis more respected, trusted, and popular than they were before these events transpired. There is clearly an upside for leaders when they are able to set their immediate self-interest aside and demonstrate care and concern for those they lead.

An interesting thing about being trusted as a leader is that you are usually given the benefit of the doubt by those you lead. In the preceding cases, if the pandemic had not been as severe as it turned out to be, people still would have believed that their leaders were doing their best, given the information they had at the time.

America's Dr. Fauci is another example of this phenomenon. Initially he urged the public not to rush out and buy masks, the idea being to protect the supply for frontline workers. Later he argued that everyone should wear a mask when out in public to help limit the spread of the virus. Generally, those who trusted him before continued to trust his perspective.

In sharp contrast, leaders with low trust scores, which include politicians in a wide range of countries, are questioned and second-guessed no matter what approach they take to problems like these. In times of rapid change and high uncertainty, leaders need the ability to adjust as situations change. They can't be too rigidly tethered to the past and previous decisions.

In stark contrast to these two successful examples, we should look at the approach taken by the United States. Dr. Anthony Fauci was director of the National Institute of Allergy and Infectious Diseases during the pandemic. He has decades of experience, has served numerous presidents, and is one of the world's leading experts on outbreaks such as COVID-19. Given his expertise and the fact that the CDC is an American entity, the United States should have been the country best equipped to handle the crisis. Unfortunately, the opposite was true. For several months in 2020,

America's results were among the worst of any industrialized nation in the world. This poor performance was due, in no small part, to the failure of those in power to listen to Dr. Fauci and act on his advice.

Uncertainty is one of the primary feelings that influences our decision to trust or not trust other people. I will explore this in more detail in chapters 5 and 6. The virus itself provoked a great deal of uncertainty worldwide; the US response, however, led to an incredible increase in that uncertainty among its citizens. There were clear disagreements among political leaders, social scientists, and public health experts on the appropriate course of action. There were notable differences in how federal, state, and local governments approached dealing with the pandemic. As a good example of how this got out of hand, at one point the governor of Georgia sued the mayor of Atlanta for having different directives than other parts of the state. These differences often appeared to be along political lines, leaving people confused over which approach was best.

The inability of the United States to agree on a unified approach to the pandemic, or to the implementation of the most basic safeguards to slow its spread, resulted in a catastrophic response. In large part, this appeared to be a trust problem. It would be difficult to list all the ways trust was undermined in the United States during that period.

The Trump administration's approach was almost diametrically opposed to that taken in New Zealand and British Columbia. In those jurisdictions, political leaders put public health experts front and center, demonstrating the faith they had in their knowledge, experience, and abilities. President Trump, meanwhile, touted his own expertise and promoted untested, dubious "treatments" despite no credible evidence of any medical expertise on his part. He diminished the public role of Dr. Fauci, the actual medical expert, and cast doubts on the expertise of the CDC and the World Health Organization. While leaders elsewhere demonstrated benevolence through heartfelt expressions of sympathy for victims of the virus, the US president made few, if any, such statements. And the integrity of the president was constantly thrown into doubt by unfulfilled promises, such as those relating to personal protective equipment and the availability of testing. He also sent contradictory messages (e.g., advocating lockdowns while supporting protests against stay-at-home orders and expressing support for mask-wearing while refusing to wear one himself).

The efforts to combat the pandemic were also undermined by a marked shift in focus. As the presidential election approached, there appeared to be a growing sense that the state of the economy would play a significant role. There was pressure to open the economy and get people back to work. The fragile nature of the US social safety net meant that many were at extreme financial risk, and stories about evictions and foreclosures became more prevalent. The focus on the economy was itself interrupted by ongoing protests about the treatment of minorities at the hands of the police. The White House shifted its election message to one of law and order as a result of violence, riots, and calls to defund the police. These shifts in focus and mixed messages further increased uncertainty and decreased the probability of collective action against COVID-19.

As we will see in chapters 5 and 6, our affective state—in particular, how we feel about the person we are deciding whether to trust—strongly influences our predisposition to trust. The intense political polarization of the United States has created a situation where large segments of the population have such antipathy toward those on the "other side" that they will find any excuse not to trust them. Given the need to work together on problems like this, the tendency to vilify and denigrate the other side makes collaboration almost impossible. Such polarization also greatly colors perceptions of outcomes. We see the same statistics about the impact of COVID-19 being interpreted in radically different ways by different groups.

As an example, the White House suggested in the summer of 2020 that the United States was doing well in the battle against the pandemic because the fatality rate of those with the virus was lower than that of many other countries. The other side argued that America was faring poorly with the pandemic because it had the highest number of cases and deaths attributed to the virus. The White House response was that case numbers were high because of aggressive testing and that fatality numbers were exaggerated. Democrats countered that public health experts and scientists were suggesting that testing was still lower than it needed to be and that the number of fatalities were, if anything, underestimated. If the parties involved, and by extension their supporters, couldn't agree on the numbers and what they even meant, it was unlikely that the collaborative response required to deal with an issue like the pandemic would ever happen.

The US health-care system also played a significant role in the prolonged presence of the COVID-19 virus and its death toll. Financial profit plays a bigger role in the US health-care system than in most other countries. Medical facilities and insurers are always mindful of the economic impacts of the services they provide. This fact is not lost on the population they serve, which often questions whether the system is acting in their best interests or in the interests of other stakeholders such as pharmaceutical firms, insurance companies, doctors, or shareholders of various companies connected to the system. Millions of Americans are uninsured or underinsured. The result is a reluctance to interact with the system at all or simply a lack of access to health care.

The US health-care system was ranked nineteenth out of twenty-eight countries measured for trust in its health-care system in 2021.[7] Only 64 percent of respondents stated that they trusted the health-care system. This lack of trust drives a reluctance to access the system during an outbreak, making the impacts of a pandemic more pronounced—and lethal. Equally concerning is the potential impact this lack of trust had on dealing with the virus long term. As I write this, several groups around the world have developed a vaccine for COVID-19. Unfortunately, as of June 2020, only 50 percent of Americans polled said they would be willing to take a vaccine when one was made available.[8] In September 2020, Trump suggested that a vaccine might be available before the presidential election. Some Democrats suggested that a vaccine rushed out by the White House shouldn't be trusted because it likely wouldn't have been adequately tested. This politicization of a potential COVID-19 vaccine was bound to negatively impact the population's already shaky enthusiasm for any vaccine offered.

A poll in October 2021 suggested that the number of Americans unwilling to be vaccinated had dropped to 16 percent. There are multiple possible factors at work here, including reported elevated levels of illness and death among the unvaccinated. Those with concerns about the vaccine witnessed others taking the vaccine and surviving. They also began to experience external pressure as government and corporate mandates compromised their freedom to travel and work.

No matter where vaccine hesitancy numbers end up over time, the efforts of various groups to undermine confidence in science in general and particularly in public health led to unnecessary suffering and death.

The under- and uninsured are almost always poor and lack the ability to physically distance themselves from others should they get sick. In the midst of a pandemic, this goes from being their problem to a problem for the entire community. It becomes increasingly difficult to get an accurate measure of how many people are sick, how many have died, and with whom they have come into contact. People lacking insurance coverage, or the necessary financial resources to seek medical attention, are faced with tough choices. They can take their chance with the virus, potentially infecting coworkers and their families, or they can seek medical attention, but in the process face long-term economic hardship.

The stark reality of this could be seen in the mass graves being dug in New York for the unclaimed bodies of those who died from the virus. Many of these bodies went unclaimed because those connected to the deceased simply couldn't afford to pay the medical bills attached to them.

Worldometer, an independent digital media company with no political, governmental, or corporate affiliations, reported that 789,155 Americans had died from the virus as of November 18, 2021.[9] The company's statistics are used by governments and media organizations around the world, including the US government, the *New York Times*, the *Financial Times*, and the British Broadcasting Corporation. As of November 2021, Worldometer listed total deaths worldwide from COVID-19 at 5.1 million.

On December 27, 2020, CNN reported that 1 in 1,000 Americans had died from COVID-19 since the nation's first reported infection in late January 2020. By January 1, 2021, the total COVID-19 cases world-wide hit 20 million (just one week earlier it had been 19 million) with close to 350,000 deaths recorded (in the US alone).

While some people may disagree with the precise numbers, which will, of course, change over time, there can be little argument that the pandemic had significant impacts worldwide. These were not limited to the direct loss of human life; there was a rise in mental health issues and long-term economic struggles for most people.

We will return to this example in the following chapters as we set out and explore the key elements of the trust model and see how they all play out in the context of COVID-19 responses.

Case Study #2: Trust and Law Enforcement

The death of George Floyd, a Black man, on May 25, 2020, in Minneapolis under the knee of a white police officer sparked protests and outrage throughout the United States and around the world. There were loud demands for significant change. The strong sentiment, widely expressed, was that police officers generally treat Blacks and visible minorities with greater violence and aggression than they do whites. It became increasingly clear that a significant portion of the population did not believe that the police were acting in the best interests of all citizens. Growing calls to defund police departments, or even abolish them outright, ensued.

In 2016 I wrote the following:

The month of July 2016 saw a remarkable heightening of tensions between the police and Black communities in the United States. The media has reported multiple police-related deaths of Black men in highly public and questionable circumstances. These events continued an apparent trend of disturbing police actions with Black casualties. The deaths triggered a series of protests and reprisal shootings targeting police officers; several officers were killed or wounded during these attacks. There have been a number of incidents in the months following this involving more unnecessary deaths, numerous protests, and heightened tensions.

To say that many of the police forces in North America face a significant lack of trust from those they serve is a profound understatement. This lack of trust in turn has led to additional unnecessary deaths and violence for police and citizens alike and there are now calls from many quarters to fix a problem that has evolved over decades. While there seems to be a general consensus that something needs to be done, there appears to be few concrete solutions.[10]

My reason for sharing this quote is to show that trust is critical for effective policing and that this issue is not new. For the last fifty years, it has been acknowledged that trust is critical to maintaining the legitimacy of any police force. In the United States, the 2015 final report of The President's Task Force on 21st Century Policing identified "building trust and legitimacy" as the first pillar for rebuilding relationships between law enforcement agencies and the communities they protect and serve.

The report outlined the need to nurture and build trust on both sides of the police/citizen divide. Decades of research and practice support the premise that without trust between police and citizens, legitimacy and the "authority to police" comes into question. It is critical, therefore, to strengthen relationships between citizens and police by building trust.

The *21st Century Policing* report offers a perspective shift, requiring law enforcement culture to embrace the role and mindset of a guardian rather than a warrior. It is not always necessary for warriors to be trusted in order to discharge their duties; guardians, on the other hand, are, or at least should be, trusted figures.

In May 2020, Canadian Prime Minister Justin Trudeau stated, "The reality is that many people in this country simply do not feel protected by the police. In fact, they're afraid of them."[11] He publicly sought concrete actions from the police and justice systems in order to move forward on eliminating systemic discrimination and making real change in Canada. "With the many disturbing reports of violence against Black Canadians and Indigenous people, we know that we need to do much more and we need to do it now," he said, adding that his government is seeking "real commitments as quickly as possible that address the root causes of these problems."[12]

Recent events in America continued to further undermine any trust that people may have had in the police. In late July 2020, federal agents showed up in Portland, Oregon, and began arresting protestors. A number of concerns were raised about the presence and actions of these federal law enforcement officers that related directly to trust. First, they were dressed in camouflage military attire with no insignia identifying the agency for which they worked. Second, they drove unmarked vehicles to transport the protestors they apprehended. Third, they were less than transparent about where they took these citizens or indeed why they were being detained. Finally, the federal agents were not under the control of, or accountable to, the local authorities who had jurisdiction in the situation they were "policing." Both civic leaders and police chiefs asked that these forces be withdrawn, stating that they appeared to be increasing tension in the area and having a profoundly negative impact on trust levels in the community.

These actions seem eerily similar to the behavior of secret police forces in developing countries with tyrannical regimes. There are ongoing disagreements among several levels of government regarding the federal government's powers, and their legitimacy, when acting in individual jurisdictions across the United States. The million-dollar question is: if varying levels of authority don't trust one another to act appropriately, how are citizens supposed to trust any of them?

Unfortunately, when trying to build trust, people often make assumptions about the uncertainty or vulnerability of others—the prospective trusters—without actually including them in the conversation. This has led to a top-down approach, where, for example, calls are made for authorities (e.g., police or government) to implement change with the objective of repairing relationships and building trust in the community. This becomes problematic, however, when these authorities do not completely understand the sources of uncertainty and vulnerability felt by community members. It quickly becomes obvious that imposing solutions aimed at building trust, without including all concerned parties developing those solutions, simply doesn't work, or at the very least it doesn't work for long.

Furthermore, although trust is a two-way street, remarkably little discussion has been devoted to the need for the police to trust those they protect. In the wake of defunding social systems, we continue to ask police officers to risk their physical and emotional well-being to serve and protect us. We equip them with lethal force, paramilitary training, and the ability to respond to things that go bump in the night. Their mandate and our expectations seem to continually grow, while at the same time the levels of uncertainty and vulnerability experienced by the police remain remarkably high, especially when they regularly put themselves in harm's way to protect others. This is particularly relevant given that their role is to keep all citizens safe. Following this thinking, the tragic and unwarranted deaths of many could be seen as failures of trust.

As already mentioned, the notion that higher levels of trust are required between the police and the communities they serve isn't new. The critical importance of trust has been argued for decades. Despite this recognition, however, frustratingly little progress has been made to improve trust levels. In fact, things appear to be headed in the wrong direction. Multiple polls confirm that trust in the police is in decline. Protests around the world are also making a clear statement that people are unhappy with the current relationship between private citizens and the police. Once again, the question remains: if we understand how much trust matters, why aren't we doing a better job building it?

Case Study #3: Climate Change

Extreme weather events are becoming increasingly common. These events include hurricanes, floods, earthquakes, and extreme heat in places such as Siberia and the Canadian Arctic that usually don't experience such temperatures. This, of course, coincides with sustained global changes in climate. These changes have led to coining a new term, *climate refugees*, sometimes called *climate migrants*. Climate refugees are people who are forced to leave their traditional homelands because the weather has become either too hot and dry or too wet and cold to sustain their normal way of life. There are widely varying estimates of how many people are currently affected, but a ReliefWeb press release stated that various forecasts predict there will be between 25 million to 1 billion environmental migrants by 2050, with 200 million being the most quoted number.[13] However, the United Nations' projections for 2050 estimate the number to be between 250 million and 1 billion.

Some projections, for instance, suggest that the Marshall Islands, a succession of volcanic islands in the Pacific Ocean between Hawaii and the Philippines, may become completely uninhabitable in the near future if inhabitants don't somehow manage to elevate their land mass. Residents of these coral atolls are faced with the prospect of moving or engaging in significant and expensive terraforming.

This and other real-life examples are consistent with a growing body of scientific evidence for anthropogenic climate change. The Intergovernmental Panel on Climate Change (IPCC) has stated that the scientific evidence supporting the warming of the climate system is unequivocal. Part of this evidence is the dramatic increase in carbon dioxide (CO_2) levels in the environment. CO_2 is a greenhouse gas that traps warm air near the earth's surface and as a result global temperatures increase, something the whole world has witnessed. Between 2014 and 2020, Earth experienced the six warmest years on record. These temperature rises have led to warming oceans, reduced snowpack, and the disappearance of primordial glaciers and ice sheets. The complex interdependence of the environment and life on our planet makes these changes cause for significant concern.

So where does trust come into this? Despite all the scientific, experiential, and practical evidence, a significant percentage of people still underestimates the significance of changes in the global climate. According to a 2018 global survey, 20 percent of respondents saw it as a minor problem and 9 percent felt it was not a problem.[14] If we can't get global consensus that there is a significant problem in the first place, it will be difficult to achieve the collective and collaborative actions required to resolve the massive challenge of global climate change.

Human beings aren't great at connecting cause and effect if those two things are not simultaneous. We see this when it comes to substance abuse, exercise, or other health-related issues that are often self-inflicted over time. For example, consumption of a Twinkie, a cigarette, or a beer may have an immediate positive (or at least pleasurable) short-term effect but can, when taken to the extreme, result in long-term negative consequences. Humanity is often beset by situations where we see short-term benefits greatly outweighed by long-term pain and consequences.

The issue of climate change is a great example of this. Actions we take now may not result in observable impacts for decades. More importantly, given the complexity and shared nature of the environment, it will be almost impossible to correlate individual actions to observable effects. This creates a challenging trust problem. We need to make sacrifices, change behaviors, and forgo some of the easy luxuries we currently enjoy to achieve results we may not live to see (or which may not be apparent to the casual observer). Not only that, we will have to rely on others (i.e., scientists, politicians, and so forth) to tell us if our efforts are making a difference. Given the struggle scientists, politicians, and other experts are currently having in getting people to believe in climate change in the first place, this will prove difficult.

Imagine, for a moment, that the incubation period for the COVID-19 virus is not fourteen days but rather, six months. This would mean that it would take 180 days for people to start showing symptoms or become aware that they were sick. In this case, our ability to track and constrain the virus would be virtually nonexistent. The complexity of dealing with the virus, if it had such a long incubation period, would simply be beyond us. Unfortunately, the level of complexity involved in dealing with environmental issues is larger by an order of magnitude.

While scientific measurements of present and past climates are (relatively) easy and compelling, climate projections remain remarkably challenging. The effort to deal with climate change has, in part, been undermined by overly aggressive or dramatic projections that have failed to become reality. This has resulted in a "crying wolf" syndrome, where people are suspicious of the validity of warnings and consequently lose trust in those who are issuing the advisories.

When it comes to climate change, people experience a number of significant vulnerabilities. Making a noticeable impact on CO_2 emissions, for instance, would require people to make substantial changes to their lives and would particularly affect first world economies. Numerous stakeholders currently benefit greatly from the status quo and are invested in blocking or delaying change. At the other end of the spectrum, certain populations are at extreme risk if climate change is not tackled with some urgency. This latter group has little in the way of resources or influence on the world stage. In a PR battle between climate refugees and multi-billion-dollar global oil companies, or incredibly wealthy oil-producing nations, the result seems a foregone conclusion. It is highly likely that complex campaigns of disinformation and supporting "scientific inquiry" are already being heavily funded by those with deep pockets (and a noteworthy absence of benevolence or integrity).

Furthermore, some sectors of society believe that climate change is a hoax—a conspiracy to close down businesses in coal, oil, gas, and other industries—or that it is a move toward socialism.

In all cases, a lack of trust is obvious and in some cases warranted. Much needs to be done to rebuild trust between various sectors of society and between "warring" factions. Scientists, environmentalists, business leaders, politicians, and the general public share a common goal of helping people survive and thrive, even though they may have differing views on how that might be achieved.

What do these big, hairy problems have in common? Without a minimum level of trust between all parties involved, it will be almost impossible for any kinds of complex, collaborative solutions to be implemented or progress made.

The trust challenge with "invisible" problems, such as COVID-19 (think microscopic virus) and climate change (it manifests itself over such a long period of time it is beyond most people's attention span or even lifespan), is difficult because those who cannot see the problem directly must put their trust in those who have the tools and ability to do so.

The crisis in policing might seem like a more straightforward issue, with a more direct connection between cause (racist cops behaving badly) and effect (disproportionate deaths of BIPOCs [Black, Indigenous, People of Color] at the hands of police), but the underlying systemic problems are much more subtle and pervasive.

Although each preceding case study talks about issues from a global or organizational level, at the end of the day all three involve uncertainty and vulnerability felt by individuals. And ultimately, it is individuals who make the decision either to trust or not trust. Big, hairy problems can't be solved until we fix the underlying lack of trust that exists between all players. To do this we need to understand the basis for that lack of trust. In the pandemic example, we saw tension between those on the health side of the equation, who were focused on dealing with the disease, and political leaders, who had to manage a broader spectrum of challenges, responsibilities, and priorities. These differing perspectives can appear contradictory to the public. This leaves people questioning who they can trust at a time when trust is based on perceived vulnerability. What complicates things further is that perception can be manipulated by one or more parties with vested interests using PR dollars.

In the policing case study, we see potential trust issues present for all parties. Moving forward will require all parties to truly understand and accept the vulnerabilities felt on both sides. Any solution will require that stakeholders come together (using a common frame of reference and language) to bring the trust issue to the forefront and have a dialogue where all voices are heard.

Collective action will also be required when dealing with the climate change argument. There are many competing perspectives, and vulnerability is felt on all sides. Major environmental challenges are a global issue and will need to be dealt with as such rather than within silos of vested interest. Sacrifices will be required to achieve results. People making those sacrifices will need to trust those asking for them and believe that the rewards will be worth the cost.

It may be discouraging to consider all the problems and barriers we face when trying to build trust. However, we need to recognize these challenges and understand why there has been such little progress, and ultimately we must explore ways to rectify the situation.

In chapter 3, we'll explore the role trust plays in being an effective leader, and then in chapter 4 I will outline some of the benefits that can be realized from having higher trust levels. Later in the book I will illustrate the trust model more fully by working through three new, specific case studies to explore how we can diagnose and resolve trust problems.

Trust Is Everywhere
(Except When It Isn't):
Key Points Review

- Organizations, communities, even economies cannot function without some level of underlying trust. Trust acts as a social lubricant.

- Trust, or its absence, is an underlying critical factor in how society deals with its biggest, "hairiest" challenges.

- We are facing a global trust crisis. Historically low levels of trust in society are also challenging the corporate environment.

- All too often, people fail to connect the challenges they are experiencing to an issue of trust.

- There is a profound lack of awareness about what trust is, who we trust, and how much we trust them. We trust people all the time; we simply trust some people more than others, or we trust them in different ways.

- The four primary barriers to building trust:

    o Overestimation of one's own trustworthiness

    o A feeling that trust is too complicated to do anything about it

    o Being "too busy" for trust-building

    o Assuming that trust takes too long to build

CHAPTER 3

The Trust Challenge for Leaders

LEADERSHIP, IN ALL ITS FORMS, FACES REMARKABLE CHALLENGES IN A world where change is one of the few constants. Leaders face a growing, shifting, diverse, and complex range of key stakeholder groups. The demands these groups make seem fluid, and the perception of what good looks like seems to be ever-evolving. The ease with which information now flows on social media means that leaders are being held accountable for opinions they had, or decisions they made, decades ago. This can be troubling because allowances aren't made for the fact that people change, as do the prevailing opinions and values of society. Values seem to continuously shift, balance, reprioritize, and equilibrate; they are the subject of constant debate, analysis, and scrutiny.

Against the backdrop of shifting values and increased scrutiny, it is not surprising that opinions differ widely on what good leadership looks like. There is growing cynicism as people wonder where all the good leaders have gone. The challenges outlined are enough to cause leaders headaches, but added to this is the frenzy and scope of the epic changes being faced by leaders and the sheer speed at which these changes are arriving. This is something we have not experienced since the Renaissance. These changes are both systemic (e.g., changing values, demographics, technology) and episodic (e.g., pandemics, extreme weather events, contentious race relations, international tensions).

In this chapter, I will explore how the challenges introduced above can make building trust more difficult and complex but also how trust is essential to success. We'll focus on three areas:

1. Multiple stakeholders with diverging interests
2. Growing cynicism around leadership
3. A profound spike in uncertainty

Multiple Stakeholders

To better illustrate the trust-based challenges we can encounter, I will use some recent events and examine them through a trust-based lens. The following case study exemplifies the struggle of dealing with multiple stakeholders, as experienced by the head of the Royal Canadian Mounted Police (RCMP). This specific example contains lessons that are relevant to all leaders.

RCMP commissioner Brenda Lucki's experience was more public than most. She faced a difficult set of issues with multiple key stakeholders observing and judging her every word and action. While your key stakeholders may not include a federal government or the people of an entire nation, they will still observe and evaluate your decisions with a mixed set of values, biases, perceptions, and expectations.

After the death of George Floyd at the hands of white police officers in the United States, police departments all over the world were under increased scrutiny. It was in June 2020 that Lucki was asked if systemic racism existed within the RCMP. Ms. Lucki's original response was that she had heard many definitions of systemic racism and was therefore uncertain how to answer the question. Many people, including members of the Canadian government, found this deflection unacceptable. As a result, the commissioner found herself facing the same question again in the following weeks.

Under pressure, she eventually acknowledged that there could be systemic racism within the RCMP. However, she then demonstrated a lack of understanding, or awareness of the importance of the question's context, when she began to equate, or compare, racism with instances of systemic discrimination in hiring practices that had been previously addressed. By way of an example, Ms. Lucki described a historic requirement for candidates applying to the RCMP to be able to long-jump six feet. She went on to say that the force had eventually realized that most people are able to jump a distance roughly equal to their height. Her point was that this meant that most of their candidates, and subsequently the officers hired, were six feet or taller. She went on to suggest that this was an example of systemic discrimination against shorter people, a demographic that disproportionately included women and ethnic groups. Once again, this response was seen as inadequate, not to mention flawed.

Eventually, Commissioner Lucki acknowledged, in a way that was deemed acceptable by stakeholders, that there was systemic racism within the RCMP. She learned the hard way that dealing with a question of this nature is far more complex than it seems on the surface. The challenge she faced was that there were three groups she wanted to appease. First, she sought to maintain the trust and engagement of those she led, which she couldn't do if she threw them under the bus by suggesting that some of their actions were racially motivated. Second, she needed to maintain, and perhaps repair, the trust of those the RCMP protects and serves in communities across the country. Third, Lucki needed to maintain the trust and respect of those in the federal government to whom she reported. To be fair, satisfying all three of these stakeholder groups when directly asked a question about systemic racism was no easy task.

So how could Commissioner Lucki have formulated a more effective response? In part, an element of transparency may well have gone a long way. She could have acknowledged that this was indeed a challenging question given its implications for the stakeholders involved. She could have stated that she was concerned about how her response would land with the officers that she leads, the communities they serve, and the political leaders to whom they report. If I had been in her shoes, I would have said something like the following:

The question you ask is more complex than it seems. A simple yes or no answer would be a disservice to those whom I lead or to those we serve and protect. The exceptional men and women I lead make significant sacrifices and serve this nation proudly. A quick look at the statistics shows that minorities in this country, especially our indigenous populations, are far poorer, less educated, and disproportionately involved in criminal activities than the white majority. Clearly, we as a society are failing them. Is there systemic racism within the Royal Canadian Mounted Police? Yes, I believe there is. Is it any better or worse than the systemic racism that exists within our society? I'm not sure. The RCMP has a proud tradition and it will strive to do better and be better. All law-abiding Canadians should feel safe in our presence. The fact that some members of our society do not feel safe is unacceptable, and the responsibility for that lies within the force's leadership. The best approach, I believe, would be an ongoing dialogue and collaboration between the RCMP and the groups in question.

This type of response would signal to all stakeholders that the leader is taking the problem seriously. It describes aspirations without laying blame on those being led for falling short.

But how does this response build trust with stakeholders? It allows Lucki to show an understanding of the issues at hand while still pushing for the best interests of those she leads and the other key stakeholders. It also demonstrates that when she faces a difficult situation, she takes accountability rather than attempting to shift the blame.

In this chapter we will look at some of the significant trust challenges leaders face on a regular basis. The preceding RCMP story is a prime example of the challenges involved in satisfying multiple stakeholders—a challenge many corporate leaders share. Leaders must consider the needs and desires of those they lead and how to help them be most effective. At the same time, corporate leaders need to balance the needs and interests of shareholders or board members. Customers and interest groups now have greater access to information about companies than ever before. In the current climate, where social media exposés are a constant source of news (both real and fake), stories about sweatshops, harmful environmental practices, shady deals, or dubious alliances are far more likely to come out and impact perceptions, influence customer decisions, and foster possible action by activists.

Leaders also need to be aware of the political realities within which they are forced to operate. Most corporate leaders will never have to face problems while under such intense public and governmental scrutiny as that faced by Commissioner Lucki; however, they are very likely to have multiple stakeholders with differing goals, objectives, and priorities. In fact, most senior leaders have to balance the interests of investors and their boards of directors against those of the people they lead.

Navigating Stakeholder Interests

Most corporate leaders have similar sets of stakeholders, including investors, board members, employees, and customers. Executives face significant challenges navigating the varying interests of these stakeholder groups, even if and when they share the same opinions or objectives; unfortunately, most often they don't.

Some shareholders and investors focus only on strong and consistent financial returns. Other shareholders are as concerned, or even more concerned, about social and ethical issues. Board members will have differing perspectives on how the company is run, its priorities, and its short- and long-term prospects. Internal politics can often play a role in the positions taken and the decisions made.

Employees will have dramatically different goals and aspirations. Some will focus on their financial remuneration, as it is a critical element to their life outside of work. Others will be motivated by challenging work or the opportunity to solve complex problems. Still other employees may find that work provides meaning to their lives and is a significant part of their identity. Some have a desire to work their way up the corporate ladder, while others may be happy simply putting in their time and earning a paycheck.

When it comes to customers, some want leading-edge technology while others want things to stay consistent and comfortable. Some want the lowest possible price while others are more focused on durability or sustainable sourcing.

Clearly, there is complexity when trying to meet the diverse needs and interests of just these four sets of key stakeholders. Unfortunately, these are not the only stakeholders that leaders have to consider. Regulators, distributors, suppliers, and others may also have vested interests. While Brenda Lucki's stakeholders at the RCMP are likely different from yours, the issues remain the same. How does a leader become trusted enough to be allowed to lead effectively? As we will see later, the challenge of meeting the needs of various stakeholders can be made even more complex when we receive misleading signals.

For now, let's look at another complex set of stakeholders. The organization More in Common conducted a year-long project and published their findings in a report titled "Hidden Tribes: A Study of America's Polarized Landscape of America." This report demonstrates that Americans are more similar than they are different. Contrary to what polls and elections indicate, the project puts forward the concept that the polarization occurring within the United States is not creating a society equally split between two sets of beliefs. The report states, "Our research uncovered a different story, one that probes underneath the issues that polarize Americans, and finds seven groups that are defined by their core beliefs rather than by their political opinions, race, class or gender."[15] The seven groups identified in the report are:

- Progressive activists,
- Traditional liberals,
- Passive liberals,
- Politically disengaged,
- Moderates,
- Traditional conservatives, and
- Devoted conservatives.

The More in Common team researched a variety of topics to gauge the opinions of the various groups. More importantly, they measured the gaps between how the groups were perceived by others and their actual opinions.

One of the topics explored was that of political correctness. A 2018 article in the *Atlantic* framed this issue as a battle between the "woke" and the resentful The belief was that this was an argument between two camps relatively equal in size. Stereotypes suggested that the "resentful" were predominantly older white men, while the "woke" were a more diverse collection of women and minorities. The reality shown by the research is that the overwhelming majority (80 percent) of Americans think political correctness is a problem in that it has gone too far. Apparently, the only group in the study who felt strongly that it wasn't an issue were the political activists who account for 8 percent of the population. However, the "noise" this group made led many leaders to believe the decisions they were making were in response to the desires of a much larger percentage of the population.

Best-selling author John Ringo popularized the phrase "get woke, go broke" in a 2018 article published on a right-wing website.[16] He was referring to the fact that when companies publicly embrace political correctness, it can often result in loss of sales. The phrase seemed to gain traction, and supporting evidence could be found in some corporate decisions that led to significant financial losses. The notion was that organizations that "virtue signal"[17] too aggressively, from a marketing and communications perspective, ran the risk of losing customers or market share to their competitors. One of the examples often cited is Gillette's 2019 toxic masculinity advertisement.

In January 2019, Gillette posted an internet ad about toxic masculinity. In the advertisement, they portrayed several stereotypical male behaviors generally defined as toxic and offered suggestions as to how men *should* act. In part, the message was intended to align with the #MeToo movement.[18] While some people liked the ad, the overwhelming majority of respondents not only disliked it but found it offensive. It's not a stretch to see that men might not want to trust, or align themselves with, a brand that basically called them toxic. Unfortunately for Gillette, those who liked the ad were not their core customers. The company's virtue signaling insulted members of its primary target market, alienating them and making it easy for Gillette's competitors to attract them as new customers. This is, in fact, what happened; several months after the ad was released, Gillette took an $8 billion write-down on its revenues. The reason the company gave to the press was that men weren't shaving as much. However, those critical of Gillette's stance had a different narrative, suggesting that an underlying "boycott Gillette" movement was hurting the company.

This wasn't the first time that Gillette's customers had felt betrayed. The company had become notorious for continually changing their razors and systems. Users were incurring increasing costs to keep up with the new products and began to feel they were being taken advantage of by Gillette. It's possible the "boycott" was just the straw that broke the camel's back—the company had squeezed its niche market to a point where its customers felt enough was enough.

From a leadership perspective, on the one side we have Gillette's leadership team telling people, including their middle managers, that people are shaving less. Others, outside the company, were saying the drop in sales was due to a boycott. It is a classic case of people either adapting various narratives to fit the evidence or twisting the evidence to fit their narrative.

In the background, managers at all levels were almost certainly aware of the dissatisfaction over the regular introduction of new shaving systems, phasing out blades for older systems, and, as a result, the increased cost to consumers. Leaders within any company have to make decisions, but to which narrative do they give credence and whom do they trust: the executive management team, their customers, the media?

The relationship between companies and their customers is complex. New competitors, frustration over product development and costs, and emerging trends in facial hair preference all likely played a role in Gillette's collapse in sales. It would appear that whoever decided on the toxic masculinity advertisements also misread the situation. For some reason, they assumed that vilifying their primary customers was a good decision; of course, it wasn't. Provoking a negative emotional response from your customers is never a good move.

People often identify with the brands they use and feel that the decisions made by those organizations reflect on them. In the Gillette example, multiple stakeholders were involved. These included advocates and critics of the #MeToo movement, those indifferent to the dispute, and, of course, customers who could fall into any of those categories.

Still, the "get woke, go broke" meme is probably oversimplified. Some companies may rush to virtue signal because they think that's what "everyone" wants (and may miss the mark, as Gillette did); but, in fact, people in general tend to like and support organizations that have a higher purpose and that are making a positive impact in the world. This is true for customers and employees alike. The challenge for a leader is to identify that higher purpose and present it in a way that isn't inflammatory or offensive to those they are attempting to serve.

How do leaders deal with this level of complexity? How do they accommodate the concerns of all their various stakeholders? The answer is, they don't, nor should they. While it is important to understand and acknowledge the perspectives of all stakeholders, attempting to be all things to all people is one of the surest paths to disappointing everyone. When I was growing up in Fort St. John, there was only one radio station. I used to joke with friends that it played just enough rock 'n' roll and just enough country music to tick off everyone. Combined with farm reports and the responsibilities of a radio station in a northern town to act as a source of community information, their programming was haphazard at best. Leaders should avoid falling into this trap.

As a leader facing stakeholders with diverse and possibly conflicting interests, what do you do? The first step is to build sufficient trust with your various stakeholders so that they give you honest answers when you ask about their needs, goals, and aspirations. You can then use this knowledge to shape the direction your organization will take and ultimately to be transparent with stakeholders about the future. This approach gives anyone uncomfortable with the organization's direction permission to speak up or find a relationship that's a better fit for them. This is one of the few ways to truly have integrity and align your actions with the values you express. In the long run, everyone is better served.

Circling back to Gillette, if the company's message was that it wanted to support women and help bring an end to sexual harassment and assault, it could have approached this goal differently. First, the company could have held focus groups to get a sense of where their customers stood on the issue. Gillette would almost certainly have discovered that the overwhelming majority of their customers disapproved of sexual assault, harassment, and bullying. It would then have been possible to create a positive message about those who weren't engaged in such behaviors. The company could have easily created a positive ad campaign: one that focused on the aspirations of the vast majority of men to be good role models, celebrating a positive rather than negative message. This would have almost certainly received more generalized support; more importantly, it would have had a better chance of changing the objectionable behavior it was confronting. Shaming people seldom changes their perceptions or behavior.

Growing Cynicism Surrounding Leadership

Much like trust in institutions, trust and faith in leaders and their leadership abilities has been in marked decline. Whether it is in the leaders of organizations we do business with or in the leaders of organizations with which we are involved, reports indicate a general decline in levels of trust. While this is troubling, it is not entirely unexpected. As mentioned previously, uncertainty plays a significant role in our decisions to trust someone. We have seen a remarkable number of global issues create dramatic spikes in uncertainty recently. This, combined with the increasing pace of change, means that trust levels are going to be under strain for any leader who isn't actively promoting and maintaining trust.

The increasing complexity of the world, especially from the growth of social media, the Internet, converging technological advancements, and globalization, has made the job of leadership remarkably challenging. The average person's perception of what makes a good leader seems incredibly broad and usually includes some element of subject matter expertise.

However, given the fast pace of change, any technical expertise a leader possesses is often obsolete within months of their promotion to a leadership position. Even if leaders do remain experts in one field, it is virtually impossible for them to be experts in all the areas of specialization of those they lead. Therefore, the revelation is that technical expertise is likely not the best criterion to use when selecting a leader. Neither should it be part of our definition of excellence when we are characterizing a good leader.

The challenge is that there is no universal definition of "good leadership," let alone leadership excellence. In the absence of a clear set of criteria for what makes a good leader, there's been a remarkably wide range of opinions. We have seen priority given to a wide variety of traits, including verbal eloquence, energy and enthusiasm, experience, physical attractiveness, gender, race, or connection to the right groups.

To complicate matters, as the world evolves, our expectations of leaders seem to be getting broader and increasingly contradictory. Ultimately, we tend to trust those who have strong abilities and demonstrate excellence in their field. Are leaders supposed to give us decisive direction? Be consensus builders? Inspire us? The answer to all of these is yes, but how are they supposed to do that in environments where those judging leadership qualities appear to agree on so little? Also, our definition of leadership excellence changes with different situations. The challenge we have is that if we don't clearly define excellence for leaders, it is almost impossible for them to strive for it.

Trust in Politics

The dramatic decline of trust in leaders has been most notable in politics, where it seems that competent, capable, and caring leaders are the exception rather than the norm. In many countries people seem to vote strategically; that is, they vote against the worst possible option rather than for the best possible candidate (leader). This is reflected in the Edelman Trust Barometer's findings that only 10 percent of people surveyed thought that governments in general were competent.[19] When people review the selection of candidates for office, a common refrain is, "Is this the best they could come up with?" How can this be the best of us? Where have all the good leaders gone?

At some point, when so many political leaders seem like such poor options, the question that needs to be asked is, "Is it us?" Have we said or done something to make the job of political leadership so unappealing that only people who shouldn't have it actually want it? When I worked as a consultant for McKinsey & Company, we asked a number of senior business leaders if they would consider running for the office of prime minister of Canada. Overwhelmingly the response was, "Why would I take the pay cut, and why on earth would I put my family through that?" Here's a thought: perhaps we are getting exactly the leadership we deserve.

In the 2016 US federal election, it appeared that Donald Trump was elected president because of what he wasn't—a politician. When Joe Biden won the 2020 federal election, it was because of who he wasn't: Donald Trump. The key point is that we don't necessarily vote for the person we trust the most; we vote for the person we fear or distrust the least.

Political campaigns, and the politicians who endorse them, have become increasingly negative and aggressive. They use this tactic because it works. The average person on the street seems inclined to seek out, and believe, the absolute worst about the individuals who lead political parties with which they don't agree. Unfortunately, this systematic undermining of an opponent leads to people distrusting not only that specific politician but politicians in general. Social media has allowed, and perhaps even endorsed, negative campaigning, making it more widespread and increasingly effective. With recent conspiracy theories, and an apparent growing disdain for the truth or facts, vilification of others no longer needs to be based in reality.

In 2016 I wrote an article on trust and politics. I suggested that politicians should stop trying to convince us that their opponents are incompetent or evil, because they had already succeeded in convincing us that all politicians were morally bankrupt. Unfortunately, looking back, those were the good old days—things have only gotten worse.

Sadly, we no longer have a clear idea of what "good" looks like—the answer, regrettably, is open to interpretation. In a Pew Research poll on positive attitudes toward America, researchers found that positive perceptions of the United States have plummeted around the world over the last few years. There seems to be a strong correlation between President Trump's "America First" mindset and the decline of the country's global reputation, not to mention the level of trust world leaders (among others) have in the US administration. This has been exacerbated by the United States as it steps away from international collaboration, which has historically been a central tenet of its foreign policy.

Many examples of recent policies have affected the way foreign partners view their relationship with the United States, some of which seem counterproductive. Economists, for instance, seem fairly consistent in their opinion that it is US citizens who end up paying for the imposition of tariffs placed on goods entering the country. The US decision to withdraw troops from the Turkish border, resulting in a large number of Kurds being attacked and executed by Turkish forces, is another occasion where the result was a degradation of trust. This is especially true after the Kurds had assisted American attempts to deal with the terrorist organization ISIS. Again, on the global stage, the US decision to pull out of the Paris climate agreement, to stop funding the World Health Organization, and to push allies in NATO to increase funding created a great deal of cynicism and eroded trust.

America asked Canada to detain Huawei senior executive Meng Wanzhou and extradite her to the United States. Canada complied and, as I write this, is in the legal process of attempting to extradite Ms. Wanzhou. In turn, China retaliated by arresting and jailing two Canadians for espionage. The United States, however, did not step up and intervene in the dispute between Canada and China, despite playing a central role in causing the political tension. In fact, America placed additional tariffs on Canadian goods. During the COVID-19 pandemic, Canada ordered a significant number of respirator masks from 3M, a US-based company. President Trump intervened and forbade 3M from shipping masks outside the country, citing the need within the United States.

There is a clear pattern of behavior that runs contrary to America's past role as international consensus builder, policymaker, and peacekeeper. Instead, the country is focusing inward with its "America First" policy. Some within the United States call this excellent leadership and point to job gains in manufacturing. Others, including Barack Obama, express concerns about the long-term impacts and America's ability to continue to influence matters on the world stage. Of course, there is a counterbalance to every action. 3M, for instance, reached an agreement to manufacture some of their masks in Canada to avoid future interference from the US government. This resulted in jobs migrating out of the United States. The challenge is that what some people perceive as good leadership, others see as appalling.

It is often difficult to understand some of the decisions politicians make. In part, the growing cynicism we feel for political leaders stems from our concerns about whose best interests they are serving. It's all too easy to find compelling narratives about their bad intentions or nefarious motivations. Getting elected is costly, so concerns become heightened when voters see the amount of time, money, and support that is required and the many promises that have to be made to ensure it is forthcoming. Problems arise, however, when outsiders begin to question the cost of that financial support in terms of how it aligns with the interests of the politician, or politicians, in question and the constituents they serve.

This has led to a strong perception that the wealthy often enjoy a disproportionately strong voice when it comes to electing a government. In a 2014 article, Martin Gilens and Benjamin I. Page stated that the United States is more like an oligarchy than a democracy and that the policies favored by the wealthy elite and powerful interest groups are more likely to be enacted than those favored by ordinary citizens.[20] After the 2016 election, a number of rebuttals suggested the results were actually more balanced, with the wealthy and the middle class both getting policies they favored. However, the poor were profoundly underrepresented when it came to policies being enacted that they favored.

Interestingly, approximately 80 percent of the time, the elites and the general population are in agreement on what they would like to see happen.[21] What isn't accounted for in these studies is the impact the media has on convincing people of what it is they really want. The media, of course, is controlled by the elite and often plays a significant role in what information is shared and how it is framed.

Growing cynicism and declining levels of trust in politicians is a problem that profoundly affects us all. In the very act of stepping forward, those willing to lead us make themselves vulnerable. They do this in a setting where excellence is greatly underdefined. What does "good" look like for a politician? It is worth considering that our definitions of leadership are so outdated that they may no longer relate well to the demands of the positions that leaders occupy. Against increasingly complex and rapidly changing situations, the effectiveness of the traditional command-and-control approach to leadership seems to be decreasing. In this new environment, political leaders may no longer see the benefit of passing themselves off as experts. They will instead allow real experts to be heard and will publicly make decisions based on their opinions. This approach would involve far more consultation and inclusion.

Historically, the perception of political leaders was that they were public servants expected to act in the best interest of those they led. Somewhere along the way, that perception eroded and people began to believe that politicians' concerns for their own self-interest dramatically outweigh their concern for those they serve. The challenge politicians now face is to overcome the stereotypes and stigma that they themselves helped create. The results of the Edelman Trust Barometer suggest that politicians are generally perceived as corrupt, morally bankrupt, and incompetent. However, they are clearly not all as hopeless as people fear.

We have recently seen some political leaders undoubtedly putting the interest of the public ahead of their own self-interest. They have done this by stepping aside to let public health experts lead the way during the pandemic and by stepping out of the spotlight. The popularity of leaders in jurisdictions that handled the 2020–2021 pandemic reasonably well has improved significantly. You will recall from chapter 2 that most of those leaders stepped back and let medical experts lead the battle against the SARS-CoV-2 virus. As an example, John Horgan, the leader of the New Democratic Party (NDP) in British Columbia, Canada, in the early spring of 2020, led a minority government that was in a virtual tie in the polls with its main opposition, the Liberal Party. Mr. Horgan decided to call an election partway through the pandemic and was rewarded with a resounding majority. This was despite complaints about calling an election during a pandemic and the fact that this broke a signed agreement he had made with the Green Party. In large part, his popularity seemed tied to the handling of the pandemic. He had allowed Dr. Bonnie Henry, British Columbia's provincial health officer, to be the face of the response and to appear to be in charge of how the province acted. She did an incredible job, and voters appreciated their leader letting the most competent person lead the effort to control the pandemic.

While politicians are front and center when it comes to distrust from the public, they are not alone. Trust in leaders and institutions, including corporations and the media (including social media), has also been in decline. Amid such growing cynicism, is it even possible for leaders to differentiate themselves or prove they are trustworthy? Can leaders even be trusted when there is such a prevalence of mistrust? Can institutions and organizations turn it around?

Trust in Corporate Leaders

The challenges faced by leaders are more complex during times of uncertainty, where it becomes harder to provide the consistency that most people crave. Corporate leaders face many of the same challenges faced by political leaders. During periods of insecurity, leaders' day-to-day actions and decisions come under increased scrutiny by their management team, shareholders, and customers. Those being led often feel extremely vulnerable to those doing the leading. This can lead to a level of paranoia as they attempt to decode their leader's behavior, which has become increasingly true as we experience more turbulence and volatility in the workplace. In addition to this, people are increasingly unsure of what their alternatives might be if their current employment were to stop for some reason.

With the rapid pace and growing complexity of change we are currently experiencing, it becomes increasingly difficult for corporate leaders to predict the exact course their company will, or should, follow. As circumstances change, the company is oftentimes required to adjust and adapt. If a leader doesn't communicate well, the shifts and adjustments can look like indecisiveness or even hypocrisy. Too many changes left unexplained can leave the organization feeling directionless and apathetic. In environments like these, a command-and-control style is particularly counterproductive. Once again, we are left wondering what "good" really looks like for a leader. In chaotic and uncertain times, what does excellence really look like for those who lead?

Rest assured that while it is difficult to lead effectively, it's not impossible. I have had the good fortune to work with some exceptional leaders. I have seen very difficult situations get better and watched leaders build strong, trusting relationships with those they lead despite declining trust levels in other parts of the organization or in society in general. In part, they do this by being consistently transparent and fully aware of the importance of building trust. They have also worked hard to understand what trust is and how it works, and they've shared this knowledge with their teams.

I have also worked with leaders whose trust scores were initially low and then have witnessed the situation rapidly and dramatically improve despite high levels of uncertainty and extremely complex environments. Clearly, it is still possible for leaders to build trust even when it seems remarkably difficult to do so. In most cases, these leaders succeed as a result of coaching that provides them with an understanding of how trust works for them in their environment.

For example, I remember working with one particular leader to get a better understanding of the challenges she was facing relating to trust with her team. I coached her using my TU trust model so that she understood the concepts and had the opportunity to explore some of its strategies. Once she was familiar with it, we introduced the model to the entire team. This allowed everyone to share the same terminology and vocabulary; we got everyone on the same page. This allowed us to discuss the elements that lead to higher trust levels and discuss what steps the leader could take moving forward.

One of the benefits of the TU model, which we will discuss in detail later, is that it makes conversations about topics like trust much easier. In part, they're easier because we initially focus on building trust by reducing uncertainty. This approach makes it less personal and threatening, as opposed to bluntly saying something like, "Why don't you trust me?"

In this case, the leader was able to take some concrete, actionable steps that led to higher trust levels. From the team's perspective, they were now prepared and equipped to handle conversations relating to trust.

Uncertainty Abounds

We live in a world of growing uncertainty. It has become progressively more difficult to predict what people, groups, or even nations will do—what actions they will take. These parties are dealing with multiple factors that will influence their behavior, such as the rate of change in our environment, whether it is technical change, change of context, or shifts in beliefs and values.

As has been mentioned previously, uncertainty plays a central role in our decision to trust. Rarely have we seen such a spike in uncertainty as what occurred in 2020. While the pace of change seems to have been constantly increasing, several events combined to make the world feel even more precarious. The "normal" sources of uncertainty included technical advancements, new product development, cultural and value changes in society, generational changes in attitudes toward work, globalization, and access to information. On top of this, however, we witnessed situational spikes in uncertainty that included the COVID-19 pandemic, climate change issues, mounting tensions between police and minorities, and escalating tensions between nations.

In circumstances where change is one of the few constants, it becomes harder for people to just focus on the things at which they are already competent. Employees can't keep doing the same thing for years on end, becoming incredibly competent and efficient at a small group of tasks. Instead, everyone is faced with a need to constantly learn, adapt, and evolve. Unfortunately, we are rarely good at things the first few times we attempt them; there is a learning curve to almost everything, and as we learn we often make mistakes.

Changing Norms and Values

Significant differences in perceptions, values, and expectations exist between different generational groups. In part, this generational diversity stems from the different experiences people have while growing up. The expectations people have for the work they do and the nature of the social contract between employers and workers have also been evolving. For example, in career advancement, younger workers today have an expectation that they will advance and achieve positions of authority faster than previous generations. In corporate environments, we are seeing higher numbers of younger people earning seats at the boardroom table and holding positions of power. This is in stark contrast to previous generations that exhorted, "You have to pay your dues."

Over the last few decades, we have seen significant changes in perceptions of social issues such as same-sex marriage, interracial couples, gender roles, language, and the nature of work and its place in our lives. Clearly, not everyone has changed at the same pace or to the same degree. As a leader, you need to understand that these changes are occurring, that not everyone is on the same page, and that you may have to tailor your responses accordingly.

For example, in October 2020 Pope Francis came out in support of same-sex civil unions. It is unlikely that all Catholics will immediately follow his lead, but this does represent a significant change in the position of the church. As a leader, Pope Francis has signaled his intent and explained his reasoning. He stated that "homosexual people have a right to be in the family. They are children of God. They have a right to a family. Nobody should be thrown out of the family or made miserable over this. What we have to make is a law of civil coexistence, for they have the right to be legally covered. I stood up for that."[22]

There will, no doubt, be other religious leaders who do not agree with Pope Francis and will continue to assert that homosexuality is a mortal sin. How do you build trust with people who hold this belief if you have gay people on your team, in your organization, or as clients? How do you build trust with those who are gay if you condone their persecution and mistreatment? Similarly, those with strong religious beliefs can feel as though they are the ones being persecuted if they are dismissed or chastised for expressing their beliefs. These are difficult waters to navigate and often require compromise and honest conversations.

My good friend Tony Simons is, in my opinion, one of the world's leading experts on the topic of integrity. He has written numerous articles and a book on behavioral integrity. For Tony, the definition of integrity is "following through on promises, and having your actions align with the values you express."[23] Integrity is one of the dimensions that we use to assess trustworthiness. This means that if you extol certain values, you need to make sure your actions line up with them if you expect to build trust with those you lead. Whether those values are around tolerance and acceptance or aligned with more traditional faith-based beliefs, your actions need to be consistent.

Stereotypes are often thrown around about the differing values of generational groups. Comparisons are made between baby boomers, Gen Xers, and millennials. Many of those differences may be attributable to their current stage of life and circumstances. I know that my priorities and beliefs are very different from what they were thirty years ago. For instance, my expectations have changed with regard to the time it takes to complete everyday activities. Using a microwave means I don't have to wait for hours for something to defrost or for the oven to heat up to cook certain foods. My patience is stretched if I have to wait for more than thirty seconds for a website to load. I expect to access information almost instantaneously (even if it might not always be accurate). The reality is that different demographic groups are bound to have different concerns and priorities. It is important to engage with them to fully understand their perspective and provide a consistent response so they know what to expect.

Change and Uncertainty

Tess is a manager in her midthirties at a tech company that has offices in forty different countries. She has worked in the industry for a decade. Her team focuses on developing learning software for large companies so they can deliver training programs to their employees on a wide range of topics. Tess was previously a team member but has recently moved into a management role. She misses the days when she only had to coordinate with her boss and a couple of teammates. Now she has to connect with an entire team consisting of twelve direct reports across multiple time zones, geographic locations, cultures, and demographics. The logistics alone are daunting.

Even when times are good, Tess has to consistently remind herself about stereotypes and the impact they could have on interpersonal interactions. Someone once told Tess that people interpret the world through stories. She sees this regularly when people make assumptions that others are lazy, rigid, unemotional, detached, mean, self-centered, disorganized, and more, based purely on their country of origin, and the stories that people have in their heads about others from various countries.

She recognizes that these "stories" have the potential to affect her as a leader and the manner in which she evaluates those she leads. They can also affect the interactions between members of her team and their perspectives of her. She even finds that the stories have the potential to creep in to how team members respond to clients and to their relationship with other parts of the organization.

Tess is also aware that being a woman in a position of authority comes with its own challenges and benefits and that these differ depending on with whom she interacts. Similarly, she recognizes that her age and experience level lead to different responses from different groups and cultures. Each time, she feels it's like a piece of a puzzle that has to be solved because her approaches and responses seem to land differently depending on the person. The learning curve of taking on managerial responsibilities has definitely been steep.

The pandemic of 2020 changed all the rules for Tess. No one knew how long it would last, what was safe, and what wasn't, and there was little guidance on how to handle it in the early days or how to try to get back to normal—or at least a new normal.

Tess didn't know how to reassure her team because she didn't know how long the pandemic would last or which changes would be permanent. Worst of all, Tess didn't know how stable her own job was or how stable her team would be moving forward. Prior to the pandemic, things had already been hectic due to the extreme speed at which technology was changing, but once COVID-19 hit, poor Tess felt as if they were all on a treadmill, constantly running but never really catching up or getting ahead. There were frequent and significant changes to their products, not to mention endless new content, all of which required new training programs. Tess was, however, happy and relieved that the company managed to avoid the seemingly obligatory reorganization happening in so many other companies, with its accompanying changes in leadership, objectives, and new personality types that she would have had to manage.

In situations like the one Tess faced, leaders can easily see the trust levels of those they lead slip into decline. Levels can decline for the organization in general and for a leader in particular. It is difficult to manage the feeling of uncertainty experienced by those you lead when you are struggling with uncertainty yourself. How can you tell people what will happen when you yourself don't know?

Tess's situation may appear particularly challenging, but given the current pace of change, such scenarios may not be all that unusual in the very near future. On a positive note, steps can be taken to build trust in settings like these, and we will explore them more fully in chapter 5 as we walk through the TU model.

Virtual Teams

Globalization and technical advancements have, in recent years, led to an increasing use of virtual teams. The COVID-19 pandemic, however, dramatically accelerated the work-from-home (WFH) trend. A number of issues follow on the heels of this trend. Working together in an office allow us to connect physically and to enjoy a shared experience; we understand what others are going through because we're going through it together. Working virtually creates a remarkable amount of uncertainty for all involved. WFH means balancing family and work in a way we've never had to do before. We may find ourselves working between interruptions and at odd hours. We may have to take multitasking to a whole new level, finding creative ways to meet the needs of our children and our bosses simultaneously. For leaders, there is the profound challenge of not being able to readily observe their team's work and provide feedback in real time. In this case communication levels need to be significantly enhanced.

Technological options are available for monitoring the behavior of others, but few organizations are set up to do that, nor does it seem like a good idea if building trust is the goal. An added challenge is that we can see what people are doing but not the context that drives some of their behaviors. Monitoring and micromanaging is bad for morale and becomes increasingly ineffective in environments where change happens quickly and there is a need to react quickly to new situations. These are all part of the strain that Tess experienced in her situation.

The Pace of Change

Leaders often react to complex environments by making frequent course corrections. The challenge for companies is that people lower in the hierarchy see this as indecisive behavior or pursuit of the "flavor of the month." This is usually because the information used to make the decisions often doesn't get communicated to these lower levels. However, this can lead to incredible change fatigue throughout the organization, resulting in people failing to respond positively to requests for change. The mindset becomes something like this: "You asked me to go left, I went left. You asked me to go right, I went right. You went back and forth several times. I'm done moving, so I'll wait here for a while and see if you come back in a month or two." Every time we ask people to go in a new direction, they have to learn new things and risk moving out of their comfort zone. They become less specialized and experienced as they learn new skills. It's uncomfortable and feels risky. In low-trust environments, responsiveness to change stops far more quickly than in high-trust ones.

A senior executive once described to me the feeling of trying to navigate change: "It feels like the senior team is in a high-end sports car and everyone else is in a trailer being towed behind. Except we've got a faulty hitch so if we accelerate too fast, or take a corner too hard, we lose them all and have to go back and start over." Change is now happening at a remarkable pace, and companies that fail to adapt become extinct very quickly.

In chapter 4 we'll take a deeper look at some of the ways that higher trust levels make a difference, along with the benefits that can be obtained when leaders get this trust thing right.

The Trust Challenge Leaders Face: Key Points Review

- Trust is particularly critical in today's rapidly changing, highly uncertain environment.

- Leaders have to balance the interests and earn the trust of multiple stakeholder populations. For corporate leaders, this includes investors, boards of directors, customers, and employees.

- Going too far to try to earn the trust of one set of stakeholders may compromise a leader's ability to earn the trust of other sets of stakeholders, each of which has its own values, biases, perceptions, and expectations.

- Much like trust in institutions, trust and faith in leaders and their leadership abilities has been in marked decline—particularly in politics, where competent, capable, and caring leaders are the exception rather than the norm.

- There is no universal definition of "good leadership," let alone leadership excellence. As the world evolves, our expectations of leaders seem to be getting broader and increasingly contradictory.

- Spikes in uncertainty in the 2020s, combined with an increasing pace of change, mean trust levels are going to be under strain for leaders who aren't actively promoting and maintaining trust.

CHAPTER 4

The Benefits of Trust

MOST PEOPLE, ESPECIALLY LEADERS, AGREE THAT TRUST IS A POSITIVE attribute. If the leader of a company or organization trusts his or her team, and if that trust is reciprocated, then productivity and success is likely to be greater than if that were not the case. If politicians gain the trust of the people, they attract more votes; if they demonstrate high levels of integrity when working with their party colleagues and the opposition, they garner more support and things get done. Community leaders, and groups in general, are more effective when they operate in a high-trust environment and deal with situations and challenges in an equitable manner.

Over the years, I have asked my students to interview leaders to get a sense of whether they think trust is important and what they do to build it. As one might expect, when interviewed, leaders will universally say that trust is either "very important" or *the* most important value needed for effective leadership. Pressed further to explain how trust can be built, those interviewed suggest a wide variety of strategies, many of which are consistent with the TU model outlined in this book. What is missing from these conversations, and from most articles and books on trust, is a more detailed description of how trust actually adds value. A valid question we might ask these leaders, therefore, is, "Trust is obviously important, but why? And, more to the point, what occurs in a trusting environment (that doesn't happen in a lower trust environment) that actually makes a difference? Specifically, what benefits can leaders expect to obtain if they successfully build more trusting environments?"

In this chapter, we'll examine situations in which higher levels of trust led to better results. For instance, in high-trust environments, changes such as new people joining the team or the introduction of new systems are met with curiosity and excitement rather than fear. Opportunities are welcomed because they offer the possibility of experiencing new things and the potential to learn and grow. In low-trust environments these same circumstances are met with suspicion, outright dread, or at best skepticism.

First, we'll examine how trust helps people become better leaders. Second, we'll explore how trust plays a part in negotiations between multiple parties by promoting dialogue, which in turn leads to better agreements. A third level of analysis will examine the role that trust plays in helping groups become successful through improved innovation, creativity, and competitive advantage. Finally, we will look at how the benefit of the doubt is present in high-trust environments and absent in low-trust environments and how that affects outcomes.

Why do successful and effective leaders consider the topic of trust so important? The answer is that to be successful, leaders have to get other people to act in a coordinated manner. This is no easy feat because they often have to encourage and convince people to invest time and energy in tasks that might not have an immediate payoff. In some cases, team members have to work with other people and teams to combine their talents to create something new. What's more, these "followers" do not usually have access to the big picture, the overall strategic direction, the challenges they might have to face, or information about the competition they might meet along the way. Clearly, a team has to have a great deal of trust and faith in its leadership in order to move forward in the face of all this uncertainty.

When we talk about the benefits of trust, the organizations that truly thrive are those where people don't just do what's required of them but rather go above and beyond. In complex environments, they strive to do what is best for their cohort, often investing personal time and other resources to make the group more effective. Doing this makes individuals vulnerable to the organization; they are making an investment against an uncertain, and sometimes unknown, future payoff. Often the financial reward is only part of the overall compensation. In high-trust environments, people also get a sense of belonging, an improved sense of self-worth, friendship, and social interaction. Being a member of an organization that is the right fit is worth far more than just financial remuneration. When people work in an environment where they consider the work they are doing meaningful, they are less likely to be enticed away to higher-paying jobs elsewhere.

The Effective Leader

There are many points of view about, and definitions of, leadership. The one I prefer comes from a *Forbes* magazine article titled "What Is Leadership?" in which Kevin Kruse writes, "Leadership is a process of social influence, which maximizes the efforts of others towards the achievement of a goal."[24] He goes on to state that "leadership stems from social influence, not authority or power. Leadership requires others, and that implies they don't need to be 'direct reports.'" This definition is a departure from the traditional command-and-control perspective of leadership that focuses on allocation of resources, setting of strategies, and creation of vision. The definition in Kruse's article strikes a more collaborative tone, indicating a shared undertaking rather than a series of directives.

The statement that leadership requires others resonates with me. The more senior our role in an organization, the less direct control we have over outcomes and the more dependent we are on those whom we lead. Leaders are not the ones hammering nails, dealing with customers, or engaging in a host of other frontline activities. They have to rely on the work and actions of others to achieve their goals and aspirations.

As an organization grows and evolves, its leaders' people skills become increasingly important and relevant, more so than their technical skills. The difference between average leaders and exceptional leaders lies in the latter's superior ability to build strong relationships. Leaders who can consistently bring all parties on side, in a common belief in their cause and direction, will consistently outperform less-skilled leaders.

Many variables can explain the success of an organization. One is the level of voluntary commitment those involved have toward the company—that is, their commitment to carry out tasks that go beyond their job description or any contractual obligation. This is called *organizational citizenship behavior* and refers to people stepping up and going beyond the basic expectations of the job. Not surprisingly, such behavior is far more prevalent in high-trust environments.

As mentioned earlier, leaders are often the only ones with an overview of the whole picture; those they lead are usually unaware of the complex interchanges that have taken place prior to their involvement. The individuals being led also have limited exposure to the information that went into, or is currently going into, the decision-making process. They have to trust their leaders enough to believe in the end goal. And they have to have enough faith to actively and enthusiastically work with people with whom they might not normally collaborate.

For example, dreaming up the initial concept for a new product requires creativity and innovation. Engineers and other product specialists then create a prototype to demonstrate its validity. Other skilled professionals are then required to build a manufacturing process that can mass-produce the product in a cost-effective way. Creative types are required to market the product and to be involved with the design to ensure that people will actually want to purchase it. Salespeople are needed to convince distributors, shopkeepers, and consumers to purchase the product. At the same time, in the background, someone needs to convince investors that the product is viable and will sell so that money can be generated to cover production costs.

In this example, a staggering array of skills, expertise, and personality types are required to ensure success. A leader needs to manage personalities, egos, opinions, and more if they are to get everyone working together as a team. At its core, effective leadership is about getting people to do the right thing at the right time—repeatedly. No one can completely predict every situation a project may run into or give guidance in advance for every decision a member of their team may be forced to make. Truly effective organizations are filled with people who are engaged and dedicated. People usually don't get that way on their own—they follow a leader they trust and in whom they have a great deal of faith.

Learning through Failure

In 1992, Sim B. Sitkin wrote an article titled "Learning Through Failure: The Strategy of Small Losses."[25] His notion was that if people push to the limits of their abilities, they will, in the process, make mistakes. If they aren't making mistakes, then they are being too passive and cautious. Any group or organization will be more effective if everyone involved is putting in their best effort. In low-trust environments, where people are fearful of making mistakes, they move slowly, especially early in a project, checking and rechecking their work. They ask others to review their work and endlessly seek feedback from superiors and colleagues. In this type of environment people fear missteps, their pace is tentative, they hesitate to make decisions, or they wait for explicit instructions rather than use initiative. Success requires risk-taking—which requires trust—as we'll see in the model in chapter 5.

Many senior leaders in organizations admit that they worry that one mistake on their part will mean severe consequences, even their termination. A leader in such an environment obviously feels vulnerable. This can lead to extreme attempts to reduce the level of uncertainty through micromanaging, constantly checking for confirmation, and exhibiting behavior that can appear obsessive-compulsive. This promotes a feeling of lack of trust in subordinates, which demotivates the entire team. These actions can create bottlenecks of remarkable proportions, which then cascade throughout the multiple departments of an organization.

Everyone makes mistakes; trying to prevent them is like trying to turn back the tide. Obviously, strategies should always be put in place to catch and reduce errors, especially serious or even potentially deadly ones (e.g., in hospital operating rooms), but rarely does a mistake made during day-to-day business prove fatal (literally or figuratively). Mistakes are a critical way of learning; they provide lessons with an edge. It's important to recognize that whenever we engage in a new skill or activity, we are bound to make mistakes. Skill and capacity improve with experience and through a balance of early successes and failures. At the beginning, that balance is weighted toward mistakes (minor "failures"), but it soon rectifies itself.

In a team setting, it's important to acknowledge mistakes, discuss what went wrong, and plan for a better result next time. Leaders need to trust the process and encourage those they lead to learn and grow. If we, as leaders, want to grow organizations that can adapt and be innovative, then we need to create environments where people are comfortable making themselves vulnerable, trying new things, and yes, possibly, making mistakes. It's hard and scary work, and unfortunately as the stakes get higher and tensions rise, it's too easy to revert to old habits such as micromanaging, fearing everything new, and punishing mistakes.

Trust Promotes Dialogue

"The intention of dialogue is to reach new understanding and, in doing so, to form a totally new basis from which to think and act."
William Isaacs, *Dialogue: The Art of Thinking Together*

It has become clear over the past several years that expressing your opinion comes with increasing levels of risk. We make ourselves vulnerable when we disagree with others or state our opinions in ways that are not widely accepted. Some people who have expressed contentious opinions have been vilified, attacked, or even "canceled" for their beliefs on social media. This is true on both sides of a wide range of issues. In fact, the polarization and fragmentation of many societies, especially in recent years, has made speaking up a hazardous activity.

The threat of being denigrated or disavowed for saying the wrong thing, or even saying the right thing in the wrong way, has made people increasingly cautious about expressing their opinions. They no longer know which individuals, or what organizations, they can trust. The problem faced by society, businesses, organizations, and leaders is that just because people are no longer expressing their opinions doesn't mean these views no longer exist. It simply means people have become more guarded about sharing them. This applies not only to hot-button issues such as politics but also to disagreements about workplace decisions.

The result is that it is difficult to have open and honest conversations or dialogue about issues where people have differing opinions. But without dialogue, greater understanding can't be fostered and minds can't be changed; positions become entrenched and heavily defended. Rather than seeking to understand the other side, people instead seek confirming evidence and look for allies to support their existing beliefs.

In higher-trust environments, differences of opinion are met with inquisitiveness and questions. Dialogue often ensues where people can express concerns and there is potential for all parties to learn something. In these settings, concerns can be addressed and minds can be changed. When people feel less vulnerable, they can tolerate greater levels of uncertainty, such as when they encounter new experiences or have conflicting opinions.

In low-trust environments this doesn't happen; people vilify the "other" and seek reassurance and support for their position from other like-minded individuals. In this case, divisions grow and positions become entrenched.

Leaders must not allow opinions to go underground. They need to foster open dialogue and conversation so that those they lead can work together toward a common goal. It isn't enough for people to pretend there aren't different opinions or goals; there actually needs to be alignment of purpose.

When things aren't going well, we would prefer that people tell us what's wrong so that we can decide whether we want to fix the situation. This doesn't mean we will always make changes to please everyone; we can't be all things to all people. Getting them to give us feedback, however, at least allows us to choose.

In 1970, Albert O. Hirschman wrote the book *Exit, Voice, and Loyalty: Responses to Decline in Firms, Organizations, and States.*[26] The main premise is to contrast the options people have when situations begin to deteriorate. Hirschman explores the contrasting perspectives of economists and political scientists to this problem. He reported that economists believe that people will simply exit the relationship, such as leave their job when they dislike their employer or shop elsewhere if they receive poor service in a store, whereas political scientists believe people will make use of their voice to push for change by providing feedback.

Hirschman's premise applies across a broad spectrum of situations. For instance, people can act in a similar way in personal relationships. When things begin to go wrong, they can either leave or explore options to try and make things better. The challenge we have when people choose to exit a relationship is that oftentimes we don't know why they left (at least, we cannot be sure about the reason and can only speculate). In this case, feedback would be extremely useful; there is immense value in being able to identify the issues that resulted in a person exiting a relationship. Armed with sufficient information, decisions can be made whether change is necessary or desirable. Organizations can never be all things to all people, but there is immense value in understanding the desires of those with whom you are in a relationship, whether that is personal or business.

Higher-trust environments encourage the use of voice because people are not afraid of being punished for expressing a differing opinion. In fact, they believe they can make a difference by speaking up. Trust promotes the use of voice; research on procedural justice shows that being heard promotes perceptions of fairness.[27] This is one of the virtuous cycles we see in higher-trust environments, where trust leads to behaviors that promote higher levels of trust.

The Power of Dialogue to Effect Change

As mentioned earlier, the death of George Floyd, an African American man, at the hands of a police officer in Minneapolis in 2020 led to worldwide protests. This act, and the profound frustration felt by many people in its wake, represented another catalyst for change in the relationship between police and those they serve. The ensuing protests raised awareness of the ongoing disconnect between the police and those they serve. It prompted support from a broad spectrum of public figures. There were symbolic acts, including toppling statues of leaders and military figures connected to the Confederacy. Other statues of individuals connected to slavery and racism were also damaged. Gestures included changing the names of sports teams and athletes "taking the knee" during the playing of the American national anthem. However, in terms of actually changing the day-to-day lives of those affected, it's unclear if any of this had a positive effect. There were calls to defund, or even abolish, police departments, with some people believing that the police were the root cause of these societal problems.

The challenge is that without some form of dialogue between the parties involved (e.g., police unions and management, civilian oversight boards, local officials, and representatives of various civilian populations), it is difficult to isolate the fundamental issues and build trust. Blanket calls to defund or abolish police departments create uncertainty, discomfort, and fear among a segment of the population who find police presence comforting. Without dialogue, no one knows what the trade-offs (e.g., between fewer police or less police funding and the potential for increased crime or antisocial behavior) might be and how that will affect all sides of the debate and the communities in question. Without discourse, those involved will fail to understand why they are seeing resistance from others or how to overcome the fear that exists behind their reticence. This uncertainty and vulnerability breed distrust.

Lasting change occurs only when there is a strong consensus among members of a group. This is not to say that everyone has to agree, but a strong majority must be in alignment for things to change and for that change to be sustainable. It is possible to force change in the short term by strong-arming those who disagree and those who are more moderate in their beliefs. However, this inevitably leads to resistance, resentment, and a backlash from those coerced into complying. Those being pressured often learn that their best course of action is to regroup, gather enough support, and fight fire with fire by using force to change things back to the way they were or to ensure that the change they were "bullied" into fails.

If we continue with the police example, we see one side pushing for defunding, or abolishing, police departments. Their perception appears to be that the police are acting in the best interests of a select few rather than all citizens. The calls for dramatic change stem from perceptions of persecution and abuse. These activists view the police as part of a system that has disproportionately focused on suppressing minority communities.

On the other side, those opposed to reductions in either the funding for police departments or the number of officers are expressing concerns about the possible escalation of crime and gun violence. This group is concerned that the only members of society benefiting from any reduction in police spending will be the criminal element.

The police themselves likely offer a third perspective. Their view is that the number of officers, the training and equipment they receive, and the funding they get combine to make them and those they serve safer.

It is unlikely that the majority of citizens will feel comfortable with dramatic cuts in police funding unless their concerns are addressed. A more acceptable conversation may be to frame policing as a reactive approach to problems that are caused, at least in part, by the current system. It may be easier to sell a proposal that calls for a gradual transition toward more preventative approaches to dealing with crime. The funding for such approaches doesn't necessarily need to come at the cost of police budgets.

For example, the United States spent over $778 billion on the military in 2020.[28] That is more than the next eight highest-spending countries *combined*. It may be worth considering that if federal funding for defense was reduced, more funds could be made available to cities for proactive crime-reduction programs.

Resistance to change seldom comes from animosity toward others; it's usually fear-based. People fear change because they feel vulnerable. Few people have so much that they aren't nervous about losing some portion of it. Therefore, if our goal is to bring about change, we are more likely to be successful if we first build trust with those who are most threatened.

The very idea of change can promote uncertainty; that uncertainty becomes more pronounced when people cannot envision what change will look like (to them) and its implications. This is where trust, once again, helps to foster conversations that allow a group to move forward collectively. Those in favor of change should be given free rein to explain why the current situation is lacking so that joint problem-solving can begin. All members of a group need to feel comfortable and safe expressing their opinions and have their concerns acknowledged.

Misunderstanding, conflict, and evil thrive in darkness. Honest and frank conversation has the potential to bring light. However, that can happen only when trust is present.

Sustainable Agreements

In negotiating an agreement, people often consider the history between the parties, the present situation, and the immediate future. What they frequently fail to consider are the long-term implications of an agreement negotiated with only the short term in mind. A ripple effect is inherent in all wins, and winning big in the short term can lead to resentment in the long term. That bad feeling can lead to hostility and a desire to get even during the next round of negotiations. In fact, being dominant has the potential to destroy a long-term relationship.

It is human nature to think short term, and this is exacerbated by the systems within which we often have to work. As humans we do many things that give us short-term pleasure and long-term pain, such as smoking, drinking excessively, eating too much—the list is long. This is especially true when there is a time lag between our actions and any consequences. At school and at work we are evaluated on short-term performance criteria. This creates a sense of urgency to focus on symptoms rather than underlying problems. In negotiations, there is a tendency to ignore long-term implications and the impact of the negotiation process and its outcome on the relationship in favor of short-term gain. Unfortunately, this desire for an immediate payoff negates the opportunity to invest now for a better payoff down the road. Working against long-term thinking, however, is the fact that a long-term perspective requires us to trust the other party. Basically, we make ourselves vulnerable in the short term and invest time, energy, and resources in the hope that all parties will be better off over time.

Consider a labor agreement negotiation. Both parties (management and labor reps/unions) are trying to advocate for the interests of those they represent while at the same time managing their relationship with the opposing side. This is complex, especially when they all have to factor in the needs and well-being of the organization that employs them. There is a lot to consider and a lot that can go wrong.

The following scenarios are illustrative composites based on situations I've witnessed in companies that have brought me in to consult on trust issues.

Scenario One

The management team at a large corporation got most of what it wanted from negotiations with an employee labor union. An objective party would definitely say management came out on top. Over the following few quarters, the corporation enjoyed slightly higher profits than they had in the past and the executive team was praised by the board of directors and shareholders.

On the other side, the negotiators for the union came under closer scrutiny and in some cases were criticized. In any case, the union was embarrassed and felt they "lost." The employees the union represented in the negotiation were frustrated and angry at receiving what they felt was a less-than-fair result. Morale began to erode, employee engagement began to fall, and productivity faltered. When the time came to renegotiate the deal, this negative attitude and feeling of "losing" dominated the thinking and attitude of the union as the union negotiators strategized and planned for what they now thought of as a rematch. The previous negotiation team was replaced with tougher and more militant negotiators. Proposals and assertions from the corporation's management were met with skepticism and disbelief. From the unions and their members' perspective, there was an overwhelming desire to make up for what they felt they had lost in the previous negotiation, even if it required extreme action such as stoppages or an all-out strike that could ruin the reputation of the company in the eyes of the public.

Scenario Two

In the second scenario, the short-term outcome was the opposite of the first, with the union negotiators scoring a big win over management and getting almost everything they had on their wish list. Unfortunately, this overextended the company's resources to the point it couldn't pursue new alternatives or opportunities. The company stagnated. A short while later, realizing they couldn't afford everything they had promised the union, management began to reduce the size of the workforce by attrition. As people left or retired, they were simply not replaced, increasing the workload for those who remained. In an attempt to manage labor costs while managing workload, the company began to hire part-time and contract workers. As time went by, the company had to consider closing shop as they could no longer afford the commitments made in the agreement.

In both scenarios, the "winners" enjoyed short-term success but ran the risk of negatively impacting their organizations. Once again, we see the potential for short-term gain leading to long-term pain, much like our discussion around climate change in chapter 2.

In labor negotiations, those involved need to consider the perspectives of all parties and what's best for the organization as a whole. When management always has the upper hand, the result is low morale, a toxic culture, and low employee engagement, all of which are costly to an organization. If labor is constantly in the driver's seat, the financial impact on a company can have long-term consequences for the future of the business and union members' jobs. It doesn't take a rocket scientist to recognize that when both parties pull together, optimal results occur. If only it were that easy.

Distributive versus Integrative Bargaining

In distributive bargaining, parties attempt to reach an agreement regarding how to share what is currently available—how best to split a finite pie. Any gains for one party come at the expense of the other party, as we saw in the preceding scenarios. Integrative bargaining, by contrast (as described in one of the best-selling and most influential books on negotiation ever published, *Getting to Yes*[29]), focuses more on the needs of the parties involved in an attempt to find collaborative solutions that can expand what is available—to grow the pie. Integrative bargaining, however, can be successful only in a high-trust environment.

For integrative bargaining to work, parties need to share information, make themselves vulnerable, and trust one another to negotiate with integrity. They also have to believe that the information being shared is complete and accurate.

The potential for a satisfactory solution is highly dependent on the time frame in question. Relationships that exist over an extended period highlight the different needs of each party at various times. More value can be created by being able to foster a relationship that has a degree of give and take. That is, the parties agree to let one of them benefit first on the understanding that the generosity will be reciprocated at a later date, when needs change. In this scenario, very high levels of trust are required.

The problem is that labor agreements usually take place at a set point in time and make broad assumptions about the future. How, then, does either party predict how its situation, or indeed the world, might change in the months and years ahead? Significant changes could leave either party feeling as if they got a poor, or less than fair, deal.

Case Study

A sporting goods company, which I'll call GoodSport, has historically managed to earn modest profits in a highly competitive market. One of its main competitors suddenly faces a significant legal issue and is forced into bankruptcy. Over the next year, GoodSport's sales boom as the company faces record demand for its products and as a result sees a massive hike in its profits.

At the height of its newfound success, GoodSport's existing labor agreement expires and management begins to negotiate a new contract. Everyone is on a high and the company identifies a need for increased production capacity to meet the new levels of demand. It increases its workforce and commits to investing capital in new machinery. Wanting to ensure good relations with employees, management agrees to generous terms during contract negotiations with the union. The new normal has been embraced by all parties.

The company now faces significant additional financial commitments based on its new reality. However, it may have given up a lot of flexibility and made itself vulnerable to changes in the marketplace. For instance, it is entirely possible that a new player could enter the marketplace by purchasing the production capacity of the now bankrupt former competitor. It is also possible that one of GoodSport's current competitors could increase capacity more effectively than GoodSport can, either through new investments or by purchasing the production capacity of the bankrupt competitor. In either case, the market supply could change dramatically. There is also the potential for changes in demand. As the reduction in supply caused by the bankruptcy results in longer wait times and potential increases in prices, consumers may begin to look for alternatives. Consumers may also consider adopting new leisure activities that don't require the purchase of products from GoodSport. Then there is always the potential for external forces such as a major economic downturn, a pandemic, or both to play their part.

If supply and demand radically change, there could be a major impact on the company, especially if it has overextended itself. The big question is, does the company have a strong enough relationship with labor to adjust and adapt if things radically change? Will labor believe management when they are told that the world has changed and management can no longer meet the commitments it made to labor? How flexible will labor be?

It's worth noting that losing in a negotiation doesn't always breed goodwill from the other side. It's why simply giving people stuff doesn't always build trust; it can instead breed dependence and contempt. If things start to go bad for the other party, the response may well be that they haven't done a very good job of managing things and that labor merely got what it deserved.

Now let's look at what the situation could have looked like if the timing had been different. The time is one year prior to the competitor going bankrupt. GoodSport is still puttering along making a small profit, gradually growing its business in a tough marketplace. The labor agreement renegotiation is handled very differently. Management is far more cautious with its plans and tougher in its negotiations, based on the economic health of the company. An agreement is reached that includes modest wage increases and very few additional benefits.

During the term of the agreement, the competitor goes bankrupt, and within a short period GoodSport begins to post record profits. In this case, the lead negotiators for the labor union face serious questions from the rank-and-file about why the agreement wasn't more flexible or built to anticipate the firm's good fortune. The question in this case is whether the relationship between labor and management is strong enough for senior management to show flexibility and reward employees based on the company's newfound success. The company could award bonuses and reduce the amount paid to shareholders, but they would have to be careful distributing any windfall. One company I know awarded flat dollar amount bonuses across the board rather than making the bonuses a percentage of salary. This upset senior, higher-paid workers who felt they deserved more.

Lasting agreements need to have built-in flexibility—no one can predict the future. There is no agreement, however good, that will completely prevent the other side from being difficult if they feel they've been treated unfairly. Success depends on a shared understanding of the importance of the relationship and a realization that all parties need to be successful for things to work long term. This requires a level of transparency and trust that allows everyone to believe that the other parties to the agreement will act in the best interests of one another and their organizations.

Trust Promotes Innovation, Creativity, and Competitive Advantage

The rapid pace of change we're experiencing today has led many companies to understand that if they don't continuously innovate, they will be eliminated by their competitors. Some companies have realized that innovation tends to happen more often when there are higher trust levels. If we think about it, innovation almost never occurs without some level of experimentation and risk-taking—and making mistakes along the way. As mentioned earlier in this chapter, in low-trust environments, people are afraid to make mistakes and hence will be afraid to innovate.

In higher-trust environments, people are more willing to share ideas and work collaboratively on projects, bringing a diverse set of skills and perspectives to bear. These types of environments facilitate the creative process and lead to more ideas. Leaders in these settings believe in their team's ability to manage itself, and leaders allow teams the autonomy to structure the approach it takes to getting work done. On the flip side, innovation can be a challenge when people feel they can't trust others not to steal or hijack their ideas or intellectual property.

This is a pattern that plays itself out over and over again in organizations and even within academia, where one of the primary goals is fundamental research, not profit. The winner-take-all systems that exist strongly discourage collaboration despite the fact that this is often the fastest and most effective way to make progress. The problem lies in the fact that ideas are the coin of the realm in academia and research centers—the rewards go to those with the best results.

People are not often willing to share stories about the blind alleys they've wandered down that could prevent others from making the same mistake, nor are they keen to share the lessons learned from failure. Research journals almost never publish an academic article unless the findings are significant and in agreement with what was initially predicted. This attitude incentivizes people to behave in ways that are motivated by self-interest, even survival, rather than for the collective good.

As the stakes rise, trust becomes more difficult and we see increasingly inappropriate behavior, including theft of intellectual property, falsification of data, or even outright fabrication. This, in part, has led to what has been termed by some as a crisis of failed replication; that is, studies that have reported allegedly significant findings that can't be successfully repeated by other scientists. One notable example of this is the work on power poses by Dana Carney and Amy Cuddy. Cuddy, in a 2012 TED talk, claimed that holding a power pose for two minutes would make you more successful in such things as negotiations and job interviews. Extensive follow-up research has consistently found that these results cannot be replicated.[30]

The challenge this presents is that genuine innovations are seldom the result of one thing, a single "Eureka!" moment; more typically, they are the result of a convergence of many things and what I can only call serendipity. By example, I would like to share my personal experience with this book. I knew I had a unique perspective on trust that I felt could help the world, but I was frustrated that I had no effective way of getting my message out to a wide audience. I had carried out extensive research over several decades and spent a great deal of time and effort applying the Trust Unlimited model in classroom settings, businesses, organizations, and government. However, challenges with my health made writing a book feel like an insurmountable task. I had a number of false starts and attempts that simply petered out.

Marin Njavro, the founder of the Luxembourg School of Business, where I teach, nudged me many times to take action. Several months before starting work on this book, he and I reengaged in conversations about taking my work and scaling it so that more people could become exposed to its message. The only way I could realistically achieve this was to pull together a creative and innovative team of people that I could trust to help me.

Eric Lott, an ex-naval officer, came into my life by way of an introduction from a mutual contact. His deep understanding of trust, team performance, and collaborative problem-solving made him a perfect project manager and thought partner. He helps me push my ideas forward and tracks the actions I take, the ideas I have, and the things I do, all of which might otherwise get lost in the maelstrom that is my life. We reached out to Mike Wicks, a best-selling author and ghostwriter, to help turn my thoughts and experiences into a form that was more broadly accessible. Through it all my longtime friend Hannah Carbone, someone I'd met working at McKinsey & Company, helped edit the chapters of the book and bring my voice out in a way I couldn't manage on my own. Hannah has done this for me for years and is a magnificent editor and a dear friend. The point I am making is that this has been a collaborative effort and wouldn't have happened had I not trusted others and shared everything I knew with them.

How Trust Facilitates Customer Relationships

Leaders and organizations that are able to propagate higher levels of trust create more resilient relationships. I refer to these as "sticky relationships": ones where customers, subordinates, and colleagues tend to land and stay. If a company hits rough water, these people are more likely to stay on board and ride out the storm together. When you consider how many factors can affect those with whom we are connected and are out of a leader's control, having a large number of sticky relationships can prove to be a significant advantage. Being less exposed to out-of-the-blue customer relationship challenges can be a huge comfort not only to a leader but to those they lead.

For instance, suppose one of your competitors develops a new product or discovers a new technology. If your relationships with your customers are superficial or transactional in nature, there is a strong possibility they will leave you in favor of your competitor's new offering. If, however, you have deep, meaningful relationships with your customers, there is a greater likelihood they will be willing to wait to see how your organization responds. Because they trust you, they are also more likely to tell you about their unmet needs in the first place, giving you a leg up on the competition when it comes to understanding what will and won't make a difference to them.

Trust is a big issue when it comes to dealing with a company—any company, especially when so many things can go wrong that can lead to a bad customer experience. Think about your own consumer experiences. How many times have you bought something and were disappointed by its quality, look, feel, delivery, or value? We all take a risk when making a purchase. We realize there is a danger that we might be disappointed, but we forge ahead in hope. When we have a satisfactory experience, we are likely to recommend the company to other people. Interestingly, however, we are more hesitant to make recommendations about products or services to people we care about, and whose relationships we value, because it feels worse if their experience is disappointing. Understandably, the more strong, trusting relationships a company has with its customers, the more likely those customers will be to make referrals and post positive reviews.

The bottom line is that higher trust levels result in more business. In the financial industry, after Bernie Madoff's Ponzi scheme was exposed and the recession took hold in 2008, trust levels dropped and it was reported that increasing numbers of investors were choosing to work with multiple advisors to spread their risk. The big question is, do you think it likely that these people spread their investments equally between their advisors? No, in my experience working with financial companies, higher-trust environments encourage people to invest a larger share of their holdings with a specific company or advisor. We see this play out in a wide variety of other industries, where customers are reluctant to have a sole source supplier for anything they truly need.

During my time as a consultant with McKinsey & Company, I was frequently amazed at how much our customers paid for our services. At one point we were charging three times more for our services than our closest competitor. On the face of it, this seems an unsustainable model. If, however, we take a moment to examine it, it isn't that difficult to find similar examples. People are willing to pay a premium for brands they trust or value. There used to be a saying, "No one ever got fired for buying IBM," the underlying message being that it's worth paying a premium for something familiar and reliable. We see this play out in the decision by some people to pay a premium for brands such as Lexus and Audi that are made by Toyota and Volkswagen. They could pay far less for a similar, or possibly even better, vehicle but are loyal to the more expensive, prestigious brand they trust.

Trust as a Differentiator

A differentiator is, as the term implies, something that sets our company, our team, or us as individuals apart from our competition. When that differentiator is something positive, it can give us a significant advantage.

Academics studying the concept of sustainable competitive advantage have come to the conclusion that the speed of technological advance, the convergence of technologies, and the growth of social media have made it difficult, if not virtually impossible, to maintain a competitive advantage for any length of time. In 1999, Richard A. D'Aveni described the way organizations in times of fast-paced change resolutely disrupted and attacked the competitive advantage of other organizations as "hyper-competition," a term that has become even more apt in the years since.[31]

Information, including whatever we are trying to do to be different or unique, becomes common knowledge almost immediately. If getting an advantage is hard, keeping it is nearly impossible. Or is it? Much depends on the nature of the advantageous differentiator. Building deep, trusting relationships is something that is difficult for competitors to copy or destroy. This is because the advantage is firmly embedded in each individual relationship.

The financial services industry is rife with copycat behavior. It serves as a prototypical example of the struggle to maintain a competitive advantage in an increasingly fast-moving and competitive landscape. The industry's regulators require transparency (to limit illegal or immoral behavior), which makes it almost impossible to prevent competitors from copying the services that financial services businesses provide. In chapter 7, I will provide a case study of how one financial services firm managed to differentiate itself by focusing on building stronger relationships with its customers.

High-trust environments can be a particularly compelling differentiator during times of volatility or unrest. Chapter 4 outlined some of the "big, hairy problems" we're facing in the world today. In uncertain times like these, the safe harbor provided by a trusted organization is incredibly appealing. Often, in times of stress people move their money to more stable investment vehicles; typically, the price of gold (which is generally trusted to hold its value) goes up dramatically when the demand for security increases. The same is true with people, companies, and organizations—the more trusted they are, the more sought after they become.

The Benefit of the Doubt

People who are trusted receive the benefit of the doubt, or at least an opportunity to explain when something goes wrong. They receive what might be called a generous interpretation of what occurred. More importantly, blame for negative events will more likely be attributed to circumstances, other people, or outside influences.

The exact same event can be interpreted differently based on how the person, company, or organization involved is perceived. For instance, if someone is a die-hard supporter of a particular politician, they will believe whatever that person says, no matter how outrageous their statements seem or how others, even experts, ridicule such politicians and categorically prove them wrong. A person's biggest fans will always give that person the benefit of the doubt—to a point, one presumes. In extreme circumstances, however, this willingness to offer benefit of the doubt can defy all rational explanation; such is the power of trust, even when it is misplaced.

Furthermore, people can experience virtually identical situations and interpret them differently based on how they feel about the people involved. In the following stories we meet two employees, both named Jenny, who bring different lived experiences to what might, to an outside observer, seem to be the same situation.

Jenny number one is waiting for her manager outside his office. Her appointment was twenty minutes ago, and she is still waiting. She begins to wonder why he is late. Her history with him has been mixed at best. There have been some positive interactions where she has experienced growth and development, but there have also been some far more tense and uncomfortable exchanges. Jenny often feels that her boss is attempting to dominate and control her. New ideas and suggestions are often met with belligerent rebukes and challenges. Sitting waiting for him, she becomes convinced that he is late on purpose or simply doesn't value being on time for her, perhaps once again establishing his dominance and her unimportance. Bottom line: this Jenny doesn't trust her manager.

Now let's explore an alternative scenario. Jenny number two is waiting for her manager outside his office. She has an appointment, but he is twenty minutes late. She begins to wonder why he is late. Her experience with him has been generally positive, and her suggestions are met with interest and appreciation. He supports her growth and development and treats her with respect. Sitting waiting for him, she becomes convinced that he has been unavoidably detained and is probably trying to get back to the office as soon as he can. She opens her notebook and decides to review her agenda for the meeting while she waits, looking forward to a positive interaction. Bottom line: this Jenny trusts her manager.

We interpret the world through the stories we tell ourselves. If we start with a negative story about the other party, it makes it more likely we will have a negative experience. Think about what happens to each Jenny when the manager eventually returns and starts the meeting. Jenny number one will be frustrated and angry. Jenny number two is likely to be ready to get straight down to productive work. How do you think the manager will react in each case? How will each meeting go? Which manager is the better leader?

When we trust people, we are more likely to respond to what they say with curiosity and acceptance, and this promotes discussion. If we mistrust someone, we are more likely to be critical and harsh, which can spark an argument. More importantly, the level of trust can affect our interpretation, leading to us being favorably disposed to those we trust. Conversely, we are likely to take offense or be dismissive of people we distrust. In the latter instance, we (often subconsciously) select evidence to confirm our negative story about them, their actions, and what they have said. And, in the former instance, we search for evidence to support our positive viewpoint.

This benefit of the doubt (or lack thereof) doesn't just extend to individuals. We see the same phenomenon with groups, individual businesses, organizations, institutions, and even nations. Research is regularly undertaken on what brands the public most or least trusts. In 2020, Morning Consult, a leader in global data intelligence, carried out a "most trusted brands" survey of corporate brands.[32] In terms of benefit of the doubt, one of the most interesting findings was that younger consumers are far more skeptical of corporate America than older ones. Age also factored into which brands were felt to be the most trusted. When asked, "How much do you trust each brand to do what is right?" consumers rated the most trusted brands overall as the United States Postal Service (USPS), Amazon, and Google, in that order. The survey then broke down its findings into Gen Z, millennials, Gen X, and baby boomers. Here there were some interesting variations in trust levels. Gen Zers rated the USPS only at number 12. Gen Xers put Netflix into 24th place. As for Boomers, Google and Netflix didn't appear in the top 25, and Amazon only reached number 11, but USPS held the number one spot in boomers' trust.

Why is trust so important? Entities that we trust get the benefit of the doubt when something goes wrong. We assume an innocent mistake has been made, and the offender is given the opportunity to make good. It takes much longer for a trusted company's reputation to erode than it would for an institution that we feel neutral or hostile toward. None of this is new; trust and the benefit of the doubt have always been important. Take the tainted Tylenol affair in 1981, where seven people died in Chicago after taking capsules laced with cyanide. Johnson & Johnson, the manufacturer of Tylenol, saw its market share drop almost overnight from 35 percent to 8 percent, which was not surprising given the circumstances. It was quickly discovered the capsules had been tampered with after they left the factory, so although the company was not to blame, it was held accountable nonetheless. What Johnson & Johnson did next, however, earned back the trust of its customers. It announced a massive recall and bought back any product people had in their medicine cabinets. Then it went further: it introduced tamper-proof containers—the first in the industry—and also introduced a new easy-to-swallow caplet that was extremely difficult, if not impossible, to taint without it being easily noticeable. These efforts cost the company more than $100 million, but Johnson & Johnson earned back the trust of its customer base—as evidenced by the fact that you probably have Tylenol in your medicine cabinet right now.

In his 2011 book *Thinking, Fast and Slow*, Daniel Kahneman outlined two systems of how people think and the heuristics and biases people use when interpreting information and making decisions.[33] In the first system, he talks about the biases of fast, intuitive, and emotional thinking and how our instinctual impressions constantly influence our thoughts and choices.

When we examine the phenomenon of benefit of the doubt, there are similarities to Kahneman's observations. Information reaches our brain and goes through a filter to ensure it fits into our vision of the world. Any analysis is subject to the biases we already have—immediately, powerfully, and subconsciously.

Many current global examples demonstrate that trust levels are at an all-time low and that the benefit of the doubt is not being extended. Conversations about systemic racism and embedded cultural biases are examples of people not being given the benefit of the doubt. These perceptions or biases often run in both directions. Current protests about the treatment of minorities by the police reveal a deep level of distrust. However, trust and distrust can be felt by all parties. For instance, the police, from their perspective, are struggling with the behavior of some people in the communities they serve. This lack of trust in the motives of some civilians can, and has, led to misunderstandings that have sometimes resulted in fatal consequences.

The polarization we are witnessing in many countries gives us a strong example of this phenomenon. People from all sides of the political spectrum have emotional stories about those with whom they disagree.

These disagreements often get in the way of productive discussion and contribute to a failure, or inability, to actively listen. People assume they already know what the other parties will say. They are also prone to hearing things that haven't actually been said but which they assume is the underlying message of the other party. This leads to profound and lasting misunderstandings, vicious cycles, biased perspectives, and, eventually, conflict. Failure to engage in meaningful dialogue results in the underlying issues never being resolved. Polarization makes trust harder because people hear only what they want to hear, and they are much more susceptible and drawn to evidence that confirms their beliefs. This sustains conflict and makes it resistant to attempts to resolve it.

Conflict and the Mechanisms that Feed It

Mutual distrust and suspicion have the potential to create conflicts that feed on themselves and escalate. Three mechanisms feed these vicious cycles. The first mechanism is our attribution of other people's intent. The second mechanism is our evaluation of harm done and the need for revenge. The final mechanism is our need for things to feel fair and just.

Mechanism One: Attribution of Intent

When two groups don't get along, each tends to attribute all kinds of ills and slights to the opposing side. Unscrupulous leaders have taken advantage of this throughout history. They simply blame the other side: unemployment is high, wages are too low, the economy sucks, the health-care system is failing, the list goes on—and it's all *their* fault. This is consistent with a general tendency to have an external locus of control ("It's not *our* fault!") when things are not going well; and if there is an opposing group to blame problems on, that's where the focus will center.

This vilification of the other party can be incredibly damaging; it often leads to destructive behaviors targeting the "bad guys." In the normal course of events, people don't consider acting this way, but when the opposing group is thought to be dreadful or even dangerous, as is the case in political campaigns, for instance, people justify and rationalize their negative actions against their opponents. Lies, smear campaigns, denigrating individuals, attacking families—it seems nothing is off limits.

Once a narrative has been created about how terrible the other party is, it seems remarkably easy to find confirming evidence. The story that people or a group tell themselves has an internal, positive effect; it creates unity, a collective response, and a level of solidarity that can under normal circumstances be hard to achieve. It also has the potential to rally others to the cause, generating support, and potentially resources, to aid in the "struggle." Unfortunately, once the powerful negative story has been created, it can be hard to find a way back or for reconciliation to occur. When the other party has been ruthlessly vilified, it becomes difficult to justify trying to find common ground and reconcile.

Mechanism Two: Evaluation of Harm

The second mechanism is how we evaluate the level of harm. Pain is subjective; to those affected it seems more real and intense than to those looking in from outside. For example, two children are playing in a sandbox and one accidentally bumps the other and causes his sand-castle to collapse. An objective observer might rate the harm done as a two on a scale of one to ten. The offender shrugs and dismisses it as nothing (perhaps a one). The victim thinks the nudge was intentional and rates it a three. The urge to get even takes over and the victim knocks over his playmate and pushes his face into the sand. Objective observers might rate this as an overreaction, perhaps a four. Our clumsy, misunderstood initiator of this little drama spits out sand and rates it a five or six (remember, the initial offense was probably rated as a one). He decides to hit the other child over the head with a toy truck. Tears flow, parents enter the scene, and both children claim the other one started it and elaborate on how awful the other child was to them. The conflict then spreads to the parents who begin to disagree with one another about an appropriate response and agree the children are no longer allowed to play together. The friendship of the two children has been at the very least stalled, possibly damaged, and potentially destroyed.

This mechanism can be seen playing out in workplaces, between governments, and in multiple locations and situations. The original victim's assessment of the pain or indignity suffered is often greater than that which the perpetrator intended or believes is the case. Therefore, when the victim retaliates based on their perception of harm done, its intensity is higher than the perpetrator believes is just or fair. The result is an escalation in the severity of responses due to each individual's perception rather than any level of objectivity. This mechanism can be witnessed during a trade war, for instance, where increasing tariffs are thought to be unfair and out of proportion to the original response. The different perspectives and resulting escalation fuel conflict.

Mechanism Three: Desire for Fairness and Justice

Fairness is subjective; it is a question that has plagued humans since the dawn of time. I can imagine cavemen Grug and Grog arguing over who got to draw on which cave wall and who got which portion of the beef-asaurus they had killed near their homestead and whether the outcome was "fair."

Research on Moral Foundations Theory proposes five foundations for understanding why humans make decisions that they feel are morally right or appropriate: care, fairness, loyalty, authority, and purity.[34] This theory has been used to attempt to understand the differences between those who support different political parties by looking at the weight they put on the five criteria.

1. *Care* is protecting others and looking after their interests.
2. *Fairness* is justice based on shared rules.
3. *Loyalty* means aligning with your group (e.g., family, region, or nation).
4. *Authority* means submitting to tradition and legitimate authority.
5. *Purity* is defined as disliking things that aren't generally accepted by society.

People with different political views exhibit different degrees of belief in, and support of, these five fundamentals; however, there is general consensus that care and fairness are important. Unfortunately, despite this general agreement that fairness is important, people often struggle to agree on what "fair" really means or what rules we should play by.

The sandbox example helps illustrate that there can be a significant difference in what is perceived as fair or just; each party sees the situation from its own point of view, with its own biases. It's not surprising that evaluating the material degree of damage done is virtually impossible. We see this clearly in long-standing disputes where the players have dramatically different ideas about how much harm has been done and can't come to agreement on an appropriate, fair, and just response.

In some particularly difficult disputes, parties ask for reparations for historical wrongs that happened decades or even hundreds of years ago that they feel are still impacting them or their communities today. Those on the other side of the dispute struggle with the fairness of being held accountable for actions that they had no part in and of being asked to make reparations to people who were not directly affected by the original wrongdoing.

It is tempting to try to restore fairness through financial reparation. However, in a book titled *Coping with the Cash*, the sustainable development research group of the Arctic Institute of North America found that settlements involving cash reparations didn't always leave the recipients any better off.[35] Usually the money disappeared in a remarkably short time frame with little significant improvement in the recipients' circumstances. Settlements such as these frequently fail to address the underlying issues that cause disparities between the affected groups and mainstream society. A more collaborative approach, one that includes programs aimed at closing the gap between the segments of the population that are struggling, regardless of the reason, might result in more success.

Justice is a tricky thing to unpack; that's why we have judges, but even they struggle and make mistakes when trying to apply the law fairly. The key to resolving conflict over the long term is that all parties need to believe a fair and just outcome was reached given the circumstances.

Research on distributive justice suggests there are three different norms that people think are fair when it comes to distributing resources: equity, equality, and need-based.

1. *Equity* means that whoever contributes the most should get the most.
2. *Equality* means that everyone gets the same.
3. A *need-based* norm means that whoever needs the most gets the most.

Of course, groups may not agree on which of these norms to apply. And even if they do agree on which one to use, they may not agree on how to apply it.

Equity requires that we all acknowledge how to value the contributions of others and compare them with our own. The challenge is that we have a tendency to overvalue our own contributions and undervalue those of others.

Need-based norms can lead to subjective judgments on how great the need is for any given group or individual. Arguments between different groups about how dire their situation is can result in a race to the bottom as different groups fight over who has been treated worse or is in greater need.

On the face of it, *equality* would seem to be the easiest to apply. While this may be the case, unfortunately it can lead to conflict if the goods being divided are not very similar or are not in quantities sufficient for everyone to get an equal share. This is a case where equality is in the eye of the beholder.

Getting the fairness conversation right is important if we are to reduce or eliminate future conflicts. Trust plays a central role here, as everyone involved needs to believe that people aren't simply gaming the system; that is, they are not promoting the use of one mechanism against another simply because it suits their best interests in the moment. Open and honest conversations are needed prior to any decisions being made, and there needs to be flexibility when reviewing outcomes. People need to feel that the rules work for the whole group, not a select few.

It would be nice if our sandbox example applied only to children. Unfortunately, similar situations can readily be seen in organizations of all shapes and sizes. These mechanisms are also prevalent in personal relationships and those between groups, religions, races, and nations. At any point in a conflict, the parties can short-circuit the escalation by taking a moment to understand the other person's perspective. Alternatively, one or both sides could give the other the benefit of the doubt. The challenge is that either option requires the communication skills of an effective and trusted leader.

In this chapter, we have identified a growing consensus that having more trust is a good thing and that higher levels of trust bring significant benefits. The challenge lies in identifying clearly how trust makes things better, why it helps, and how to build trust, which we will deal with in more detail in the following chapter.

People sometimes ask how one becomes a trust expert. In chapter 5, I'll share a bit about the path I took to develop my perspective on trust and how it works. For now, suffice it to say that it's a journey that doesn't really have a fixed end point. I am still learning and growing with every client, engagement, or project.

The Benefits of Trust:
Key Points Review

- Trust is a positive attribute—the higher the level of trust, the better an organization will function, especially in times of uncertainty.

- Higher levels of trust lead to better performance, improved creativity and innovation, greater returns to shareholders, better employee engagement, and healthier customer retention.

- Leaders and organizations that are able to propagate higher levels of trust create more resilient relationships—ones where customers, subordinates, and colleagues tend to land and stay. Such relationships are difficult for competitors to copy or destroy and hence can be a key source of competitive advantage.

- Higher-trust environments encourage the use of voice (e.g., people are not afraid of being punished for expressing a differing opinion). This can lead to virtuous cycles where trust leads to behaviors that in turn promote higher levels of trust.

- In negotiations, trust leads to better agreements by encouraging dialogue.

- In higher-trust environments people are more willing to share ideas and work collaboratively on projects, bringing a diverse set of skills and perspectives to their work.

CHAPTER 5

Introducing the
TU Trust Model

In the last four chapters, my goal was to raise awareness of how important trust is, the impact it has on all our lives, and how it is dramatically in decline. I hope that I have also managed to give you a new, more enlightened perspective on trust. In this chapter I will formally introduce the elements of the TU trust model and describe how they come together. What follows is the culmination of more than two decades of research, both for my doctoral thesis and as a result of working in the trust field as a consultant and author.

First, let me remind you of my definition of trust: *Trust is the willingness to make yourself vulnerable to another when you can't completely predict how they will act.* Within this definition, uncertainty, vulnerability, and choice are present. If any one of these elements is missing, then we're not really talking about a trust situation. Let me explain:

- If there is no *vulnerability*, then you don't really care what happens and indifference would be a better description than trust.
- If there is no *uncertainty*, then you know what's going to happen and trust isn't required.

- If we have no *choice,* then we aren't actually trusting; we either have confidence in the other party or we don't, but "trust" doesn't really come into play.

This definition of trust is a variant of the one provided by my friend Roger Mayer and his colleagues in their seminal work "An Integrative Model of Organizational Trust" in 1995.[36] Using this definition, we can now start thinking about how people make the decisions to trust someone else.

The Bases of Trust

Before I delve deeper into building trust, let's briefly explore the rationale people use when deciding whether to trust another person. When people are deciding whether they should trust someone, they ask themselves two fundamental questions:

- How likely am I to be harmed (i.e., perceived *uncertainty*)?
- If I am harmed, how badly will it hurt (i.e., perceived *vulnerability*)?

Figure 1: Bases of Trust

When deciding whether or not to trust someone, we ask ourselves two fundamental questions:

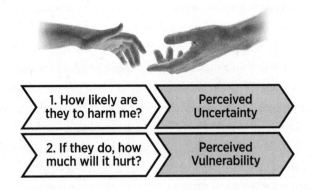

| 1. How likely are they to harm me? | Perceived Uncertainty |
| 2. If they do, how much will it hurt? | Perceived Vulnerability |

Our perceptions of uncertainty and vulnerability form the basis on which the trust decision is made. You will notice that I frequently use the word *perceived* when I describe the model. The reason for this is that presented with identical situations that require a trust decision, some people will choose to trust, and others will not—based on their respective perceptions of the degree of uncertainty and the amount of vulnerability present.

Uncertainty and vulnerability combine to give us a level of perceived risk. In any situation, each of us has a unique level of risk with which we are comfortable (our risk threshold). We then assess the level of risk involved (our perception of the risk). Once out of our comfort zone, we decide not to trust. We base this decision on our personal risk threshold and our evaluation of the risk involved.

Figure 2: Uncertainty and Vulnerability Interaction

If the perceived risk level is **higher** than a person's threshold, they will decide not to trust you.

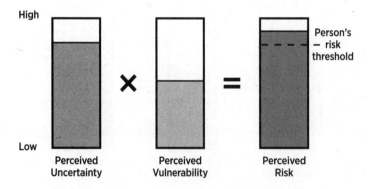

We trust some people and we don't trust others, even in otherwise identical situations. This is based on how uncertain and vulnerable we feel at a specific moment with that particular person. In fact, we may well experience different risk thresholds for the same person in different settings. For example, people may be more comfortable taking risks, or be more willing to trust, in their personal lives than they are in their work lives, or vice versa.

Our risk threshold, or willingness to trust, comes from a combination of our cultural background, personal traits, and experiences. Consider your friends and family: Are some of them far more trusting than others? Although one's risk threshold evolves over time, it tends to be stable within a given set of circumstances. For example, we may always trust doctors but have difficulty trusting realtors or insurance salespeople.

Framing the trust decision this way makes the concept of building trust fairly simple. We try to understand where the other person's uncertainty and vulnerability are and take steps to reduce them. In figure 3 you will see that we simply reduce the level of perceived uncertainty while the level of vulnerability stays constant. This results in the level of perceived risk dropping from beyond the risk threshold (see Figure 2) to beneath it in Figure 3.

Figure 3: Reduce Perceived Uncertainty

When perceived risk level is **lower** than a person's threshold, they will decide to trust you.

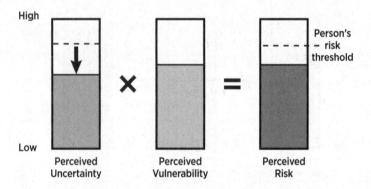

While techniques exist and can be taught to influence people's willingness to trust, I've never been comfortable advocating them. My intent is not to teach you methods by which you can take advantage of others but rather how to close the gap between how much you should be trusted and how much people actually trust you. In other words, I'm here to help you learn how to be more trustworthy rather than to teach you how to make people more trusting.

Once we have decided to trust someone, we then experience the outcome of that decision, the assessment of which is often subjective. Obviously, outcomes can be seen as a success, a failure, or something in between. With each evaluation we gain information for our next interaction with the same, or similar, people or organizations.

Figure 4: The Cognitive Trust Model

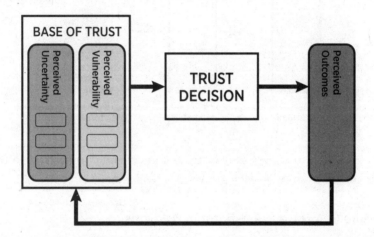

Our relationships evolve over time and can become deeper. Imagine Cindy is the receptionist at my office building. I meet Cindy every day and become familiar with her. I'm comfortable making small talk, even sharing some information that I wouldn't with a complete stranger. Although I "know" Cindy, I still don't know much about her; it is a somewhat fragile, or superficial, relationship. Although these positive experiences begin to reduce any uncertainty I might have about her, they do so only to a point. To further reduce any remaining uncertainty and win my deeper trust, she may need to make efforts that go beyond those of simple interactions.

The early relationship with Cindy was a shallow one in which there was a high level of uncertainty. This high level of uncertainty means that we can tolerate only a small range of vulnerability and still fall beneath the risk threshold we are comfortable with.

Figure 5: Getting to Know One Another

As we get to know more about one another, uncertainty goes down and we're willing to be more vulnerable—relationships are shallow and still somewhat unstable at this stage.

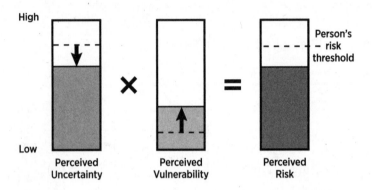

As we get to know Cindy better, our uncertainty begins to go down. We are now comfortable with a slightly broader range of vulnerability.

Figure 6: A Normal Relationship Develops

Most normal relationships have moderate levels of uncertainty and moderate levels of vulnerability, allowing trust (and stability).

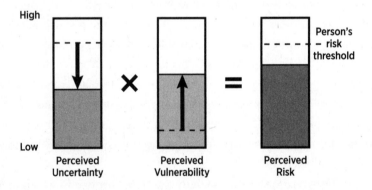

Cindy will need to figure out how to significantly reduce my uncertainty for us to have a deeper relationship, like the one depicted by the bar graph in Figure 7. In this case I have extremely low uncertainty, so the range of vulnerability I can tolerate is extremely broad.

Figure 7: A Deeper Relationship May Develop

In deep relationships, uncertainty is very low and we're willing to be very vulnerable with one another—the relationship is very stable, and we're willing to trust one another in a broad range of situations.

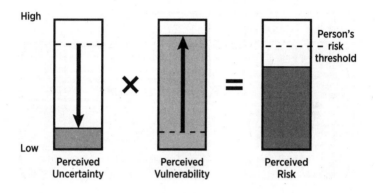

The majority of existing literature on the topic of trust treats people as if they were rational actors. Now, if you've ever dated someone or had children, you know that people aren't always rational; readers of books and articles on trust that assume rationality in people might justifiably wonder if the authors have ever actually met real people. The fact that current conversations surrounding trust models almost always fail to talk about emotions is likely one of the reasons anyone trying to intervene in long-term disputes, which are often loaded with emotional baggage, finds it so difficult. Simply liking or disliking a person can have a profound impact on our evaluation of them and our assessment of interactions with them. This means that we need to account for how our feelings influence our perceptions of the bases of trust (i.e., uncertainty, vulnerability) and our perception of the outcomes from our interactions with others. We will explore this in further detail later in this chapter.

Our feelings act like a filter and influence our perceptions and reactions. The more extreme our emotions become, the less rational we are.

Love is blind—and so is hate. If we like someone, we are more likely to view them positively: we search for reasons to trust them and are generally more likely to trust them. If we dislike them, the converse is true. This is how con artists are so effective; they have a knack for getting people to like them immediately.

Figure 8: The Full Trust Model

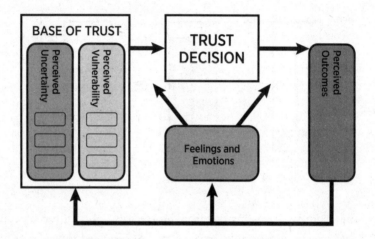

Our perception of an outcome also has the potential to positively or negatively impact our feelings. We appreciate those with whom we have positive interactions, making us like them. The reverse is true for those with whom we have negative interactions; we tend to dislike those who make our lives difficult. Feelings can thus further reinforce the positive or negative feedback loops we saw when talking about perceptions of outcomes.

Building Trust

As we explore the trust model in more detail, you will see that building trust with someone requires reducing their perceived levels of uncertainty or vulnerability to a point where their level of perceived risk goes below their risk threshold.

If we are to engender trust, we need to have a deeper understanding of the elements involved so that we understand where we need to focus our efforts. I think of these elements, and their subcomponents, as a series of levers. We all have the ability to build trust; some are simply better at evoking it in people than others. Those who aren't very good at building trust pull the same lever over and over again, hoping it will line up with the problem. Those who are a little better use multiple levers. Those who are more experienced use multiple levers and know when to pull which one. I'll spend the rest of this chapter talking about the potential levers that can be pulled, and then in chapter 6 we'll explore how to actually pull them.

Perceptions of uncertainty and vulnerability are the bases on which the trust decision gets made. To effectively build trust we need to better understand where perceptions of uncertainty and vulnerability come from and then examine how to take steps to reduce them. I'll begin by describing the core elements of uncertainty, followed by elements of vulnerability, and close out by showing how outcomes and feelings fit into the picture.

Uncertainty

To reduce uncertainty for someone making a trust decision, we first need to understand its origin. Some uncertainty is attached to the individual seeking to be trusted (the trustee). We may be unsure of their motivations, abilities, or intentions. The majority of existing trust literature focuses on this area. The big question is, What drives our perceptions of the trustworthiness of someone else?

Existing research on the individual is incredibly important and helpful, but it is somewhat incomplete. We often trust people without knowing anything about them as individuals. Our society and culture actually require us to have a certain level of trust in individuals we don't know personally (e.g., doctors, police officers, ride-share drivers) in order to function effectively. Hence, context also needs to be considered when we attempt to build trust. Our understanding of an individual and their context combine to drive our perceptions of uncertainty. Early in our interactions with someone, the context is more responsible for our perceptions of uncertainty, as we will discuss in more depth later. As we get to know the other person, however, the weight starts to shift more toward the individual, which is where we'll start.

Individual Uncertainty

A great deal of trust research focuses on individual uncertainty and its impact on trust. The most often cited work is Mayer's "An Integrative Model of Organizational Trust," which I mentioned earlier. It was foundational in the development of my own trust model. Mayer and his colleagues identified three main traits that drove perceptions of an individual's trustworthiness: benevolence, integrity, and ability.

Figure 9: Qualities of Individual Trustworthiness

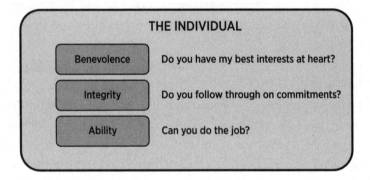

Benevolence

Benevolence is having someone's best interests at heart. If I think you are benevolent toward me, I believe that you will take actions that are in my best interest that give you no direct, short-term benefits. An example might be a volunteer at a soup kitchen or someone who puts your name forward for an award.

The expectation that someone else will act in our best interests helps reduce our uncertainty about how they will behave. This can be extremely powerful in settings where we are unsure about a specific situation. We believe that no matter what happens, the other person will try to look out for us. Research suggests that benevolence is the most impactful lever when people evaluate their leaders.

When I work with parenting groups I often ask, "Who here has their kids' best interests at heart?" As you'd expect, everybody's hands go up. However, when I change the question and ask, "How many of your kids would say you have their best interests at heart?" only about a third of parents put up their hands. If our benevolence isn't blatantly apparent to our own kids, where it should be a given, how do we make it apparent in situations outside the home—for example, when we are a leader, in the workplace or in society, benevolently juggling a wide variety of people's different interests?

It is not uncommon to believe we are acting benevolently toward another person but the other person does not see it that way at all. A student in one of my classes told me that she always had her partner's best interest at heart. I asked her what that looked like, and she replied, "I tell him what to do." When I asked her how that was received by her partner, she paused for a moment of reflection and then said, "Not very well." Let me give you another example of intended benevolence not landing well. Imagine you noticed me dining at a restaurant, about to dig in to a huge, decadent dessert. Concerned about my health, you stop and say, with a frown on your face, "Darryl, you're not really going to eat that, are you?" Your intent may well be benevolent, but chances are I won't perceive it that way!

While I was volunteering in one of Allison Rees's exceptional classes on parenting, I was struck by one of the topics. She was talking about personality traits and how they aren't completely under our control. She raised the excellent point that each trait has elements that we will find positive or negative when dealing with the person who displays them. One of the traits she mentioned was distractibility.

This reminds me of one of my favorite stories. My youngest son, Alexander, is highly distractible. Research on traits suggests that there are positive and negative elements associated with any trait, and one of Alexander's traits is that he is extremely sensitive to other people and situations, giving him tremendous empathy and a remarkable sense of humor. However, this also adversely affects his punctuality. One day, when I was picking him up from school, he was even later than usual. The other kids had all left, several teachers had left, and still there was no sign of him. I had plenty of time to reflect. I was frustrated and not sure how to respond. As Alexander finally emerged from the school, I realized that people had been yelling at him for being late all his life and still it hadn't changed his behavior. Reflecting on Allison's wise counsel, I realized that this behavior wasn't intentional; it was part of who he is, part of his wiring. I realized in that moment that my choice was to either accept him for who he was or continue to fight what was inevitably a losing battle. When Alexander approached, he looked dejected and upset and said, "I'm sorry I'm late, Dad." I looked at him and said, "Buddy, you're worth the wait."

In that moment I realized it was true: nothing mattered to me more than he did. Whoever was waiting for me next wasn't as important as him. The next person would have to wait for us if we were late. Alexander's response was immediate relief. The feeling that he was being accepted for who he was, all that he was, removed some of his anxiety. That acceptance and appreciation of my son was benevolence, and it landed that way with him.

The challenge lies in how we demonstrate our benevolence in a way that actually lands as we intend. A good place to start is not to assume what is in the other person's best interest but rather to engage with them directly to get a better understanding of what their best interests are. Being able to understand what matters most to someone else, or what success looks like for them, allows us to actively move forward. If we've included them in the conversation, we can be transparent about our benevolent intentions; this will leave less room for any misunderstanding.

Integrity

I use the definition of integrity provided by my good friend Tony Simons, who teaches at the Cornell School of Hotel Administration. He has written numerous articles about behavioral integrity as well as the book *The Integrity Dividend*.[37] Tony defines integrity as following through on our promises and taking actions that align with the values we profess. Much like benevolence, displaying higher levels of integrity makes it easier for others to predict our behavior; this in turn reduces their uncertainty and makes it easier for them to trust us.

If we consistently follow through on our promises, it makes it easier for people to rely on us. If others understand what our values are and see us act in a way that is consistent with those values, it becomes easier for them to predict what we will do in the future, thus reducing their uncertainty about us.

We seem to consistently fall down in a few ways when it comes to following through on promises. There are explicit promises that we make, and there are also implicit promises that relate to people's expectations of us. These implicit promises can lead to misunderstandings if we aren't aware of those expectations or how they might arise from the situation or the role we are in.

For example, imagine an employee asking his manager to clear some vacation time for him. The manager says she will get right on it. The subordinate might interpret this as getting an answer in a day or two. The manager, however, has a process to follow, and her time line is more like two weeks. When the employee doesn't get an answer within two days, he believes the manager has broken her promise. The manager, on the other hand, is expediting the vacation request as quickly as she can, but in the eyes of the employee her integrity has taken a hit.

Such misunderstandings tend to become more frequent when we are interacting across cultures—something we'll explore more when we talk about the role of context in uncertainty.

A common challenge facing many people is a temptation to over-promise. This predisposition seems to be particularly hard to resist when things have gone awry, and we find ourselves saying things such as, "I'll never do that again" or, "That won't happen again." These assurances are virtually doomed to fail from the moment they are uttered. I try not to make promises about things that aren't completely within my control. This often means being careful to make promises only about my own actions rather than outcomes.

To strengthen the perception that our actions align with our values, we first need to be very clear on those values. Statements about corporate values, in particular, seem to lend themselves to perceptions of hypocrisy rather than integrity. Many organizations come up with a set of core values and often feature them on their websites or on sales and promotional literature. Unfortunately, websites and promotional collateral are often the only places those values reside. What's worse is that the people working for or with these organizations often make inside jokes about their apparent hypocrisy.

I worked with a telecom company in Canada that had a well-known tagline. While consulting with the company, I asked, "What does it mean?" There were six people in the room, and only one of them actually knew the intent of the slogan. It is important to understand the promises you are making to your customers and how those promises are being interpreted. Keep in mind that these were senior executives inside the organization. If they didn't know what the tagline meant, how likely was it that external stakeholders had any idea?

Any disconnect can affect how your customers rate your integrity.

Leaders take actions, make decisions, and set strategy. The struggle they often face is that people interpret the world through stories. All of a leader's behaviors are being observed by other people, each of whom has a story they are using to interpret those actions. If the leader doesn't take the extra step to explain how their actions align with the values they are expressing, they can often get wildly diverging opinions about their integrity.

We also see failures in integrity when leaders create rules or give direction and then don't follow them. During the COVID-19 pandemic, we saw a remarkable number of examples of this in Canada. Numerous politicians actively and publicly told people to stay home and not visit loved ones over holiday periods, only to go on vacations with their own families to warmer climates. This "do as I say, not as I do" approach is a sure way to detrimentally affect people's perceptions of one's integrity.

Ability

If we profess ability, we are telling people we have the competence to do what we say we will do. This is often a favorite lever to pull when people are trying to win others over and earn their trust: "I have this much experience, these credentials, this many customers." When people make such comments, they are attempting to show others they are capable. Often, however, when I work with organizations and senior executives, I find that this trait, despite its popularity, is often profoundly underdefined.

When I stand in front of a group of senior executives and ask, "Who is an excellent leader?" all hands go up. When I ask them what that means, however, an uncomfortable silence often follows. At a client meeting with a financial services company, senior executives, middle managers, and frontline staff were all in attendance. I asked the group, "If I divide you into three groups by position, do you think all three would come back with the same definition of an excellent middle manager?" They told me they didn't think they would get the same answer even within each group, let alone between the groups.

If we can't clearly define what excellence (ability) is for an organization, or for a given role within it, then how do we recruit for, train, evaluate, or communicate it? How can we strive to be excellent if we haven't reached a shared understanding of the definition of excellence? Furthermore, who should be involved in defining excellence in the first place?

I work as a coach, facilitator, and teacher. If I wanted to define excellence in any of those roles, I could likely come up with some parameters that I thought were important. But is my own perspective the only one that I should adopt? Other professionals in a similar line of work to me may have a valuable perspective on what excellence looks like in this role. Including them may give me greater insight into what good really looks like. Those who hire me and those I serve also have valid and valuable perspectives on what excellence looks like in each of those roles.

By now I think you will agree that it can be difficult to define excellence. Sometimes we rely too heavily on measuring outcomes instead of measuring what is within the control of the person being assessed. My son Thomas was on a baseball team, and early one season he said, "Dad, I don't think we're going to be very good this year." We had a long conversation, and I suggested that he define success in terms of things he could control. He came back to me with a list of things of which he had control. These included his own work ethic, improvements in his skills, and how he showed up as a teammate and leader. In essence, he was defining what excellence looked like as a teammate and player so that he could strive for it without being distracted by the noise of things outside his control by inappropriately being given blame (or credit) for such things.

While working with a CEO and his VP of sales, I asked them both how they saw excellence in the VP's role. They looked at each other and agreed that meeting or exceeding sales targets was the measure they used. I responded by asking them how that worked, given that the market was incredibly competitive. Wasn't it possible that the VP could be the best sales executive in the world, and his results far better than anyone else's would have been under the circumstances, even if he missed his targets? Conversely, what if the market were overflowing with opportunity, and even the worst sales executive in the world could have hit their targets with virtually no effort?

In this example, excellence had been defined by outcomes, which to a significant extent were outside the VP's control. We then started to discuss what elements of the VP's tasks were within his control. How could we measure those, and what did excellence really look like?

We tend to rely heavily on perceptions of ability when assessing others. When we hire or promote people, we often focus on ability as the primary variable. We sift through job applicants' resumes or look at transcripts to see how well they've performed in the past. But despite our heavy reliance on ability, we are not always good at identifying or measuring it. When making new hires, organizations often give preference to candidates who achieved excellent grades at Ivy League schools. Indeed, there are reasons to justify this preference: these students have demonstrated that they are able to excel in stable, structured environments and that they can absorb traditional education. Unfortunately, given the speed of change in society, such stable, structured environments are becoming less common, and there often isn't the time or the structure for traditional education within organizations. The question we have to ask, in this case, is whether our measurement of ability is truly relevant.

I recently had the pleasure of joining a workshop with my friend and colleague David Obstfeld. David had organized the workshop to help develop social skills and social capital for a group of first-generation university students from California State University, Fullerton. The majority of the students present were working full-time while attending school; many of them were minorities and supporting their families.

These students had remarkable stories to tell. They had experienced significant challenges in life yet they persevered. They showed resilience, grit, and determination. In an environment where change is constant and things don't always go our way, might this not be a better example of ability than a perfect grade point average from an elite institution?

In general, MBA programs might serve their students better if they helped them develop benevolence and integrity (and taught them how to demonstrate those traits) rather than just focusing on ability.

These examples illustrate how hard it can be to identify, assess, or measure ability in others, even in areas where we may have a reasonable amount of expertise or experience ourselves. Our inability to recognize or define excellence in other people's performances will likely compromise our perceptions of their abilities when we are making the decision to trust them to undertake a particular role or job. Equally, it may not be obvious how we can demonstrate our own ability to those whose trust we are trying to earn. We will explore this further in chapter 6.

Our uncertainty about someone as an individual lessens as our perception of their benevolence, integrity, or ability becomes more favorable. As our uncertainty is reduced, we are more willing to make ourselves vulnerable to them—in other words, to make the decision to trust them.

As we've discussed, the trust decision is based on perceptions of uncertainty and vulnerability. In this section we've covered the individual traits that promote perceptions of trustworthiness. If we believe the other person is benevolent, we are more likely to believe they will try to look out for our interests no matter what happens. If we believe they have integrity, it is easier to predict what they will do based on their values and commitments. If we believe they have ability, we believe they have the skill to do what is required and won't let us down by making mistakes.

In chapter 6, we'll learn how to pull these three levers (perceptions of benevolence, integrity, and ability) to reduce other people's uncertainty about our own benevolence, integrity, and ability and hence increase the likelihood that they will decide to trust us. Later in this chapter we will look at the role context plays in affecting the perceptions of uncertainty that inform the trust decision.

Vulnerability

When making the decision whether to trust someone, the second question we ask ourselves is, "If I'm harmed, how badly will it hurt?" This is our level of perceived vulnerability and is the second basis for the trust decision. Vulnerability can be a fuzzy concept, one that is hard to quantify. Our levels of vulnerability in a situation are extremely subjective. We can have dramatically different perspectives about what is at stake, and the value we place on it, depending on the players and the situation.

When I was a doctoral student, some friends asked me to play poker. The stake for the evening was twenty dollars. I was not, and still am not, a good poker player. I barely knew the rules, and the prospect of losing my stake, even though it was for a fun evening with some good friends, had me feeling sick to my stomach. The feeling of vulnerability was fairly high because I simply didn't have much money at the time—I was a typical poor, starving student. Some years later, when I became a consultant with McKinsey & Company, spending twenty dollars to spend a few hours playing poker with friends would have been a no-brainer (my level of perceived vulnerability would have been incredibly low). Something as measurable as money can create a dramatically different level of perceived vulnerability for different people or for the same people at different points in their lives.

If something as quantifiable as money can result in substantially different valuations, how different might our perceptions of vulnerability be for things like our reputation, our honor, or our relationships? Our perceived level of vulnerability can increase exponentially if we think that more than one thing is at stake in any given interaction. For example, in the poker story, I was thinking that not only would I lose my money but my friends would realize I'm an idiot. Alternatively, what if we think that the outcome from the trust decision will lead to a series of things that are linked together? I'll lose my money, my friends will realize I'm an idiot, and then they'll stop hanging out with me. I'll live a life of isolation because they'll tell everyone else I'm an idiot. Perceptions of vulnerability can have a tendency to escalate dramatically.

Shifting the focus, let's look at how and why other people feel vulnerable. First, we need to try to understand what is at stake for them, or more precisely what they perceive is at stake. What do they think will happen if they trust me and I don't follow through? What is the worst-case scenario in their mind? To do this we have to appreciate how vulnerable they feel by learning how they value what is at stake.

Scarcity plays a role in a person's evaluation of how valuable something is to them. Remember my twenty dollars meant more to me when I was a student, and money was scarce, and far less when I was a well-paid consultant. In one of my favorite movies, *Tombstone* (the 1993 remake), Doc Holliday is asked why he is helping Wyatt Earp in his search for the outlaw gang, the Cowboys. Holliday replies that Earp is his friend. One of the cowboys responds that he has plenty of friends, but they aren't worth dying for, to which Doc replies, "But Wyatt is my only friend." The scarcity increased the value of the friendship.

The value we place on all sorts of things can depend on cultural norms, values, and our own personal preferences. I value above almost anything else the relationships I have with my two sons and their welfare. There is very little I would not be willing to forgo to maintain my relationships with them or to see them do well. The fact is, we all have things that are special to us for one reason or another. The challenge is that it's not always easy for strangers to know what those special things are or what has or doesn't have a deeper meaning to us. Often the only way we can truly understand how someone else values these things is to either ask them or spend time observing and paying attention to the choices they make.

The subjective nature of what is at stake, and how it is valued, can make it challenging to understand and measure the other person's feelings of vulnerability. Another major factor is that people can have misperceptions about the level of harm they truly face. We can witness an actual level of vulnerability that has been compounded by exaggerated perceptions of potential harm.

Numerous people underestimate the level of vulnerability they face when posting personal information on social media. Others overestimate how vulnerable they are to the COVID-19 vaccine. Their belief appears to be that they are not just at risk of suffering from side effects but are also at risk of losing their freedom or part of their identity.

Perceived Outcomes

Just as I intentionally used the word *perceived* when talking about elements of individual uncertainty, I also use it when I talk about outcomes because the same event can be experienced in dramatically different ways by different people. Their perception of what went on can differ depending on their mood, their comfort level, their point of view, the people they are with, or even the way the situation is presented.

For instance, take the toppling of Saddam Hussein's statue when American forces occupied Iraq. If you watched the event on CNN, they showed a closely cropped picture of a jubilant crowd packed around the statue cheering as a rope pulled the statue over. The story line was that Iraqis were overjoyed at the US presence and the toppling of Hussein's regime. However, if you watched the same event on Al Jazeera, you would have seen a wide-angle shot that revealed a relatively small crowd clustered around the statue and a US military vehicle attached to the rope that was dragging the statue off its foundation. The story line in this case was that most Iraqis were not thrilled with the US occupation of their country and its interference in their country's leadership.

A third perspective was supplied by Canadian news channels. They showed both versions of the video and explained that there was an element of truth in both sets of accounts. They reported that many Iraqis were thrilled that Saddam had been ousted, but given that he had not yet been captured, they remained fearful he would return and were reluctant to demonstrate their enthusiasm openly. There were also segments of the population that were rightfully concerned about what his removal would mean for them and how it would affect the stability of the country.

We tend to evaluate the outcomes of our interactions with other people in a couple of ways. First, we assess the success of the interaction: Was the interaction positive, negative, or somewhere in between? Second, we attribute credit or blame for the outcome. Was the other person responsible for the outcome, or was it primarily due to circumstances outside that person's control?

As I mentioned earlier, people interpret the world through stories. They search for confirming evidence of those stories and use them to form a perspective on what has happened. This is particularly true when we look at perceptions of outcomes. Someone with a positive narrative about another party is more likely to see the outcome of an interaction with them as positive. They are also more likely to view them as responsible for that positive outcome. This can be the start of a virtuous cycle, part of the positive feedback loop mentioned above.

The Role Emotions Play

How we feel emotionally toward someone can have a profound impact on how we evaluate them. I was one of the first academics to begin including emotions in a trust model. It is still very rare for academic or popular press books to consider people's emotions when discussing the issue of trust. Unfortunately, this means that most trust models treat people as if they are rational actors—which, as noted, is certainly not always the case (and may in fact be the exception rather than the rule).

The stronger our emotions become, the less rational we are, and the more pronounced our biases become. At our emotional extremes, we tend not to be very rational at all. Existing trust models do not properly account for this irrationality. If these models treat extremely emotional people as rational actors, they are doomed to fail.

Emotions tend to be at the root of some of our most persistent disputes. Often conflicts last so long that no one even remembers how they started. Given the extent to which the parties involved are often suffering, outsiders are often baffled as to why the disputes continue. To build trust in such hostile environments, we first have to reset everyone's emotional state, calming them to a point where reason has a chance to take hold. At that point, we can start applying the more rational elements of the model. Even in settings where emotions aren't as extreme, we need to be aware of them when trying to build trust with others.

As I said earlier, when we like someone we have a positive story about them. We search for confirming evidence of that story and are more likely to trust them. When it comes time to evaluate our interactions with people we like, we are more likely to view those interactions positively, once again confirming our story about them. If we see the outcome of the interaction as positive, we are more likely to give them credit for that positive outcome. If the outcome can't be seen as anything but negative, we likely blame the outcome on the situation (the context) rather than the person we like. This whole process can often cause us to like these people even more, creating a virtuous cycle.

And the reverse is true; when we dislike someone, we have a negative story about them. We search for confirming evidence of that story and are less likely to trust them. When it comes time to evaluate our interactions with people we dislike, we are more likely to view those outcomes negatively and blame the people for the bad experience. If the outcome can't be seen as anything but positive, then we are more likely to believe the outcome was caused by the situation (the context). Alternatively, we may suspect that the other person did something positive only to set us up for something negative down the road. This whole process can often cause us to dislike the other person even more and lead to vicious cycles.

This phenomenon can be seen when someone fanatically supports a political figure or political party. Whatever the media reports, whatever other people say, even when supported by evidence, people construct their internal (and often external) narrative to fit the positive or negative perspective that has become entrenched. The more extreme our emotions become, the less rational we are; this is why long-term disputes and divisions are so resilient to solutions.

The Importance of Context

While many people think of the trust decision as primarily an evaluation of an individual's trustworthiness, the context surrounding the decision can have a profound impact on the perceptions that inform the decision at multiple levels. We often trust or mistrust people without knowing much about them as individuals. We often stereotype people, oversimplifying our judgments about them to justify our actions. The actions we take might not only be informed by our biased judgments but may also help elicit the responses we expect. Our biases and stereotypes may have their roots in personal experiences, but they can also be fueled by misperceptions, strong external voices, and a powerful narrative that we find evidence to support, even if it seems irrational to those around us.

As we explore each of the elements of the trust model in more detail, we will see that contextual factors can play as important a role as individual ones.

The Importance of Context to Perceived Uncertainty

I think of context as the rules of the game. It's the setting in which we are embedded, and it often deeply affects our behavior. I used to ask participants in my classes and workshops, "If you could be anywhere, doing anything, with anyone, right now, how many of you would be sitting here listening to me?" Overwhelmingly, people were easily able to think of somewhere they would rather be than sharing their time with me. I would then ask, "So why are you here?" The answer was often because they had to be, based on their job, their pursuit of a degree, or a relationship in their life they wanted to strengthen. Often the answer was their context. I eventually stopped asking—the answers weren't good for my self-esteem.

The inclusion of context allows us to understand why we trust, or mistrust, some people as soon as we interact with them. Rather than trying to figure out whether we trust them as individuals, we instead trust their role and the constraints placed on them within that role. Context can also be specific to a particular location or situation. The example I often use is a doctor's office. We sit in a room with a strange bed, maybe a couple of chairs, and some diplomas on the wall. A person enters in a white coat pulling on some latex gloves and asks us to take off our clothes. The odd part is that we usually do what they ask, even if we've never met them before. But what if we had the same two people, wearing the same clothes, and changed only the setting? Imagine instead that it's a gas station bathroom; the scenario instantly goes from plausible to downright creepy.

Figure 10: Context (Individual)

In deep relationships, uncertainty is very low and we're willing to be very vulnerable with one another—the relationship is very stable, and we're willing to trust one another in a broad range of situations.

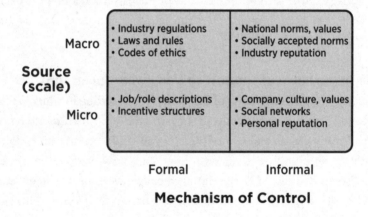

We can break down elements of context in a two-by-two matrix with mechanisms of control on the horizontal axis and scale of analysis on the vertical axis. There are formal and informal mechanisms of social control that constrain our actions, with a host of these mechanisms constraining our behavior every day. A few examples of *formal* mechanisms that are on the micro scale include job descriptions, evaluations, employment contracts, and local by-laws. Formal mechanisms that are more macro in nature include federal or regional laws, professional codes of conduct, and tax structures. *Informal* elements of context on the micro scale include personal relationships, our reputation, and group membership.

Informal elements of context that are more macro include cultural norms, values, national identity, and religious values. Understanding how we are constrained by these elements of context—or how we are perceived to be so constrained—can reduce uncertainty for others and help build trust.

How particular contexts affect our likelihood to trust may vary significantly based on our own personal context and experiences. For example, while I was attending graduate school in North Carolina, one of my colleagues arrived at school and seemed concerned. I asked him what was wrong, and he said that he'd had an uncomfortable trip to school. Apparently, a police car had followed him most of the way to the university. As a white male Canadian, I was somewhat confused; in my perception, there is no safer place on earth than standing next to a member of the Royal Canadian Mounted Police. However, as a Black man living in the southern United States, my friend had a very different perspective. Our contextual relationships with law enforcement, and hence our likelihood of trusting police officers, were dramatically different.

I could write another book, or at least a series of articles, just on formal and informal mechanisms of social control, but for now let me summarize them. Formal mechanisms tend to be more clearly defined, rigid, and reactive rather than proactive. Informal mechanisms often don't have the same direct power or immediate consequences as formal mechanisms, but they are often more flexible and have the potential to be proactive rather than reactive. Societies often incorporate a blend of formal and informal mechanisms that allow them to function in the face of complexity.

We are complex beings, seldom completely defined by any one element of our context. I am an executive coach, a teacher, and a scholar. These titles, however, don't completely define me; they provide understanding for only part of my context. I am also a father who loves his two sons above all else, which shapes my behaviors and priorities in many ways. I am a Canadian who loves his country, its history, and its people. This doesn't mean I disrespect other nations or nationalities—far from it—but it does help me understand how people can come to love something as abstract as their nation. I am happy to celebrate their love of their own country and countrymen, and I do not feel diminished or threatened by it. I care deeply about the individuals I meet and with whom I interact; I feel fortunate that my work often helps make a positive impact in their lives. This is my personal context—the situation in which I exist. There may be some elements of my context that might conflict with others, but by making clear which things are most important to me, I also help reduce uncertainty for others.

Many of the macro elements of context in today's society are in a state of flux because of the sheer pace of change that underlies so much of what we're talking about in this book: technological change, climate change, changes in values, and also extraordinary situational changes such as the COVID-19 pandemic. While these elements of the context within which we live are outside of our direct control, they do have an impact on our ability to build trust because they lead to higher levels of uncertainty. In chapter 6 we'll explore how to mitigate this issue.

Importance of Context to Perceived Vulnerability

We have already seen how the context of the person attempting to gain trust (the trustee) and the context of the person doing the trusting (the truster) can influence perceptions of uncertainty. The context of the truster can also influence their perceptions of vulnerability. It is important that we try to understand the other person's context when we are trying to build trust with them.

When I wrote about vulnerability earlier, I pointed out that scarcity can influence how much we value something. When there aren't as many opportunities available, we will feel more vulnerable. When the COVID-19 pandemic started having profound effects on employment opportunities, people started to feel increasing levels of vulnerability. Statistics showed significant unemployment levels and companies were struggling. This led many people to perceive that it wasn't an ideal time to be looking for a job, making them feel more vulnerable.

Context can influence our perceptions of vulnerability in other ways. Singing in the shower may be well within your comfort zone. Being asked to sing on stage might be a different matter. Trying something new can feel uncomfortable; being asked to do so in front of someone you're trying to impress can be excruciating. Revealing sensitive information about ourselves to anyone can be a challenge, but doing so in front of our parents might feel impossible. For instance, a teenager coming out to his or her parents would feel less vulnerable if their parents were open-minded and knowledgeable about LGBTQ issues and more so if they were vocally biased against such lifestyles.

Importance of Context to Perceived Outcomes

Part of how we interpret outcomes depends on the context that we, and others, are experiencing. Did the other person do what they did because they had to or because they chose to? Were there rules in place that dictated their behavior? Often our perceptions of other people's intentions, and external factors, play a significant role in how we evaluate them.

Earlier I mentioned my conversation with a CEO and his VP of sales, where I asked them what a good outcome would look like for the VP. The response from both was that "good" looked like the VP meeting or exceeding his sales targets for the year. I asked them if that definition or perspective would change if something happened to dramatically increase or decrease the demand for their product. We don't have to work too hard to imagine the following scenario: a global pandemic hits and dramatically, and detrimentally, affects the demand for their products (since they are not selling face masks, toilet paper, or disinfectant wipes). The definition of a good outcome may no longer be determined by absolute sales numbers but rather by something else, perhaps market share.

Importance of Context to Feelings

We can have emotional responses to others based on our perceptions of their context. While we often have a cognitive response to people based on their roles, we may also have an emotional response. The role of frontline workers during the pandemic has caused many of us to appreciate them more than we once did. We may well have an even more positive emotional response than usual to people involved in health care.

We often see emotional reactions to entire groups of people as a result of world events or our experiences. After the terrorist attack in the United States on September 11, 2001, there was a strong backlash against Muslims or people who looked like they might be Muslim. The origination of the COVID-19 pandemic has led to an emotional, irrational backlash against Asians. If we are trying to build trust with others, we need to understand how our context may trigger an emotional response from them that isn't rational.

Conclusion

This chapter has laid out the model for how people decide whether to trust others. It has also discussed the various levers we can pull to increase someone's likelihood of deciding to trust us. The focus here has been on explaining a framework of how the trust decision gets made and how perceptions of uncertainty, vulnerability, and perceived outcomes feed into that decision, including the effects of context, emotions, and feelings. In chapter 6, I'll lay out some steps you can take to diagnose where the trust problem lies, along with some examples of approaches you can take to pull these levers effectively.

Introducing the TU Trust Model:
Key Points Review

- Trust is the willingness (choice) to make yourself vulnerable to another person when you can't completely predict how they will act (uncertainty).

- Perceptions of uncertainty and vulnerability combine to give a level of perceived risk; a person will trust if their perceived risk is lower than their personal risk threshold. Building trust with someone requires reducing their perceived levels of uncertainty or vulnerability to a point where their level of perceived risk goes below their risk threshold.

- The bases of trust (uncertainty and vulnerability) arise both from elements specific to the individual and from contextual elements.

- The elements of individual uncertainty are benevolence (looking out for another's best interests), integrity (following through on promises and acting congruently with one's values), and ability (competence to deliver against expectations).

- While many people think of the trust decision as primarily an evaluation of an individual's trustworthiness, the context also has a profound impact on the perceptions that inform the decision. Context can influence uncertainty through both formal and informal mechanisms and at both the micro and macro scale.

- A person's perceptions of vulnerability depend on what's at stake and how much it's worth to them.

- The outcomes of a trust decision feed back to influence future trust decisions.

- Feelings (positive or negative) about a person or organization to be trusted influence the truster's perceptions of the elements of individual uncertainty and outcomes. Outcomes can in turn influence feelings, resulting in virtuous or vicious cycles.

CHAPTER 6

Fifty Ways to Love Your Lever: Using the Trust Model

EVERYBODY HAS THE ABILITY TO BUILD TRUST—SOME PEOPLE ARE simply a lot better at it than others. The question is why, and what can you do to improve? In the previous chapter I broke down the trust model into its subcomponents. A good way to think about it is as a series of levers you need to pull when you are trying to build trust with someone. My trust model has ten levers.

1. Benevolence
2. Integrity
3. Ability
4. Vulnerability
5. Perceived Outcomes
6. Feelings
7. Context (Uncertainty)
8. Context (Vulnerability)
9. Context (Outcomes)
10. Context (Feelings)

Figure 11: Trust Levers

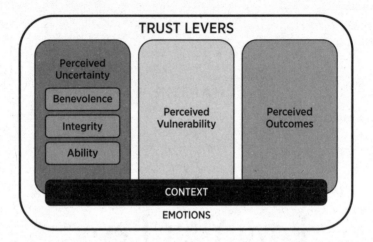

As discussed in chapter 5, the TU trust model provides a framework for trust-building; in this chapter I discuss each trust lever and how it connects to the model. Ultimately, the skill lies in pulling the right lever at the right time, which is at the point at which the gap in trust between you and the other person is due to that particular lever. Now we'll diagnose "trust gaps" by asking questions related to the different elements of the model, identify the available levers, and provide some general suggestions about how to pull each one.

Pulling these levers may feel a little unnatural at first, and it may take some time and effort to get comfortable identifying and solving trust gaps. Think of it like a new exercise routine where your muscles aren't used to the strain and pattern you are putting them through. We all pull these levers differently based on our past experiences and personalities, so feel free to alter or adapt the suggestions below to suit your specific needs.

When people first see the trust model, they often state that it's obvious. I've had people say to me, "It's common sense; of course this is how trust works!" However, they soon discover that it is challenging to apply the model to their own relationships and trust problems. In this chapter, I will give you some guidance and concrete examples to help you apply the model and build trust.

"Ask, Listen, Respond" as Emotional Intelligence

One of the mantras I use when teaching people how to build trust is "ask, listen, respond." Always include the other party when you are trying to discover and diagnose a trust gap. Through open dialogue with another person, we can begin to determine which levers may or may not be effective with a given party in a given situation.

When we approach trust problems, we often do so from a place of incomplete information and less than full awareness of what is in our own best interests or even what we would like the situation to look like. Sometimes, simply asking the right questions can signal to the other person that the relationship has value and that our aim is to make it better. We have to bear in mind that the other person may feel a sense of vulnerability when answering such questions. There is no guarantee that the person will have the answers we seek or that they will be willing to share such answers with us if they do. However, initiating a conversation is usually a central element in any attempt to build trust.

Daniel Goleman suggests that there are three kinds of empathy: cognitive, emotional, and compassionate.[38] *Cognitive* empathy allows us to understand how others think. This type of empathy can allow us to communicate with others in a way that demonstrates an intellectual understanding of the situation. *Emotional* empathy is an understanding of how others feel and allows us to navigate potential emotional responses. With emotional empathy we can elicit positive responses and avoid triggering negative ones. These two elements allow us to understand others and present ourselves to them in the best possible way. *Compassionate* empathy involves actually caring about others and taking action to help.

The first two elements of empathy equip us to be successful in communicating with other people, but they can be used positively or negatively because of our potential lack of caring. The third type of empathy, compassionate empathy, means we actually care about the other and have their best interests at heart; in other words, we have benevolence. The "ask, listen, respond" mantra has elements of these empathic archetypes baked into it. When we ask and truly listen, we are more likely to understand how others are thinking and feeling.

Pulling the Benevolence Lever

> **Definition of Benevolence**
> Benevolence is having someone's best interests at heart and acting in their best interests, even if it's not in your own immediate best interests to do so.

We often struggle to demonstrate our benevolence to others when we don't correctly identify or understand what is actually in their best interest. Even when we attempt to be benevolent, it doesn't always land that way because our efforts aren't framed or interpreted as we intended. We can run into trouble when we try to act in another's best interests, but they see it differently. It is, therefore, useful to discover whether someone thinks we are truly acting in their best interests—that is, in a benevolent manner. Asking the following questions will help start that conversation:

- What matters most to you?
- What does success look like for you?
- What would it look like to you if I were acting in your best interests?
- What can I do for you that would actually be helpful?
- I try to do things that I think are in your best interests; here are some examples. Do you see it that way?

These questions will help start a conversation that involves the other person to determine what is in their best interests and will help avoid any misinterpretation. If people are comfortable sharing what success looks like for them or what matters most to them, you can begin to take active steps toward helping them achieve those things. However, it is important to be transparent when you are taking actions that are intended to be benevolent to ensure others also interpret your actions as benevolence.

Imagine an employee says that they would like to advance to the next level professionally. You can start by asking questions such as, "What is it about that level that appeals to you?" and "Is this part of a formal progression plan you see for yourself?" You can also let them know the steps they will have to take or stages they will need to pass through to reach their goal. In future conversations, you can remind them about their aspirations and how the feedback you are giving them is related to those objectives. It is good to focus your feedback directly on their specific aspirations. The next step is to provide them with opportunities to demonstrate competence at tasks associated with that new role. Consider sending them for training that would help prepare them for that next level. Working with them in this way allows you to hold them to a higher standard than their peers because you are preparing them for the responsibilities of a more senior role.

It's important, and perhaps a little counterintuitive, to recognize that benevolence isn't always about being nice. Sometimes it involves holding people accountable or giving them tough feedback to help them reach their goals. How they interpret these actions is what matters. If they believe you are on their side and that you have their best interests at heart, they will be more likely to trust you and therefore accept your message more readily.

I was in a team meeting once with a group of people working for a large global organization. In casual conversation, one of the team members mentioned that she loved to travel. She stated with some enthusiasm that she had already visited dozens of countries. During the workshop I asked her boss how he thought he might display benevolence to her. The boss was stumped—and so was the employee (it's surprising how often this happens). Cutting to the chase, I suggested that the boss should start preparing his employee for a role within the company where travel was part of her job. It was a global company and there were several potential roles that would be a good fit for the employee and the firm. It was a "Eureka" moment for them; they immediately began talking about possible roles and the steps needed to make it a reality.

Now, there may be times when people are reluctant to tell you what matters most to them or what they feel is in their best interests. In this case, they may feel that by revealing these things they may be making themselves too vulnerable—that if they share what matters most to them, you may use that knowledge to take advantage of them. In short, they may not trust you enough to have an honest conversation about what matters most to them.

In situations like these, my advice is often to start by clearly stating that you would like to build a stronger relationship, letting the person know that your intent is to act in their best interests. If they are still uncomfortable sharing what matters most to them, you can consider their situation and make some educated guesses. You can then test your assumptions by telling them what you believe matters to them and act accordingly. In this case, as you engage in actions aimed at what you assume are their best interests, let them know that the actions you are taking are intended to help them. Keep communication lines open, and they will at some point open up about what matters to them.

For example, suppose that a leader, Kelly, is trying to build trust with her direct report, Stan. Stan seems reluctant to complain or raise any problems he might be experiencing. He appears to be an introvert and struggles to talk with his colleagues. He prefers to keep his head down and just do his work. Kelly tries to get Stan to have a conversation about what matters most to him or what success would look like for him. During this conversation, she gets the strong sense that what Stan would like most is not to be having this conversation.

Making the assumption that Stan, like most of her employees, would like to move up through the organization, Kelly decides to let him know that she is going to move ahead with trying to act in his best interest with that goal in mind. She also lets him know that he is free to let her know at any point if her perception isn't accurate and to let her know what success might actually look like for him.

Kelly enrolls Stan in a training program and tells him that this is intended to help him prepare for career advancement, again making it clear this is consistent with her assumptions about his aspirations. Stan still says nothing to disillusion her. Kelly then begins giving Stan the opportunity to prepare some reports that are more involved than is usual for his role. Once again, Kelly lets Stan know that these "stretch" tasks are aligned with her perceptions of where he would like to go. Stan completes the reports and talks with Kelly about some of the tougher parts. Based on his experience of Kelly trying to help him, and her benevolence, Stan reveals that he struggles with public speaking and wonders if he could try presenting the reports to a small group of people. Kelly sets up a small trial run for Stan and at the same time signs him up for a course on making presentations and public speaking.

Throughout this example, Kelly reduced Stan's uncertainty by explaining, and then following through on, her intentions to be benevolent. Eventually Stan opened up and shared something work-related that he would like to improve his skills. Had Kelly begun with offering public speaking classes, Stan may have frozen. Instead, Kelly showed that she intended to be benevolent and worked toward that until Stan trusted her enough to give her the opening to work with him directly toward his self-identified best interests.

Pulling the Integrity Lever

> **Definition of Integrity**
> Integrity is following through on our promises and acting in ways that align with the values that we express—in other words, not just "talking the talk" but "walking the walk."

Integrity is very much a perception issue. People create their own subjective reality based on what they see and hear and the stories they tell themselves. This means that how they view something you have done (or not done), or said (or not said), may not be objective. You may, in fact, be acting with the highest integrity, but someone else may simply not see it that way. This perception gap needs to be bridged, as before, with the "ask, listen, respond" mantra.

When you suspect another person's perception about your integrity is not lining up with objective reality, you can ask some of the following questions to help you understand where there are gaps:

- What promises do you think I've made?

- Do you believe I follow through on my promises?
- What are your expectations of me?
- Do you know what values I think are most important?
- Do you think I or the organization acts in a way that is consistent with our values?
- Can you think of areas where we don't live up to those values?

Be very careful about the promises you make. Research (and common sense) tell us it is better to underpromise and overdeliver. People will rarely complain if you overdeliver. In a similar vein, it is often better to promise things that are within your control rather than make promises about outcomes. It is far safer to make commitments about the things that you will personally undertake and the effort you will personally make.

One way to safely make promises is to create a systematic approach to situations that occur fairly often: for example, welcoming a new member to your team. Following a consistent process will allow your behavior and the situation to be more predictable and provide an opportunity to demonstrate your integrity by consistently and effectively orienting the new hire.

Being transparent when you believe you have followed through on a promise is an excellent way to reduce the possibility of misunderstandings. For example, after a conversation with someone, I often promise to send them some follow-up materials. In my email I will say, "As promised, here are the materials I said I would send." This allows the other party to let me know if they feel I had promised something else that I didn't completely follow through on.

When it comes to demonstrating integrity through the alignment of our actions and our values, we need to act intentionally. First, identify your core leadership values—how do you want to lead? Second, when taking any action, be thoughtful and intentional and ensure the action aligns with your values. Third, be sure to tell a clear story about how your actions link to your values. This will reduce the chance of a perception gap where the other person interprets things through their own lens.

Failure to follow through on the values expressed by an organization, or a leader often results in profound employee cynicism and disengagement. A leader should be able to tell a story that clearly shows how decisions are consistent with the values expressed.

Another way that leaders end up with their integrity questioned is when they exhibit a "do as I say, not as I do" attitude. When the rules apply only to some people and not to others, skepticism about the reasons for, and validity of, those rules starts to grow, resulting in a decline in trust levels.

Pulling the Ability Lever

> **Definition of Ability**
> Ability is having the competence to do what you say you will do; "excellence" is another way of referring to high levels of ability.

As I mentioned in chapter 5, the ability lever is the one that people most commonly use when trying to build trust. They believe that if they list all their credentials, the person sitting opposite will "trust" them. Ability is a common evaluation tool in hiring and promoting people. People talk about their credentials, status, experience, and history in an attempt to convey aptitude or excellence. The challenge, as I discussed in the previous chapter, is that it is difficult to define excellence. Worse, we often make assumptions about what other people think excellence means.

A key question is, Who should define excellence? Obviously, it makes sense to figure out who the stakeholders are before building a definition of excellence. As a leader, you can start with self-reflection and conversation with peers. To gain a broader perspective, you should add those to whom you report and the people you lead. This should help you create a list of credentials, actions, traits, or values that are required to demonstrate ability, based on the varied perceptions of the stakeholders involved.

Here are a few questions you might ask yourself and the relevant stakeholders:

- What does excellence look like in my role?
- What are the traits of an excellent leader?
- What are the essential skills of an excellent leader?
- Think of great leaders you've known or heard of; what made them great?

As an example, when I teach workshops or classes, I ask participants what excellence would look like in my role as an instructor. I usually get responses that include things such as a deep understanding of the material, the ability to share it with them in a way they can understand, application of the material in ways that are relevant to them, and the ability to engage them by being somewhat entertaining.

If I then think about what my employers would define as excellent, it would likely include a number of elements that aren't on my students' lists. My bosses would probably prefer that there are few, if any, complaints from students; that I complete administrative tasks in a timely manner; and that my teaching generates interest so that it improves their or the organization's reputation, making it easier to attract future students.

From my perspective and that of my peers, excellence includes elements from the stakeholders from whom I've already sought input but it also includes additional, distinct elements. I believe my performance has been excellent when participants not only understand what I'm trying to teach but actually apply it. I think I achieve excellence when I can enable someone to change the way they see and interact with the world. I have a passion for what I do. I care deeply about making an impact and improving the lives of those with whom I'm privileged to work. This review of my own and my stakeholders' perceptions of excellence allows me to figure out those elements of ability that are critical to me.

In conclusion, the first step in pulling the ability lever effectively is to define excellence properly. This will involve conversations with your key stakeholders about what excellence looks like for each of them. Since we can rarely be all things to all people, once we have a comprehensive list of the elements of excellence, the next step is to create our own list by deciding which elements are most critical and prioritizing them. The final step is to figure out how to demonstrate these elements of excellence effectively to those whose trust we are seeking to earn.

Pulling the Vulnerability Lever

Definition of Vulnerability
Perceived vulnerability is an assessment of what is at stake and how it is valued; it's what a person may (or thinks they may) lose in a given situation.

We feel vulnerable when we believe something of value is at stake: when we are in danger of losing money, a relationship, a job, and so on. How vulnerable we feel depends on how highly we value the thing we believe is at risk.

Including vulnerability in our trust model allows us to talk about the depth of a relationship. The deeper our relationship, the less uncertainty we feel and the more vulnerability we can tolerate. Early in relationships, uncertainty is usually high; this means the level of vulnerability we can tolerate is low.

Whatever the status of a relationship, whether it is shallow or deep, we can always be mindful of the level of vulnerability the other party feels and take steps to reduce those perceptions of vulnerability to make trusting us easier for them. As I mentioned in chapter 5, perceptions of vulnerability are incredibly subjective. To understand how vulnerable the other feels, we need to ask questions such as:

- What do you think is at stake here?
- How easy would it be for you to replace what you might lose?
- If something goes wrong here, will that have implications anywhere else for you?
- Is there a way I could make you feel more comfortable?

When we try to reduce someone's perception of vulnerability, we need to be aware that these perceptions are generated by a combination of an objective level of vulnerability and their subjective view that very likely contains misperceptions. If the person is unaware of how vulnerable they truly are, they can either overestimate or underestimate their actual level of vulnerability. Either situation can lead to problems.

People with inflated perceptions of their level of vulnerability are less likely to trust, even in situations where it may help them. Reducing exaggerated perceptions of vulnerability in these situations can help people make more rational decisions.

Conversely, people who are unaware of how vulnerable they really are may be inadvertently exposing themselves to more harm than they realize. For instance, if you purchased a cute vintage British MG Midget but the seller did not warn you that the spare parts were hard to come by and also very expensive, you might in retrospect blame the seller for not giving you a heads-up that this was the case. The bottom line is that you were more vulnerable than you at first realized.

In situations like this, as the seller, we could increase the buyer's trust level by making sure they are aware of the possible consequences of their purchase. This is, admittedly, a longer-term perspective, as it might mean they don't buy the vehicle immediately or we have to take steps to help them reduce their vulnerability before we can proceed. While there are elements of benevolence or integrity inherent in this approach, it also helps us understand and potentially help the other party manage their vulnerability.

If we can get a sense of the vulnerability someone feels they are experiencing and then compare notes (i.e., compare their understanding of how vulnerable they are with our perception of their vulnerability), we can act as a sounding board and hopefully reach agreement on the true level of vulnerability.

Reducing the Stakes

A person's perception of vulnerability stems, at least in part, from what he or she believes is at stake. On a positive note, it is possible for us to help reduce what others feel is at stake each time we interact with them. Companies do this with generous return policies and try-it-before-you-buy-it programs, for instance. Free samples are a way to reduce what is at stake. Many ice cream stores allow you to taste a sample of a flavor before you purchase a cone. Thinking about trying rum raisin ice cream for the first time? Don't buy a double scoop waffle cone only to discover you hate it; try a small sample first.

Like many online learning platforms, Trust Unlimited offers free materials and content in the blog section of its website. My company is also developing courses that require different levels of investment of time and money for participants.

The intent is to allow people to make an informed decision about whether they want to put the time, energy, and money into investing in a full course. This reduces uncertainty and vulnerability so it's easier for people to make a decision based on an understood level of risk. There is transparency around expectations, the cost of the course, and how much work will be involved.

In these examples, the level of vulnerability is rarely reduced to zero. People still have to invest time to watch a free video and there will be some mental effort required. In the ice cream example, you are still eating a mouthful of rum raisin ice cream, which you might hate, and you may also face judgment from others about how long you are taking to make your decision.

Understanding the Value

Another element of perceived vulnerability is how people value what they believe is at stake. In part, this valuation is driven by scarcity (e.g., friends, money, jobs). As leaders, we can reduce perceptions surrounding the value of what is at stake by educating and raising awareness of alternatives or even creating alternatives. Similarly, we can offer insurance policies that will protect the other party in the event something goes wrong.

Leaders can take steps to reduce perceptions of vulnerability by developing their employees, highlighting their skills, and promoting their abilities within the organization. This might open up more opportunities for alternative employment for your team members should you have to reduce your department head count, for instance. Helping those you lead learn new skills and gain accreditations make them more in demand, internally and externally. These steps can reduce scarcity by generating other opportunities and hence make those you lead less vulnerable.

Unlinking Outcomes

Our perceptions of vulnerability, and our actual vulnerability, can be increased by the impact an interaction might have on future interactions. For instance, you might be concerned that making a comment in a meeting, disagreeing with someone above you in the hierarchy, or providing honest feedback about, or to, your boss may be damaging later.

These examples provide just a glimpse of how we often connect potential outcomes to influence our perceptions of vulnerability. A great example of linked outcomes is in a gangster movie where the hero is grilling some hoodlum and they say, "I can't tell you. If I tell you, they'll hurt me." Giving one person what they want will lead to harm from another.

The first step to unlinking outcomes is to think about what other consequences the third party might face. In a labor negotiation, all participating parties have people they represent who are not at the table. It is rare that these situations are onetime events. As we saw in chapter 4, winning big in one negotiation can lead to hard feelings and resentment, which lead to difficult working relationships and vindictive behavior in the next negotiation. Being aware that the parties present will need to go back to talk to those they represent should lead to a shared interest in creating a situation where all parties can tell a positive story.

Some of the concern about linked outcomes involves a fear of loss of reputation. This concern can be alleviated by guarantees of anonymity. We see this when employees are allowed to fill out anonymous surveys, or with brainstorming sessions or focus groups, where the identities of those involved are concealed. We can also put rules in place to guarantee confidentiality.

Pulling the Perceived Outcomes Lever

> **Definition of Perceived Outcomes**
> Perceived outcomes are an evaluation of what happened as well as attribution of credit or blame.

It is important to manage people's perceptions of outcomes because these perceptions have a significant impact on their decision whether to trust you in the future. One of the struggles you will often face is that rather than thinking ahead about what outcome they would consider to be "positive" or "negative," people tend to make that determination only after the fact. This can lead different people evaluating the same experience to have dramatically different perceptions of it.

When my sons were young, we played a game called Kerplunk. The game involves marbles suspended on sticks in a cylinder. Each player takes a turn and removes a stick. If any marbles fall through the spaces between the sticks during a player's turn, they accumulate in a small tray. My youngest son decided that, for him, winning meant collecting the most marbles. My oldest son decided that winning meant collecting the fewest marbles. I decided that winning meant having two happy sons. The end result was that everyone felt like they won. However, had others been playing the game, they may well have had different notions of what was a good or bad outcome.

The best strategy, therefore, is to define what success looks like in any given interaction before it occurs. This will allow you to strategically focus your efforts and resources toward a shared understanding of what success looks like. Taking this approach will significantly increase the likelihood of success. By knowing what a successful outcome looks like (to them), each involved party will be less likely in retrospect to wish they had done things differently.

Here are some questions you can ask people before they make the decision to trust you, and most importantly, before an outcome occurs:

- What would success (in this interaction or our relationship more generally) look like for you?
- What are some of the criteria you use to measure success?
- Does the outcome of this exchange impact other things for you? If it does, what are they, and how will this help or possibly hinder?
- What would your best-case scenario look like?

You will need to work closely with the person whose trust you are trying to earn to create a shared narrative for how the outcome will, or will not, be consistent with your joint objectives. Working together reduces the probability of dramatically different perceptions of the outcome. It also helps you prepare for success in future interactions with the same person.

For example, we often see a misalignment of expectations when it comes to youth athletics. For one parent, the outcome is either good or bad depending on whether their child's team won. For another it is the improvement in their child's skill and development that defines a good outcome. A third parent might have the perspective that sports are intended to help children develop a whole slew of social skills and develop sustainable habits that lead to healthier lives.

Of course, in reality it is rare for anyone to fall into only one of these three camps. Few parents want their kids to learn that cheating or hurting others is acceptable as long as you win. Others are fine with their kids losing every game as long as no one's feelings get hurt.

In groups, the highest level of success is among those who agree on what "good" looks like before they start. This is equally true within organizations of all kinds.

Pulling the Feelings Lever

> **Definition of Feelings**
> Feelings (as relevant to the trust model) are liking or disliking another person or group.

Our emotions (the way we feel) can have an overwhelming impact on our assessment of others and our evaluation of their actions. This impact can be either positive or negative, and it becomes more pronounced depending on the depth of the emotions we are experiencing in any particular situation. Indeed, emotional states can create situations that appear to defy reason. These situations are difficult for outsiders to understand if they are viewed only through a rational lens. Resolutions to these types of situations are difficult to find if people haven't dealt with the emotions that are driving them.

Before you can attempt to resolve situations that are loaded with emotion, you first need to correctly identify that the issues you are facing are tied to feelings. In extreme situations this is relatively easy. If someone is angry or sad, or they love or hate someone, they will find it difficult to hide their true emotions. However, when things are not so extreme, people often hide their feelings if they can to avoid any judgment. When considering how people feel about us, introspection can be a valuable tool.

Asking direct questions about someone's emotions can be challenging because it can be seen as provocative; it can also trigger feelings in ourselves. For example, if we ask people whether they like (or dislike) us, it can make them feel uncomfortable. To avoid this, a better, more introspective approach might be to ask ourselves:

- Is there a negative history between us?
- Am I close to someone they care about?
- Are they jealous or envious of my position at work or of me personally?
- How do I feel about the person with whom I am trying to build trust?
- Do I know how they feel about me?
- Are they comparing me with someone they dislike or whom they are prejudiced against?
- Might they have stereotypes or biases against me or people like me?

These questions can help us identify possible issues related to feelings prior to having a conversation with someone.

If you are anticipating negative emotions when dealing with someone, you need to see if you can make those feelings more neutral. One effective way to achieve this is to share something about yourself with the other party. It is more difficult to dislike someone once you know them. For example, a flashy car races by you and then drifts into your lane cutting you off, and you call the anonymous driver an imbecile (or worse). A few minutes later you see them a few paces ahead of you walking into the local coffee shop; they courteously hold the door open for you and you recognize them as the father of one of your son's friends. Do your feelings toward them change? It is more challenging to dislike people based on stereotypes and false narratives if we know them.

If you try to put yourself in the other person's shoes and understand the situation from their perspective, it can reduce the emotional charge that exists. Saying something like, "I'm trying to understand your perspective, is this what you are saying/feeling?" has the potential to lead to a more open conversation. Demonstrating a desire to understand and improve things will often lead to a reciprocal approach from the other person.

We tend to like people who are similar to us. Sharing personal information can help you discover common areas of interest or common beliefs. Asking questions can also help you find common ground. Once you've found areas of common interest, try to focus on those areas and make them more relatable for the other person. In this way the other person will feel you "hear" them and that the two of you are more connected.

We also tend to like people who like us. Letting people know that you appreciate them or respect them tends to lead to a response in kind. Commenting on someone else's strengths, or the things that you think make them special, will evoke a positive response in all but the most difficult cases.

Recently, I was a guest lecturer for a virtual course called Mad Love. It was for married couples who were looking to strengthen their relationships. I began by explaining the concept of excellence, but instead of focusing on what excellence looked like in terms of a marital partner and what could be improved, I asked them to identify an area in which their partner was already strong and to share with the group something they really appreciated about their partner. At the end of the exercise the couples looked noticeably happier, and it was very clear from the Zoom screens that during the lecture they had physically moved closer together.

What Is Context?

> **Definition of Context**
> Context (with respect to the trust model) is the formal and informal mechanisms of social control that influence our behavior.

I think of context as the rules of the game: the formal and informal mechanisms of social control that influence people's behavior. By understanding context from this perspective, we can better understand the range of possible actions others might take and thereby reduce uncertainty.

Context also plays roles in other areas. It is the background against which we evaluate and respond to everything. It serves as a proxy for our experiences and expectations. A situation's context can make us feel more or less vulnerable, it can provoke emotional responses, and it can profoundly impact our perception of an outcome.

My friend Paul Saurette was fond of saying that "context is not your fault, but it is your problem." We often don't have control over other people's history or preferences. We don't know all of their trigger points or to whom they compare themselves. If, however, we can make an effort to better understand where they're coming from (i.e., their context), we will more likely avoid missteps and build trust. In turn, by being more transparent with our own context, we can make it easier for other people to predict our behavior. In both cases, an increased awareness of context helps build trust.

Pulling the Context (Uncertainty) Lever

Definition of Context (Uncertainty)
Context (uncertainty) is the "rules of the game": the formal and informal mechanisms, at the micro and macro scale, that constrain our behavior.

When I talk about the uncertainty aspect of context, I am talking about helping other people understand the constraints you are facing. Once they recognize the context in which you are operating, it is easier for them to predict your behavior and reduce their uncertainty.

Asking context-related questions allows you to share information with others that in turn helps you identify things you have in common. Asking generic questions about their context will allow you to look for examples. These might include:

- Where are you from?
- What do you do for a living?
- What brings you here today?
- What types of hobbies do you have?

Simple questions to be sure, but they allow the other person to identify with you. Just these four questions can offer many opportunities to connect. I teach a lot of international students, and not so long ago I had a couple of Romanian students. I mentioned that my grandparents on my father's side of the family were from Romania, and this gave me an opening to ask them questions and share a part of myself.

Asking these types of questions also plants a seed. By asking about someone else, you open a conversation to how much (or how little) they know about you. You can then begin asking clarifying questions about people's understanding of your context and how it constrains you. These questions might include:

- Do you know what my role is?
- Do you understand how I get evaluated?

- Have you had experience with someone in my position before? How did that go?
- What are your expectations of me?

How do you build trust using this context? In part, you can clarify for others how you are constrained. Let them know what, in a *formal context*, you can or can't do for them. This reduces uncertainty and builds trust. Your context has multiple facets so you can discover areas of overlap where you share common ground. This allows you to feel kinship or a camaraderie (informal context) that makes it feel like you can understand one another better. This again reduces uncertainty.

When I was working with a group of first-generation university students who were predominantly minorities at Cal State Fullerton Social Capital Academy, I shared my background and history. As you read in chapter 1, my history includes some challenging experiences. Once I had laid out the challenges I faced and the resilience I had shown, the students saw me in a different light. I was no longer a privileged white male academic. I was now someone who had faced challenges and overcome them—someone to whom they could relate. This allowed me to talk to them on a different level and increased the impact of my words and teaching.

In this way, we can actually change or reinforce the context that constrains our actions in order to help reduce uncertainty and build trust. We can do this with formal elements of the context by introducing new rules, policies, and procedures or by entering into contracts. We can change the way we evaluate performance to try to encourage different behaviors. If we don't have the ability to change some of the formal elements of the context, we can lean on the informal elements to constrain our own behavior.

You can make changes within the informal elements of the context by making public commitments or introducing people to your network of friends and colleagues, with the result that any bad behavior would directly impact your reputation. For example, imagine I introduced you to my mentor and told him I was doing business with you. If I shared his email address with you, you would have an open line of communication to tell him if I ever behaved poorly. This puts pressure on me to act appropriately because my reputation with my mentor is very important.

There are a number of ways we can constrain ourselves informally. Examples include making public commitments to a large group of people, making private commitments to important people, putting up a peace bond (e.g., if I don't follow through on my commitment, I will donate fifty dollars to a charity of your choice), or sharing information that we don't want shared with others, to be released if we don't keep our promises.

Pulling the Context (Vulnerability) Lever

> **Definition of Context (Vulnerability)**
> Context (vulnerability) is the elements of the truster's situation that make them feel more or less vulnerable.

When I talk about the context aspect of vulnerability, we are trying to understand the context of the person with whom one is trying to build trust. That is, does their context make them more or less vulnerable? As discussed in chapter 5, a person's vulnerability is based on what someone thinks is at stake and how they value it. Context can influence our perceptions of vulnerability, and this mostly happens through how we value what is at stake. Our environment can be rich with plenty of opportunities, or it can be scarce with few options. The scarcer something is, the more valuable it becomes and the harder it is to replace. For example, if unemployment is high, then jobs are scarce and people will feel more vulnerable if their job is threatened.

The example I used in chapter 5 was singing in the shower versus singing in front of a huge crowd. The setting alone can make us feel more vulnerable. It's one thing for some unfortunate soul to pass by the bathroom while I'm belting out show tunes, but subjecting a crowd of people to that experience seems overly cruel. What if someone records the event and shares it with others? How much damage would I potentially do and what would the long-term consequences be? People who heard me sing might wish they were deaf or become traumatized by the thought that I might sing again. There could be ripple effects or linked outcomes related to the experience. While most of this seems like vulnerability for those exposed, it is also a very real concern for me.

Questions you can ask others when assessing their vulnerability are generally centered on what they think is at stake and how they value it. For example:

- What do you think is at stake here?
- How easy would it be for you to replace that scarce item?
- Is there a way I could make you feel more comfortable?

People will always have some level of discomfort in scarce environments, where resources and opportunities (e.g., food, jobs, shelter, safety) are hard to come by. The best way to reduce a person's vulnerability is to provide them with options or help them increase their probability of success—whatever that looks like to them. If we consider the employment example, we can help people make themselves more valuable through training, development, and identifying job opportunities. This could also mean introducing them to other people in the organization and allowing them to succeed. This may make them more attractive within the company and reduce their vulnerability by giving them increased flexibility to move to other roles in the organization should something happen to their current position. In addition, if they are forced to leave the organization, they will be far more attractive in a potentially tough job market. Furthermore, the stronger network they have built within the company will help them find new leads.

In terms of contextual vulnerability, there are steps you can take to reduce people's perceived vulnerability. You can allow them to slowly and gradually increase the amount of exposure they face. If we go back to my singing example, we could expose a couple of brave souls to my singing and allow them to leave if they can bear it no longer, or offer them therapy. Who knows, there may be a niche of people who actually appreciate my singing—masochists, perhaps?

Pulling the Context (Perceived Outcomes) Lever

> **Definition of Context (Outcomes)**
> Context (outcomes) is the external comparisons that the truster can make either with their own previous outcomes or with others with whom they compare themselves.

When talking about the perceived outcomes aspect of context, you need to be aware of the constraints on the person attempting to build trust and the context of the person who is doing the trusting.

When someone evaluates an outcome, they base their findings on a number of criteria, including how well something went relative to something else. On a personal level it might be how they performed in relation to a competitor or colleague. There is a psychological construct called relative deprivation theory. It suggests that people are happy as long as they feel they are doing at least as well as those around them. This construct helps us understand why people who appear to have virtually nothing can still be happy, and those who, objectively, have more than most can feel miserable. While this may not be a complete explanation, it is usually part of the equation.

When I'm grading assignments for my students, many are concerned not only with how well they did but how well they did relative to their classmates. We see this play itself out in many settings because such a comparison gives us a sense of how well we *really* did. Was the task easy or hard? Knowing how others did helps us calibrate our own performance.

Another way people evaluate outcomes is through their perception of the other party's intent. It's one thing to assess whether someone has been helpful or harmful, but the motivation for that help or harm also plays into their evaluation of the outcome. Did the other party have any alternatives? What rules were they playing by when they acted? Did they help or harm because they wanted to or because they had to?

When you are trying to build trust, there may also be situations where people perceive your actions incorrectly. For instance, if in your initial interactions with someone you show kindness, it can be mistaken for weakness. In these instances, you may find that you have to reset the other person's perceptions by establishing boundaries. You may also need to impose consequences for those who seek to take advantage of you, so that your kindness is correctly interpreted.

Here are some of the questions you might ask relating to the context of perceived outcomes:

- What would a good outcome look like for you?
- With what or with whom will you compare your results?
- Do you understand what my options and constraints are?

You can manage outcome perceptions within a given context by being clear about the constraints you are under, along with the possible actions that are open to you. A successful strategy to maintain trust is to clarify what you can and can't do. You have to be transparent around the outcome experienced by the person you are dealing with, compared to other similar situations. The key is to explain that you have tried to act in the person's best interests. In cases where the outcome did not fully benefit the person, you need to explain that you did your best considering your constraints. This honest and open course of action goes a long way to building and maintaining trust.

I mentioned the theory of relative deprivation, which is essentially how people's perceptions of their performances are influenced by their peer groups. The challenge is that often they are not comparing themselves to the right group.

Remember my earlier example of the company that provided everyone in the company the same flat bonus? In that case, some of those earning higher salaries were disappointed with this decision. They felt that bonuses should have been a percentage of compensation rather than equally distributed. We need to be aware that inevitably comparisons such as these will be made. As leaders we need to be able to provide appropriate context by making them aware of multiple reference groups. We also need to be able to communicate other possible options that were considered. In this instance it would seem that getting money versus not getting money is a good thing. However, higher earners' negative reactions to the outcome of not getting paid more than everyone else might have been anticipated and dealt with before the announcement was even made. Managing expectations is critical to the management of perceived outcomes.

Pulling the Context (Feelings) Lever

Definition of Context (Feelings)
Context (feelings) is the history and experience of the truster that may provoke emotional response to phrases, gestures, or symbols.

People can exhibit strong emotional responses to symbols or group membership. These responses can be immediate and overpowering, negative or positive. For many, the swastika provokes an immediate negative response; for others it can be statues and flags from the Civil War South in the United States.

Many symbols evoke powerful positive emotional responses too, one of the most common being one's national flag. When I was living and studying in the United States, I experienced moments of homesickness for Canada. On one occasion, I remember watching an episode of a television series called *Due South* about a member of the Royal Canadian Mounted Police living and working in Chicago as part of the staff of the Canadian embassy. There was a scene in one episode where a group of Mounties parachute into a remote location to rescue the series' main characters. The parachutes looked like Canadian flags, and my response was positive, immediate, and emotional.

Emotions can also be triggered by gestures, phrases, and general language. Groups will often signal membership with one another in these ways. Such actions may also exclude others from membership and thus serve to separate rather than unite us. Another consideration, particularly with hand gestures, is that what can be innocuous in one country can be insulting in another. Even nodding one's head can be misinterpreted depending on your nationality. Talk about mixed signals.

Here are a few questions that can help you navigate context as it relates to feelings:

- Does the other party belong to groups with which they strongly identify?
- How do they signal that to the world?
- Are there symbols or gestures that might have significant meaning for them?
- Are there groups that they strongly dislike (e.g., political parties, religious groups, activist groups)?

You need to be aware of the cues you are sending and how they may affect those with whom you are interacting. Some people wear certain symbols to signal to others that they are in the same tribe or to broadcast their beliefs or status to others (e.g., a cross, a yarmulke, tribal tattoos, academic robes). If our goal is to build trust, we need to be aware of, and intentional with, these types of signals.

You can also get into significant trouble for falsely signaling that you are part of a group to which you don't actually belong. This becomes an integrity violation if we pretend we are something we aren't.

Some of those who write and speak about trust frequently talk about being "authentic." But others might hear, "Accept my being authentic" to mean, "You must accept me as I am." When we saw the crowd of people storming the US Capitol building on January 6, 2021, they certainly appeared authentic. While this helped them build trust with their followers, it did little to build trust with those outside that in-group. Similarly, wearing symbols that provoke those who do not agree with your stance will make it profoundly harder to establish trust with them.

While working with a company that had a history of difficult labor relations, I was asked to spend some time working with senior executives and leaders from the unions. This was a challenging engagement as emotions were running high for all parties—they didn't like each other. Compounding this was the fact that the next round of negotiations for a new labor agreement was rapidly approaching.

At the start of the session, I took some time to outline how I understood each parties' perspectives. I made it clear I wasn't biased toward any of them and understood their positions, so they wouldn't automatically dislike me and discount the message I was trying to share.

I told everyone that I had worked with senior executives in a range of capacities in the past, so I understood their concerns. I also told everyone that my father was a welder who had been a member of a union for decades. I let them know that I had personally experienced situations where people had been treated unfairly by management, and I understood the need for organized labor. I also made clear to everyone that I wasn't on anyone's side and that I would hold all parties accountable.

By taking these steps, I short-circuited any "story" those in the room might have had in their heads that I was in any way biased toward or against either side. This helped avoid any emotional response. Once all parties knew I wasn't going to play favorites, I was able to tell them that my intent was to give them a framework that would promote conversation. As the session progressed, I included all the parties equally and I attempted to evoke empathy on both sides.

As an example, one of the union representatives commented on the fact that the workers tended to be long-term employees, but senior management seemed to have high turnover. For him, this signaled the workers' commitment to the company and cast doubt on the senior executives' commitment. I asked him if he thought senior executives were well compensated and if the job was prestigious. He said it was. I then asked him what he thought that suggested about the nature of the senior management job. He paused for a moment, looked at me and said, showing some newfound empathy, "I guess that means it's a pretty tough job."

Understand, Align, Diagnose, Resolve, Evaluate

When someone comes to me asking for help with a trust problem, I go through a multistep process. I try to *understand* the people and the problem, *align* myself with their goals, *diagnose* where the trust gaps are, help them formulate a response to *resolve* the problem, and then *evaluate* whether any progress has been made. Signs of a strengthening relationship can generally be seen after just one pass through this process. However, it often takes multiple attempts to deepen and strengthen a long-term relationship.

My first objective in this process is to *understand* the situation and the people involved. Once I have achieved that, I delve deeper into what has happened in the past, identify the gaps in trust, and determine what, if anything, has changed over time. This involves listening to all parties' stories and their perspectives on how they got to the current point. In some ways this is like executive coaching; in coaching it is necessary to gain an understanding and awareness of the person being coached, but here we also have to make an effort to understand how all parties are interpreting the situation. When I am working with an individual, I need to have empathy not only for them but also for the party or parties with whom they are trying to solve a trust problem.

Stage two is to *align* myself with my client. What goals do they have? What does good look like to them? What would change if they enjoyed higher trust levels? It is the same process when you are trying to bridge gaps in trust: you need to understand or anticipate the goals of the other party.

For example, I worked with a manager who was struggling with one of her direct reports; she and her employee seemed always to be in conflict. The first thing I did was to identify the manager's motives. Was she trying to get rid of the employee? In this case, that was not her objective; what she wanted was to help them do better and succeed. Then I asked the manager a series of questions: What skills does this person have? Have they been placed in a position where they have an opportunity to succeed? Have you had a conversation about what success looks like for them? Once the manager engaged with her employee, she discovered that he felt no one was supporting him, and he felt isolated. That simple discovery led to the manager changing her internal story. She began communicating with her direct report differently and positioning him to be more successful. This in turn led to better performance from the employee and a new openness to coaching and development. The employee went from being a constant source of conflict to a useful and helpful member of the leader's team.

Once I have gained an understanding of the situation, the people involved, and their goals, I move on to step three and, using the TU trust model laid out in chapter 5, I *diagnose* the trust gaps and what approaches might be taken to make things better. This is where pulling the right levers, as described in this chapter, is important to help *resolve* the problem.

Finally, I need to *evaluate* how my efforts landed. As most relationships experience more than one trust gap, it's important to evaluate the effectiveness of the actions taken and whether any of the steps need to be repeated. Building trusting relationships is complex and may require several trips through this process.

Pulling It All Together

Let's look at a trust gap case scenario. You are a new leader attempting to get off to a good start with your direct reports. The first thing you will want is to convince your new team that you can do the job. An excellent way to do this is to understand the perspectives of those you lead and your team's most important stakeholders. Part of this journey will include learning whose trust you need and what achieving higher trust levels will lead to for you and your team. Next you will need to engage in an empathetic exercise to align yourself with the needs and perspectives of the people with whom you want to strengthen your relationships. This exercise will likely involve a series of conversations with those you lead and representatives of the stakeholders in question. Finally, diagnose any gaps. Are there questions surrounding your ability, benevolence, or integrity? Do your people understand your context? Have there been events that have led to perceptions of vulnerability for those you lead or your other stakeholders?

Once the diagnosis step is finished, it's time to start thinking about which levers to pull. Some may have direct experience working with you, but others might think they know you based only on your reputation or history. An excellent start is to share with them your background and credentials and to explain your vision for where things are going. This is pulling the ability lever. While rarely sufficient on its own, a certain baseline of ability is a necessary condition of being trusted.

Having read this book, you now know that the best next step is to pull the benevolence lever. This is the strongest lever for leaders to use with the people who answer to them. Pulling this lever means actively trying to understand what your team members feel are their best interests. To do this, you create opportunities for people to share what matters to them and what success looks like for them, and you then include them in a conversation about how you can help them reach the success they aspire to.

None of your efforts will be effective if people don't believe that you will follow through, so you must endeavor to demonstrate your integrity. One way to ensure this is to make promises relating to efforts, not outcomes that are outside your control. Then you check in with your team members regularly to see whether you both agree that a promise has been followed through to its conclusion. At all times you are transparent about your values and how your actions align with those values. You are, in effect, creating a shared narrative so that everyone's story is similar.

As you grow in experience within your new role, you gain a better understanding of the context in which you and your team are embedded. You provoke conversations about that context so that everyone has a shared understanding of the formal and informal rules that guide your decisions. As the rules evolve, you are clear with your team about how the changes will impact your decisions and actions. When necessary, you create new rules that help reduce uncertainty and make the behavior of you and your team easier to predict.

Over time you will recognize the different levers you can pull and when, and you can practice all of them.

Recovering after a Violation of Trust

I often get asked how we can recover trust after things have gone wrong. The breakdown can be between individuals, countries, a company and a customer, or individuals and their government. Groups can become alienated, resulting in people within a group struggling to interact because of a strong narrative or a strained relationship. Some turn into ongoing feuds ranging in scale from individual relationships (divorced couples, estranged siblings) to long-running disputes between nation-states (e.g., India and Pakistan, Palestine and Israel). While the latter provided interesting cases related to hostile environments I featured in my original PhD thesis, this book is focused more on one-on-one relationships that have gone awry.

The first question I ask when a relationship has gone from trusting to not trusting is, "What has changed?" If we review things through the lens of the trust model, we can ask specific questions about what has changed, such as:

- Are there increased levels of uncertainty?
- If so, do they come from us as individuals or has the context changed?
- Has there been a change in the perceived levels of vulnerability?
- Was there a recent event that had an unexpected outcome?
- Have feelings changed?

It is unlikely that a betrayal of trust will affect just one of the bases of trust. Following a trust violation, people often feel an increased level of vulnerability. As their perception of the person's benevolence, integrity, or ability takes a hit, their perceived level of uncertainty will increase. Depending on the type of violation that has occurred, there can also be an emotional response.

A violation of someone's trust will usually manifest itself as disappointment in the way things worked out and in the other person involved. The person whose trust was violated often experiences a sense of betrayal, a feeling that things didn't go the way they expected or thought they should. When trying to rebuild trust, you need to make an effort to understand the story that is being told by the person with whom you are attempting to rebuild trust.

Once you have identified the gaps that have been created, you need to take steps to explain and repair the damage. A level of empathy is required. You need to understand the story the other person is telling themselves about what happened, the role you played, and the level of responsibility they believe you should bear. Consider how the person was harmed and what the implications are for them.

If you are to recover and regain the trust that has been lost, you need to acknowledge what happened and recognize (and accept) how it impacted the other party. Allow them space to agree with, or to correct, your perceptions surrounding the situation and the harm they feel they experienced. An expression of remorse coupled with a clear understanding of how they were harmed can go a long way toward resetting emotional states.

The next step is to explain why you feel the failure occurred. What are the reasons behind what the other party experienced? What is your story? What can you do to make up for what has happened?

I am sure you can come up with examples of significant trust violations from your own experiences. Use these to practice the skills you have learned so far in this chapter. However, I suggest you start with something that is more disappointing than devastating. The following case study demonstrates a type of trust violation that many people have experienced.

Jackie's boss had been hinting for a while that she was in line for promotion. She had been working hard, getting good feedback, and going above and beyond to justify that she was worthy of the step up. But when the promotion was announced, it was given to someone else. After the initial shock, Jackie began to wonder what went wrong. Was it something she'd said or not said? Was her boss just taking advantage of her and lying to get her to work harder? Or was there something more sinister at work? Did the person promoted get preferential treatment because they "knew" the right people? All these stories flooded Jackie's brain, and a sense of outrage and betrayal started to build. The voices in her head convinced her that she should have got the promotion, that she deserved it, that it was stolen from her.

Jackie's performance and productivity quickly slipped, and her boss immediately recognized his part in causing the problem and his need to rebuild the relationship. He invited Jackie into his office and said, "I know you expected to get the promotion, and I can only imagine how disappointed you must be. I've seen the extra work you've been doing and how well you are performing. I know that while I didn't ever tell you explicitly that the promotion was yours, I can see how you thought that would be the case."

His next step was to acknowledge the harm that he might have done. Once again, he showed empathy by saying, "I can imagine you were already seeing yourself in your new role. I'm so sorry. I really thought you were going to get the promotion. I know that most of your colleagues were thinking you were going to be moving up. If it were me, I'd be furious. You have every right to be angry with the organization and with me. However, I hope we can move past this and look constructively at your future with the company."

This stage of the conversation would allow Jackie either to agree with her boss's assessment or to correct him. Possibly she could add things he wasn't aware of. Perhaps the promotion had implications for others in Jackie's family or other decisions were being made based on the expected increase in salary. Another area of potential vulnerability could be Jackie's expectations about the future in the form of a shaken belief in her role with, and value to, the company. Will she *ever* get promoted? Is this a signal that the company or her boss doesn't believe in her?

The next step in this situation was for the boss to try to understand the story that Jackie was telling him and explain why he failed to follow through. Asking about Jackie's perspective could include questions such as:

- What do you think the criteria were for the promotion?
- Why do you think you didn't get the job?
- Why do you think the other person got the job?
- Is there anything you can think of that they have and you don't?

It may be a challenge to get direct answers to difficult questions like these, particularly given that Jackie's trust levels have likely been shaken pretty badly. It may take some probing, prompting, or guessing on the part of the boss.

Now it is the time for the boss to share his version of what happened and try to take steps to reduce the likelihood of it happening again. For the purposes of this example, let's assume the boss really did think Jackie was the best candidate for the promotion when he was were giving her hints to that effect and encouraging her. It was only during the formal decision-making process that other leaders weighed in and not only made the boss aware of another candidate for the position but successfully lobbied on that candidate's behalf with people further up the corporate ladder.

This reveals what may have been gaps in Jackie's understanding of the context; she may have believed the boss was the sole decision-maker. It may suggest a gap in Jackie's perceptions surrounding her boss's integrity. He made promises, albeit implied ones, on which he couldn't follow through. She may also have concerns about her boss's ability (or lack thereof) to influence those higher up in the organization on behalf of those he leads.

To address these concerns, the boss needs to take action and begin raising Jackie's profile so that other decision-makers are also aware of her skills and work ethic. The boss needs to clarify how the decision-making process takes place and have a conversation with Jackie about how they will jointly prepare for the next promotion opportunity. He should also approach senior leadership about the issue and see if there are other mechanisms they can put in place to reward Jackie to show her she is valued.

There are many possible ways this story could have gone, and it highlights a remarkable variety of ways that we can let people down or damage the trust they have in us.

In this chapter, I provided you with an overview of the ten trust levers you can pull to bridge the trust gaps we all experience in our lives and careers. Knowing which lever to pull, and when to pull it, won't come naturally at first. Be patient; I guarantee that with a little practice you will begin to recognize real-life situations where pulling one of the levers will benefit a relationship or help rebuild trust. Don't be afraid to experiment, even though it might feel strange at first. And feel free to adapt my suggestions to meet specific situations. Treat the information in this chapter and in chapter 5 like a workbook—use an applied approach and work through the trust model.

The TU trust model has been comprehensively tried and tested, as you will see in the case studies that follow. Each case study describes a unique trust problem and how I used it to close trust gaps. The studies range from helping the military in Afghanistan to build trust in hostile environments, to reducing uncertainty and increasing customer confidence at a leading financial planning company, to working with more than five hundred leaders at one of the world's leading software producers to build a more trusting work environment.

Fifty Ways to Love Your Lever: Key Points Review

- Everybody has the ability to build trust—some people are simply a lot better at it than others.

- The TU trust model has ten levers: benevolence, integrity, ability, vulnerability, perceived outcome, emotions, context (uncertainty), context (vulnerability), context (outcomes), context (feelings).

- The skill lies in pulling the right lever at the right time, which is at the point at which there is a gap in trust between you and the other person.

- To build trust, ask, listen, and then respond. Open dialogue helps determine which levers may or may not be effective with a specific person in a particular situation.

- Solving a trust problem: understand the people and the problem, align yourself with their goals, diagnose where the trust gaps are, help them formulate a response, and then evaluate progress. Note: it often takes multiple attempts to deepen and strengthen a long-term relationship.

- The strongest lever for leaders is the benevolence lever. Actively try to understand what your team members feel are their best interests. Create opportunities for people to share what matters to them, what success looks like for them, and then include them in a conversation about how you can help them reach the success to which they aspire.

- None of your efforts will be effective if people don't believe that you will follow through, so you must endeavor to demonstrate your integrity. Make promises relating to efforts, not outcomes that are outside your control.

CHAPTER 7

Repairing a Trust Deficit: A Future Needs Case Study

THE FINANCIAL SERVICES SECTOR DOESN'T SCORE HIGHLY WHEN assessed for trustworthiness. According to the Edelman Trust Barometer, trust in this sector declined in twenty of the twenty-seven countries where it was measured between 2020 and 2021. Historically, it has been the least trusted of all sectors measured. For example, in 2019 Edelman reported that trust in financial services was at an all-time high (since 2012) but it was still the least-trusted sector they measured. As I write this in late summer 2021, trust in the sector is the lowest it's been since 2016 among the general population and the lowest since 2018 among the informed public.

While people may view financial professionals as being smart and capable, they don't believe they always display integrity or work in the best interests of their clients. There is a strong belief that they are in fact primarily looking out for themselves. Evidence abounds to support this narrative. Media reports regularly feature nefarious schemes and illegal or at least dubious behavior within financial services organizations.

Building trust benefits leaders in all fields and is a powerful tool for helping them excel regardless of the industry. I am convinced, however, that there are few sectors where the connection between success and higher trust levels is more immediate, clear, and direct than in financial services. When financial service providers start building higher trust levels with those they serve, there is virtually no lag or ambiguity with respect to improved performance. My research shows very clearly that when consumers decide to commit their savings to a financial advisor or company, the primary driver for that decision is trust.

Whenever I have asked the question about what excellence looks like in the financial services sector, the response has always focused on financial returns. Although understandable, the challenge for the industry is that financial returns are often difficult to accurately measure, let alone predict. Looking back at which funds have performed well in the past rarely predicts which will do well in the future. It is a common disclaimer in the mutual fund industry: "Past performance is no guarantee of future returns."

Do higher rates of returns truly define excellence? Or would consistency of returns be a better indicator when assessing a mutual fund provider or financial advisor? When many of the factors that drive outcomes are beyond the control of a financial services professional, focusing on outcomes can often be a detriment to defining excellence, especially with respect to any single financial product. However, providers and advisors do have control over the process they use to make the most informed decisions regarding their products and services. Perhaps this decision-making process should be the focus for defining excellence.

Financial markets are inherently unpredictable. A financial advisor's value proposition is that he or she is prepared and willing to put work into researching the markets to make the best possible estimates of future market developments, while working with clients to build a portfolio that hedges against the unpredictability of the market.

Arrow: My First Trust Unlimited Client

Almost twenty years ago, I was approached by a friend and former McKinsey & Company colleague. He was working as the head of strategy for a financial services company in Canada and wanted me to speak at a group corporate retreat. I will refer to the company as "Arrow" to protect its identity. The purpose of the retreat was to reimagine its market position. The company was searching for a way to differentiate itself from its competitors. I had been asked to speak about sustainable competitive advantage.

Sustainable competitive advantage is generally defined as an advantage that competitors can't copy. The challenge with the financial services market is that it's hard to create products that other people can't copy. Industry regulators require considerable transparency when it comes to financial products and services to protect consumers from disreputable behavior.

If you think about it, there is little that you can't copy about a financial product. As I mentioned in chapter 1, when I thought about Arrow, I realized that I could buy one share of every fund they sold and have solid information on how those funds were structured. At that point, I could easily recreate the fund without having to pay a fund advisor to build the fund in the first place. I shared this observation with my audience and suggested that the only truly sustainable advantage would be to build deep, trust-based, long-term relationships with their financial advisor clients, who in turn helped investors build their portfolios. These relationships would be difficult to copy and would differentiate them from the competition. My presentation was well received, and I was invited back to provide more detail on how this might look on the ground. I subsequently developed a training workshop for the Arrow sales team to show them how they could become better at building trust with their financial advisor clients.

A Little Historical Perspective

There was a wave of investment activity in the mid- to late 1990s related to the Internet and associated high-tech ventures. It was referred to as the dot-com bubble and led to significant growth in financial markets. Between 1995 and March 2000 the Nasdaq rose by roughly 400 percent. People entered the stock market in droves. Organizations began creating an online presence and normal rates of returns were no longer enough.

Financial sector companies took more risks to demonstrate greater growth to attract more investors. Workers flocked to the high-tech sector, all expecting to get rich. It looked a great deal like a modern-day gold rush, with people entering the market who had never previously considered investing.

Inevitably, the dot-com bubble bust, when it came, also had a profound impact. From March 2000, when it peaked, to late 2002, the market tumbled by 78 percent. Now people viewed financial markets with skepticism and were pulling their money out like crazy. People working in the financial services sector, who had thought themselves skilled when markets were surging, now realized how little power they actually had to manage or control their clients' returns. Some financial advisors struggled profoundly with the realization that they were getting paid well while their clients were losing significant sums of money.

Inside Arrow

Scott felt like he was going to throw up. He had just gotten off the phone with his long-time client Susan. Scott was a financial advisor with thirty years' experience, and he had just explained to Susan that a significant portion of the money she had set aside for her daughter's university expenses was simply gone. Clients had been calling him all week. Some were angry, some depressed, and others, like Susan, in tearful shock. He felt like muting his phone and hiding under his desk.

Susan's story was tough, but some of his other clients were even worse off; many had invested more than they could reasonably afford to lose. Bankruptcies were being declared, cars and houses repossessed. An argument could be made that Scott had warned his clients about these risks, but had he pushed the point home enough? The markets had been going up so fast that everyone who wasn't investing felt like a fool. It was like they were losing because they weren't winning as fast as everyone else they knew. The siren song of the market had lured many of Scott's clients in too deep.

Scott was struggling a lot with guilt. While the markets had been surging, he had felt in control. He had felt good about himself; he was helping his clients achieve their dreams and earning great money in the process. All that remained was the money he was still earning while riding his clients' life savings into the dirt. He now realized that it was easy to believe that he was solely responsible for his clients' financial success during the good times and not the market. Now he was scrambling to preserve what was left of his clients' money—and their confidence in him and the markets.

Conspicuous by their absence were the companies that had created the funds in which he had invested his clients' money. Where were those folks now that everything seemed to be going down the tubes? Just a few months ago they were plying him with tickets to hockey games, inviting him to lunches at trendy restaurants, and providing support for his client presentations and wine and cheese soirees. They always seemed to have some new fund to offer or a glossy presentation folder outlining the next great investment opportunity. And now? Crickets.

Things changed when the dot-com bubble burst. Investors and their advisors (like Scott) had gone from feeling immortal to feeling all too human, and many struggled psychologically. It became obvious that while they thought they had their clients' best interests at heart, the roles they played were not as significant as they imagined.

This dawning reality prompted Arrow to research how financial advisors operated. What they discovered was that many of them were destroying their client investors' wealth by frequently switching funds or investments. One of the reasons was that many were compensated on a per-transaction basis rather than on how well or poorly their investments were performing. The incentive structure was not aligned with the best interests of clients. If Scott, for example, worked for a bank and provided investment advice to its clients, it's possible that the bank would instruct Scott to have 40 percent of each of his portfolios made up of the bank's own investment products. Obviously, this is great for the bank, which would collect fees both for Scott's services and for the financial products they had developed. Although this could potentially work out okay for the investor, one could question whether the bank's products were the best for the client.

The way financial advisors such as Scott are compensated can be remarkably complex and opaque. This complexity and opacity sometimes seems to be intentional. There is an advantage when clients aren't aware of all the facts and don't know exactly how financial advisors get paid. As mentioned, some advisors are remunerated based on transactions. This creates a strong incentive for them to make trades even when those trades may not be good for the investor's overall returns. These misaligned incentives cause investors to question whether they are getting good advice from their financial advisors. Arrow's research also revealed that an investor with more than a million dollars invested would, on average, have 3.5 financial advisors. This diversification indicated that investors don't completely trust a single advisor. Ironically, while financial advisors frequently tell people to diversify their investments, they don't like people having multiple advisors.

For Arrow there was opportunity. Understanding how their clients (financial advisors) were constrained helped them adopt a new perspective. They realized that while some financial advisors were not allowed to invest more with them than they currently were, the rules could change in the future. Arrow also started taking measures to adjust their own context so it more closely aligned with the best interest of their clients. As a result, they started redefining what "good" meant and how they would evaluate and compensate their sales force.

We began having conversations with Arrow's clients about what an excellent service provider looked like from their perspective. Arrow started sharing examples of the research and effort that went into selecting the companies that went into its various funds. Part of being an excellent service provider also meant trying to bring some clarity to the complexity of the markets and helping advisors become better informed so they could ultimately pass along that same information to their clients.

In an environment of overwhelming complexity, Arrow's approach was to simplify and align its objectives with its stated values. To this end the company communicated its intentions to the financial advisors and made changes to the sales incentives so that they aligned more effectively with the goal of serving clients rather than maximizing short-term sales.

Once I started working with Arrow, there were many things to figure out. In part, the sales team had to learn a new set of skills relating to building trust, but I also needed to have several strategic conversations and problem-solving sessions with management. My previous work on trust had been a blend of academic research and practical experiences; I now had to translate all that into practical solutions for Arrow and its team.

First, I approached my friend and mentor Frederick "Fritz" Mayer. Together, we turned my doctoral thesis into a two-day workshop. Fritz had served on my thesis committee so he understood the model well; as I have said before, he's one of the smartest people and most gifted educators I've ever met. We turned the material into modules that I could use to teach others how trust works, covering the same framework and elements described in this book.

My goal was to not only improve the one-on-one trust-building skills of Arrow's sales and marketing team but also to change the financial advisors' perspectives on how much they trusted Arrow's entire organization.

I actively communicated with the leadership group on a regular basis to help them problem-solve. We walked through the various elements of the model and talked about how to demonstrate benevolence, integrity, and ability in order to reduce perceptions of uncertainty; how to address contextual elements of uncertainty; and how to reduce the levels of vulnerability perceived and experienced by their clients, the financial advisors to whom Arrow was trying to sell mutual funds.

Vulnerability

Let's now look at the other half of the trust equation, vulnerability. From Arrow's clients' perspective, their major area of vulnerability was the risk of losing reputation or relationships. One of the best ways to attract new business in the financial services field is by getting referrals from existing clients. Giving clients bad advice or choosing the wrong products could mean losing those referrals and losing business. This would, of course, have short- and long-term ramifications.

Given financial advisors' incentive/compensation structures, an advisor might not be vulnerable to financial loss in the short term, even if their clients' portfolios lose money (as we saw, Scott kept getting paid even when Susan's portfolio tanked). Nevertheless, advisors who are acting in good faith and trying to keep up their fiduciary duties to their clients will still be vulnerable, psychologically if nothing else, to the vagaries of the stock market and the performance of their clients' portfolios.

When we first think of vulnerability within the context of financial services, we usually think about money. This is a reasonable perception. Most of us certainly value money, and it's easy to quantify, but this falls far short of fully describing the vulnerabilities people experience when it comes to financial matters. Money represents something far beyond merely a number. It is their and their family's future. It represents their hopes and dreams of a future life or of having an impact in the world. That is where the true vulnerability lies. For example, as we saw at the beginning of the chapter, for Susan it wasn't just the money—it was her daughter's college education on the line.

An element of self-esteem is also included in someone's perceptions of vulnerability. Most people have a feeling of accomplishment when they are financially secure, more so if they have had to work hard to achieve it. On the other hand, people fear making a mistake and the inevitable hit their self-esteem will take if they have to admit they made poor investment choices. Even more pronounced is the fear of being made a fool of, that they will be the victim of a con and swindled.

The professional reputation and sense of self-worth of a financial advisor is dependent on making good financial decisions, not just for themselves but also for their clients. This results in a high level of vulnerability. Working with Arrow, I needed to address the company's clients' perceptions of vulnerability. Together, we focused our energies on the areas over which the company had some level of control: for instance, on building strong relationships.

Advisors who focus solely on returns find themselves extremely vulnerable to the vagaries and volatility of the market. By helping them understand how to focus instead on clients' needs and building relationships with them, we were able to reduce that vulnerability. As their client base became less influenced by short-term fluctuations and more focused on having an advisor who had their interest at heart, their sense of vulnerability lessened.

We followed a similar approach with Arrow, encouraging the company to focus its energies on its relationship with financial advisors and the processes it used to better serve its customers to create stable long-term relationships.

Benevolence

Historically, the frontline sales staff at Arrow had followed the "good buddy" sales approach, giving their customers (financial advisors working with frontline investors) perks such as meals, sponsorships, and expensive tickets to events. However, during the period I was working with Arrow, there were growing concerns about the optics of mutual fund companies doing this. It was easy to connect the dots between benefits received by financial advisors to those advisors promoting those mutual fund companies' financial products to their investor clients.

Back at Arrow, I suggested a major shift of thinking and approach. Instead of trying to get clients to sell more of Arrow's products to investors, the sales team would pull back the lens and consider an alignment of the best interests of all concerned. In practice, this meant helping the financial advisors grow their total book size (i.e., the amount of money they managed on behalf of their investor clients). My reasoning was that if an Arrow salesperson had 10 percent of an advisor's business and the salesperson helped the advisor double their book value, they would in fact be doubling Arrow's product sales. This was far more efficient than trying to squeeze an extra percentage point in the share of their existing book value. The added benefit was that it was highly likely that helping advisors be more successful would promote higher trust levels, which in turn would result in the mutual fund salespeople enjoying not just the same share of a larger book but an increased share of the advisor's book. Clarifying the overlap and alignment of the best interests of both parties helped change behavior patterns for Arrow's sales force. Arrow's mutual fund sellers began having more focused conversations on the needs of their clients' customers and focused on information that could help them thrive. They began talking with their clients about trust and how important it was for attracting and developing the type of relationships with their own clients that helped drive success.

The insight that growing their clients' business would directly benefit the mutual fund sellers also led to a more dramatic change in behavior at Arrow. Instead of attempting to sell only their own products, they shifted to what I like to call a "Miracle on Wall Street" approach. If you've ever watched *Miracle on 34th Street,* you will remember Santa telling customers they could get a better deal at one of Macy's competitors. He was almost fired by Macy's before the company realized his refreshing honesty increased customer loyalty. Arrow began providing advice on how to structure a portfolio of investments to best meet the needs of frontline investors (their clients' clients). They would make recommendations about the best products in different asset classes that usually included a group of options. If they didn't think their product was the best in that class of assets, they would tell the advisors as much and recommend another product for them. They also began providing training sessions for clients where they shared information about how various products were constructed.

In addition, Arrow started providing free training sessions across the country to help financial advisors maintain their credentials by meeting their industry's ongoing education requirements. While the sessions did include information about how Arrow's funds were created, they also included training on how to attract and better serve investors. This material included a basic overview of elements of the trust model so that financial advisors could apply the model to their customers.

In short, Arrow began taking steps to address their clients' needs rather than solely focusing on selling more product. At one point, a senior manager turned to me and asked, "We are investing a lot of time and resources into our clients; how do we then ask them for their business?" My response was, "You won't have to. Once you have their trust, they will want to do business with you." I told Arrow that demand for its training and support services would soon exceed supply; once this state was reached it would be able to focus on clients who wanted their involvement and who demonstrated it by purchasing more of its products.

In the end, the focus on a relational approach to their clients rather than a sales-first approach had tremendous impact, so much so that Arrow started recommending that their financial advisor clients use the same approach with their own customers.

Integrity

As we've seen, organizations (and individuals) demonstrate integrity when they follow through on their promises and if their actions align with the values they express. This does not always happen, however; organizations often experience integrity gaps between sales and marketing, other departments, and management. Frequently, this is due to the people in sales and marketing making promises that the rest of the organization fails, or is unable, to keep. Marketing materials often make promises that aren't clear and are therefore open to interpretation by prospective customers. This results in different expectations in different groups.

Arrow had an integrity problem, but it wasn't the fault of sales or marketing; it came from someone involved in the production of its financial products. It had a fund that I will call Big Blue that was supposed to be populated with stable, predictable blue chip funds; it was intended to provide stable growth. However, the fund manager became frustrated because, despite solid returns, the fund wasn't attracting as many investors as he expected. Tech stocks were generating higher than normal returns, so steady growth funds just weren't sexy enough. In an attempt to increase the level of growth of his fund, he started slipping in more volatile tech stocks. When the dot-com bubble burst and tech stocks plummeted in value, Big Blue went down the toilet.

The Big Blue decline was a significant problem for Arrow while I was working with the company. Many financial advisors try to provide their customers with a balanced portfolio. They balance riskier investments, that will hopefully promote stronger growth, with stable, safe investments to mitigate risk. Moving tech funds into Big Blue had upset that balance; it left Arrow's clients in a position where they were subjecting their customers to far more risk exposure than they intended. Inevitably, many of Arrow's clients felt they had been burned and that an implied promise had been broken. Arrow's frontline sales team had to deal with fallout from a problem they had not created.

I helped prepare a response that included explaining what had happened, why it happened, and what steps were being taken to prevent it from happening again. The Big Blue fund manager was fired and procedures were put in place to more closely monitor funds. Part of this response included a new corporate message focused more directly on the best interests of its clients. The actions taken to show benevolence provided support for that message. Arrow's ongoing investment in tools, research, and delivery of training also showed an alignment between the message it was sharing and the actions it was taking.

Arrow's marketing and sales departments were all included in the trust training that TU delivered. This meant that messaging and behavior was consistent throughout the organization. Over the subsequent months, Arrow managed to demonstrate heightened levels of integrity with a renewed consistency in behavior. This, combined with an explanation for what had happened with Big Blue and the steps that had been taken to prevent it from happening again, significantly reduced uncertainty for Arrow's clients.

Ability

Ability is the competence to follow through on promises made. When I first began working with Arrow, I was certain that one of the fringe benefits would be finding a really good financial advisor. In reality, I discovered that there wasn't a strong correlation between assets under management and competence. A "good" advisor was deemed to be one who had a high volume of assets under management. To me, all this meant was that was a good salesperson, not that they were necessarily doing a stellar job for their investor clients.

Working closely with its clients, Arrow had helped them redefine excellence for themselves. By sharing its training, research, products, and tools, the company had helped its clients become more professional with the investors they served. In the eyes of its clients, Arrow became the definition of mutual fund company excellence.

The Result

With the dot-com bubble bursting, financial markets were in turmoil. Markets were in full retreat and people were pulling out what was left of their money as quickly as they could. Against this difficult backdrop, I faced the task of helping Arrow convince a wide range of skeptical financial advisors that the company could be trusted, and that's exactly what I achieved.

After working with TU for eighteen months, Arrow hired a professional survey firm and found that trust had become the primary driver of the purchasing decision for its clients. The survey company also determined that Arrow was, after following TU's advice, dramatically more trusted than any of its competitors, having started as a middle of the pack organization looking for ways to differentiate itself from the competition.

Arrow gained a significant market share and, over the following two years, captured 75 percent of every new dollar that came into the mutual fund industry. It was dominating the Canadian market in a way that none of its sibling firms in other geographic markets were doing, despite their common ownership group and approach. As a result, Arrow's American parent company began sending teams from all over the world to Canada to try to understand and ultimately emulate its success.

Unfortunately, every member of the leadership group I was working with at Arrow moved on to new opportunities and a new leadership group took the helm. Unfamiliar with the trust- and relationship-based approach that was working so well, but at the same time determined to get credit for how well things were going, they got rid of everyone who had been involved with the previous regime (including my company). Arrow moved away from what had worked so well and reverted to the traditional "good buddy" sales approach. After an all too brief two-year stay at the top of its industry, the company slowly sank back into the churn of mediocrity.

My experience with Arrow was a deeply influential one for me and for my company. I learned an incredible amount about training as well as practical, applied problem-solving. The experience also showed me that the model worked in the real world. It wasn't perfect—in actual practice, no theoretical model ever is—but I had witnessed the incredible impact it had in a difficult and complex environment.

Although I never intended it to be, working with Arrow turned out to be a form of natural experiment. My intervention resulted in dramatic change. The other companies owned by the same corporation in other countries, along with Arrow's competitors in Canada, were like control groups in this experiment. Arrow witnessed amazing growth in market share and assets under management during a turbulent period, thanks to TU's intervention—a growth that was not shared by its sibling companies in other geographies that did not have the opportunity to work with TU. What's more, once Arrow's sales and marketing activities and corporate philosophy went back to business as usual, so did its results.

Repairing a Trust Deficit:
Key Points Review

- Building trust benefits leaders in all fields and is a powerful tool for helping them excel regardless of the industry. There are few sectors, however, where the connection between higher trust levels and success is more immediate, clear, and direct than in financial services.

- When many of the factors that drive outcomes are beyond your control, focusing on outcomes can often be a detriment to defining excellence; instead, address clients' perceptions of vulnerability by focusing on areas over which you have some control, such as building strong relationships.

- Aligning the best interests of all concerned helps build trust.

- Adopting the "Miracle on Wall Street" approach builds loyalty.

CHAPTER 8

Building Trust with the Locals in Afghanistan: A Diagnostic Case Study

ON A BRUTALLY HOT DAY IN 2011, MAJOR JOHN LEAHY WALKED INTO A small village in rural Afghanistan and set down his weapons.

As a senior officer in the Canadian Armed Forces, Major Leahy was tasked with trying to build trust with the local population—a task that hadn't proven to be easy. Building trust meant being able to help the locals with irrigation systems, roads, and new construction projects. This could happen only if Leahy was confident there were no insurgents in the area while his troops were helping the community. Without trust, his troops would be in constant danger. Getting reliable information from villagers Leahy could trust was paramount.

Leahy took off his helmet and extended his hand to the headman of the village. This was new behavior for the major, and his fellow soldiers grew uneasy. Their superior officer's vulnerability was off the scale. If anybody in the village was working with the Taliban, the situation could go south very quickly. The calculated risk Leahy was taking was the first step in building trust with the village. He was making himself more human by making himself vulnerable. He'd recalled conversations around building trust and knew that one person with a gun looks a lot like another person with a gun. He needed to differentiate himself and do it in a way that demonstrated that he was benign.

The major stood before the headman in the village square and asked him if the Taliban were active in the area. He knew the man would say no. They always did. It didn't mean anything. Leahy then asked the headman to show him around the village, after which they would return to the square and he would loudly declare that the headman was his friend. Leahy knew that if there were Taliban close by, the headman would not agree to the tour—the risk to him would be too great. If there were no insurgents nearby, the headman would gladly show Leahy around because it would raise his status in the area.

Vulnerability in this situation was high for all parties—the locals, the NGOs, and the military—even though the Canadian troops were there for what were, from their perspective, benevolent purposes.

The Background

To understand the situation on the ground in Afghanistan, one needs to see things from the locals' perspectives. For instance, farmers were placed in an almost impossible position. Many didn't want to grow poppy—a crop used to manufacture illegal drugs—not least because it was contrary to their religious beliefs. In addition, harvesting the crop was extremely hard, backbreaking work. However, the poppy is a tough plant capable of surviving in the harsh local conditions and requires little water.

Other crops needed reliable irrigation systems, which raised another problem—irrigation systems look like infrastructure. Infrastructure was a target both for insurgents and sometimes for those hunting them. The farmers' harvested vegetables needed to be taken to market, which meant running into multiple roadblocks, both militia and bandits. Often, these were the same people in different uniforms. This meant paying bribes— which reduced profit. Should a farmer fail to sell all his merchandise at the market, he would be forced to pay more bribes on the return journey.

Customers at the market knew this and would barter heavily, especially toward the end of the day. Poppy buyers, however, would come directly to the farmer—no trip to the market required.

Most farmers needed loans to set up and maintain their operations. However, at the time, the only loans that were available were for growing poppy because the organizations loaning the money were sure to get their money back.

Farmers were backed into a corner. Think about it from their perspective: Looking to the past, if all you saw were a litany of broken promises and corruption from just about everyone in authority, how willing would you be to make yourself and your family vulnerable though investments in irrigation systems and perilous trips to the market when the easier route was to plant poppy?

Let's back up a little and take a closer look at Major Leahy's predicament. Afghanistan is a multiethnic and tribal society, and its people have been stuck in what seems like a perpetual loop. A country or a faction invades, attempts to establish some type of partial rule, and is either displaced or leaves. Repeat. The Afghan people and the country seemed in stasis and had reverted to survival mode.

Canadian military involvement began as part of the US-led Operation Enduring Freedom (OEF), America's global war on terrorism launched in response to the 9/11 attacks. OEF's primary goal was to deal with al-Qaeda and the Taliban regime that had harbored members of Osama bin Laden's organization. Later, Canada's involvement came under the umbrella of the United Nations Assistance Mission in Afghanistan (UNAMA). The focus of this mission was to rebuild Afghanistan.

At the time Major Leahy walked into that village, things weren't going very well. The country was still a mess, and little reliable infrastructure had been built. To make things worse, the Taliban had not been brought under control. Complicating the Canadian mission further was the fact that members of the local population were unwilling to invest time and energy into projects when the future payoff was uncertain.

Leahy realized that not all the insurgents his troops were facing were religious zealots; many were acting out of sheer desperation. Afghan men were not allowed to get married, have children, or own property if they didn't have a job; unfortunately, unemployment levels were exceptionally high. Given this economic environment, if the Taliban offered a young man $20 to plant a roadside bomb, the likelihood was that he would accept the lucrative opportunity. The Taliban could, in this light, be seen as a potential employer by the young man rather than a cause of his problems.

When Major Leahy approached me in 2010 to diagnose the trust issues at play, there was no end in sight for his mission. He told me that although international forces had been in the country for years, there had been virtually no economic development. The general feeling was that this was due to a lack of trust, for the most part, between the general population and their leaders. People didn't want to invest time or energy unless they could see an immediate payoff. I could understand their reticence: Why construct roads and buildings that would become targets for one faction or another to destroy?

This reluctance was also seen with respect to job skills training. It seemed futile to learn to repair vehicles when it was unlikely any of your fellow villagers would be able to afford a vehicle, or to pay for repairs even if they had a vehicle. There was little motivation to plant crops that required irrigation systems or to attend school because to do so one had to make oneself vulnerable. Investing in the future (e.g., in an irrigation system whose benefits pay off much later) is an act of trust. And learning new skills made you more interesting to the insurgents—people with whom you did not wish to become involved.

The Canadian military's strategy was to try to build pockets of safety and stability where trust could develop. If that could be achieved, economic development might begin to take hold. If that occurred then there would be other, feasible alternatives for young men desperate for work that did not involve working for insurgents. All this would foster an increase in commerce, which in turn would stimulate social life and a return to some semblance of normalcy. With more to lose, citizens would hopefully be less likely to partner with insurgents.

To begin creating these areas of safety and stability, the military needed to have intel about insurgent activity in the areas they were trying to protect, to safeguard its troops. This was why it was so important for Major Leahy to build open, trust-based relationships with the headmen of the villages.

If this could be achieved, the Canadian troops could return home and leave the Afghans in a more stable environment where they could thrive and plan for the future. In turn, this would enable a healthier and natural progression for their society.

Unpacking the Story: Context

This case study is an attempt to show how you can use the Trust Unlimited model to understand and diagnose a complex problem such as the one in Afghanistan. It will focus on the role played by context and the persistent gaps that were likely experienced in the domains of benevolence, integrity, and perceived outcomes.

As mentioned earlier, there were two separate missions in Afghanistan: OEF and UNAMA. The former was set up to eliminate the Taliban and al-Qaeda; the latter focused on rebuilding Afghanistan and pushing toward a more peaceful and stable future for the region. However, it generally wasn't obvious to the local population which troops were on which mission. The actions of one group could positively or negatively impact perceptions of all groups.

The multiple missions made it incredibly difficult for frontline forces (that is, those most engaged with locals) to consistently demonstrate integrity toward these people. There is no doubt that individual soldiers felt they were acting with integrity. However, high-level decisions made by both OEF and UNAMA affected things on the ground. From the locals' perspectives, an individual soldier's actions could cast doubt on his integrity; any soldier's individual actions might appear inconsistent with prior promises or commitments because of conflicting orders given by different senior officers on different missions.

Integrity was obviously a significant and ongoing challenge to building trust. Without consistency, you can't display integrity. We display integrity by following through on our promises and taking actions that align with our values, making our behavior easier to predict.

In Afghanistan, this required collaboration and communication at the most senior levels of the missions in order to ensure there was consistency across all regions. Promises made by one member of the coalition would need to become the responsibility of all members. Values needed to be consistent and clearly communicated across all missions.

In this context, the traditional approaches to building trust, such as displaying individual traits underlying trustworthiness, were hard to implement. While individual soldiers might demonstrate benevolence, integrity, and ability, they were not around long enough for these traits to have a significant impact. Afghanistan has been a revolving door of would-be conquerors and saviors who come, make promises, and leave. As far as the locals were concerned, these latest missions were no different.

The level of consistency, coordination, and sophistication required to demonstrate collective integrity would be difficult for the armed forces of a single nation to implement, let alone an international group. As we will see, coordinated action is vital when it comes to demonstrating integrity.

In much of the Western world, we are used to strong central governments. We are accustomed to laws that generally are obeyed, police forces that tend to apply the rules, and a system of justice that, for the most part, works as we expect it to. We rely heavily on the formal elements of social control. When someone tells you that they will follow through on something because it's their job or because you have a contract, you believe it will happen. This simply isn't the case in places such as Afghanistan, where the central government had difficulty controlling things within the capital, let alone anywhere else in the country.

Where there is a weakness or absence of formal mechanisms of social control, the need for informal elements becomes more important. Family connections, shared religion, shared friends, and similar backgrounds have far greater weight than political or legal structures. When people want to get something done, they have to develop strong relationships with people who can advocate on their behalf and influence others. At the same time that UNAMA personnel were trying to build trust while providing support for the new government, OEF troops were actively hunting Taliban insurgents, which often involved kidnapping Afghans for detention and interrogation. These conflicting messages were bound to create confusion.

Diagnosis

My usual five-step approach to a challenge like this is to understand, diagnose, align, resolve, and assess. Unfortunately, in this case my brief was to engage in only the first two steps. The situation had been going on for decades and no resolution was in sight. The Canadian military realized that its window of opportunity for finding a resolution had closed. Troops had been in place too long without sufficient, measurable progress to build the needed credibility with the local population. I was engaged to help the Canadian military learn, and better understand, a potential alternative approach for analogous future situations.

Working with Major Leahy, I soon realized that, early in a relationship, context carries more weight in developing trust than our individual traits. This makes sense given that we don't know much about the other person as an individual at that early stage. Hence, the focus needs to be more on the systems and rules we put in place and less on individual behavior.

Further complicating this particular situation was the transience of military personnel. Individuals continually arrived, stayed for a period, and left. Even if they did want to demonstrate the individual elements of trustworthiness, it was the combined military units who needed to develop trust by demonstrating benevolence, integrity, and ability collectively, not just individual soldiers.

My next step was to take a closer look at the roles that vulnerability, benevolence, and integrity played in building trust in this hostile environment.

The first thing I believed the military needed to do was to understand the nature of the vulnerability felt by all stakeholders. Military personnel understood their own vulnerability, but the locals were living in conditions of great scarcity, and losing just a little of what they had was threatening to them. The Afghans were, and many still are, in an extremely vulnerable situation. It was likely they knew people in the Taliban or at the least people connected to them. To help the troops they would be putting themselves and their families at risk, especially once the military pulled out and the Taliban inevitably returned. When that happened, the Taliban would hunt them down and execute them. During the early summer of 2021, the Canadian and US governments bowed to pressure to help thousands of Afghan translators at risk from Taliban reprisals relocate with their families. Unfortunately, it is too late for the hundreds who already died in targeted killings.

Every nation or faction that has ever taken control in Afghanistan almost certainly promoted a narrative about how they were serving the best interests of the people involved, both externally (to the local population and other stakeholders) and internally (within the groups that took power). In truth, they may well have believed that they were serving the best interests of Afghanistan. In 1979 the Soviets arrived promising to modernize the country. The Taliban followed them, promising to show the population the light of Islam. Then military groups from the West arrived, promising to free locals from the harsh Taliban regime. While many may have told good stories to themselves about how they were serving the best interests of the Afghan people, it seems that few actually asked the locals what they really wanted.

There is a long and troubled history of strife between various factions within Afghanistan. Against this backdrop, it is reasonable to expect that some attempts to promote the best interests of certain segments of the population will be seen as harmful by other segments of the population. It would be easy to get bogged down in a discussion of right versus wrong, or morality, but the issue I was tasked to diagnose was building trust with the locals in Afghanistan. The reasons for building trust were to promote economic development and reduce the number of insurgents. To achieve this, those involved needed to see things from the perspective of the local population. It is counterproductive to try to impose one's own values and norms on people who live in a world of uncertainty and who face a unique set of circumstances that make them increasingly vulnerable.

I could see that there was a gap between what those trying to "help" the Afghans believed was benevolent and what the local population perceived as benevolent. Any communication that argued for the best interests of the Afghan population—particularly in the long term—was likely met with skepticism, regardless of the purveyor's true intentions.

A Potential Way Forward

I've always wondered what the Afghan people would have said if someone had simply asked them what mattered most to them and then asked how to help them get there. It was my suspicion that, given the high levels of unemployment and constant conflict, the Afghans would have said what mattered was to live a peaceful life where their society could evolve naturally without overwhelming interference. (Of course, that may also be simply my own projections biased by my Western mindset.)

Given that benevolence or its perceived lack was an ongoing barrier to building trust with locals, I feel that the best approach would have been to develop programs that helped locals find success on their own terms. After conversations about what mattered most to the locals and what success looked like to them, concrete actions to address these concerns and aspirations could have been put in place.

As my role was limited to diagnosis, I don't have all the details about what happened after my contract ended. I do know that microloans have been used with great success in a number of developing countries, and they might have worked in Afghanistan, especially given the difficulty Afghan farmers had in getting financing for anything other than a poppy crop. Other initiatives might have included constructing communal warehouses close to markets or regular protection convoys to escort farmers to market. The cost and risks involved with offering these loans would have been higher than in more stable environments, but considering the trade-off, the powers that be would have needed to factor in the cost to police the global fallout of poppy production and the value of the lives of the troops on the ground.

Afghanistan's economy is primarily agricultural. Support for this industry could have been provided through education, farming equipment that could be shared within given regions, and the creation and maintenance of irrigation systems. Such approaches would have shown benevolence in ways that might have been harder to misinterpret. Teaching the locals to deliver and maintain these programs independently could have delivered both short- and long-term benefits.

Perceived Outcomes

Another challenge when building trust with the Afghans was that different populations had dramatically different perspectives on what a good outcome looked like. The Afghan people are not a monolithic entity. Much like any country, there are dramatically different perspectives and values across different sectors of the population. In Afghanistan, there are several different religious beliefs and different perspectives on the same religious beliefs. What some might consider a good outcome, others will consider an outrage.

Our perception of outcomes is often based on a long history of experience with related interactions. Individual soldiers or military units may not have much understanding of the Afghan people, but Afghans have had wide-ranging interactions, over time, with various occupiers and would-be helpers who have filled similar roles. This means that any military group trying to build trust in the country had to deal with an extensive and often painful history that was outside of their control. As has been said about various aspects of trust-building, even though it's not your fault, it's still your problem.

Building trust with the locals in Afghanistan would have taken an understanding of their perceptions about past experiences. What were the good and bad elements of previous regimes? How did this time seem the same and how was it different? Once we knew their story and what a good outcome looked like, we could have taken steps to be transparent and intentional about future outcomes. We also could have had conversations that potentially distanced us from previous negative experiences.

This case study is intended to show how my trust model can be used to identify gaps. In this case, the model provided a lens and a perspective on the problems faced by the military in its attempt to build trust with the locals and promote economic development.

Upon reflection, we can see clearly that the local population in Afghanistan experienced extremely high levels of uncertainty and vulnerability. To trust in these circumstances, they had to make themselves even more vulnerable. This was a significant challenge. The multilayered, multiple military forces, with their different missions and objectives, layered as they were on top of a complex local dynamic, made for an incredibly challenging environment in which to attempt to build stronger relationships. All stakeholders had significant exposure.

The locals were caught between two warring factions—the Taliban (the last oppressors) and the forces from the West (the new oppressors). Both sides were pressuring them for assistance and both sides threatened punishment if they were betrayed. The occupying military from the West were kidnapping and questioning locals they thought had information about the insurgents. The insurgents were pressuring the locals to join forces with them and help them plant roadside bombs. These pressures, on top of the daily struggles of obtaining food, clothing, and shelter in a location with extreme unemployment, must have been overwhelming.

Given the vulnerability already being experienced by the locals, it would have been hard to expect them to make themselves even more vulnerable by trusting anyone. With so little margin for error, trusting the wrong person or group could have proven fatal. This extreme level of vulnerability allows little tolerance for uncertainty. Someone trying to follow through on a promise but not doing it in a timely matter could result in terrible consequences. An example of this played out in late August 2021 when the United States pulled out of Afghanistan. Within weeks the Taliban took over, negating over twenty years of blood, sweat, and toil. An incredible price was paid by those who served and by the Afghans who believed change was possible.

This environment led to a reluctance by the locals to engage in anything but spot market exchanges, where they could provide something and immediately be provided something in return, avoiding the additional vulnerability of a delayed benefit. It would be unrealistic to expect the population to go beyond this, and venture into longer-term, trust-based transactions, unless steps were taken to reduce their vulnerability.

The occupying soldiers also faced significant levels of vulnerability. They were targets of the insurgents and were at risk of being injured or killed. They also faced the very real risk of emotional trauma associated with losing a close comrade, being forced to harm others, or experiencing prolonged stress and tension.

August 2021

As I write this, on August 15, 2021, Taliban fighters walked into Kabul with ease. The Afghan military, trained and equipped by the United States, capitulated immediately, giving up the majority of the country without a fight and allowing the Taliban to take over control.

The Taliban immediately began making promises about the welfare of the Afghan people. A spokesperson attempted to assure the world that women would have rights under their rule, although to what extent was unclear. The Taliban obviously felt some level of vulnerability to even have made such a promise. However, few observers believed the Taliban's statement, and evidence quickly began to emerge that, even assuming the regime was genuinely willing to relax its total control on women, it would struggle to follow through on such a promise. Edicts were issued telling Afghan women to stay in their homes for the time being, as Taliban fighters had not yet been trained in how to deal with them.

The Taliban faced other areas of vulnerability, not least from the rise of ISIS K, a group that feels the Taliban isn't extreme enough. Many of the followers of ISIS K originally came from the ranks of the Taliban. Their defection, combined with the fractured and splintered nature of the country in general, suggest that the Taliban may need to walk a narrower line than was generally perceived. When those who are seemingly "devoted" to the Taliban are presented with different opportunities, their loyalty will be tested.

I worked with the Canadian military to begin the process of attempting to build trust with the Afghan people. The aspiration was to help rebuild the country to a point where it wouldn't be as vulnerable to the return of the Taliban. Clearly, in the end, the mission was not successful.

Building Trust with the Locals in Afghanistan: Key Points Review

- The Trust Unlimited model can be used to understand and diagnose problems as complex as those faced by military missions in Afghanistan.

- Early in a relationship, context carries more weight in developing trust than our individual traits. However, a complicated context may hamper our ability to display individual trustworthiness.

- When different stakeholders have different perspectives on what constitutes a favorable outcome, building trust is particularly challenging.

- Building trust requires an understanding of the other parties' perceptions and past experiences.

CHAPTER 9

Organizations of the Future

Leadership challenges in our ever-changing world continue to increase. The COVID-19 pandemic forced many organizations to adopt a more virtual mode of operating, greatly accelerating the adoption of technical advances that make remote work feasible. In the coming years many will maintain at least some level of hybrid operation. As the pace of change continues unabated, it will be accompanied by heightened levels of uncertainty.

The blurring of borders and the shrinking of the world will result in many leaders being forced to consider an increasingly complex array of issues. In today's global environment, it will become increasingly challenging to rely on shared backgrounds or history to provide us with shortcuts to building better relationships. Leaders will need to become skilled at dealing with a range of people with whom they have little in common, both those they lead and stakeholders to whom they are accountable.

As we discussed earlier in this book, one way to build trust is to reduce uncertainty. The most common way people handle this is by pulling the ability lever: "Trust me, I know what I'm doing." The question one has to ask is, How well does that work across cultural boundaries in terms of defining leadership excellence? Different cultures have very different expectations of their leaders. In an evolving future, the definition of excellence within an organization may change dramatically over increasingly shorter periods of time, and especially when the organization operates across multiple regions and cultures that may themselves be shifting and evolving ever more rapidly. Moving forward, pulling the ability lever to build trust is going to require a far more active and participative approach. We won't be as able to rely on experience because we will often be forging into unknown territory where past experience is less relevant. New types of skills will become more valued—the skills of knowing how to change and adapt to new situations, and building consensus across diverse populations.

In chapter 6, we discussed integrity as another lever for reducing uncertainty; this entails following through on your promises, and demonstrating consistency between your values and the actions you take. If the current pace of change continues or accelerates, keeping promises over longer time frames will become challenging. For instance, companies that promised pay raises prior to the pandemic in 2020 may have had to rescind them. Promises surrounding expansion, or other operations and the opportunities provided by them, could get sidelined by extreme weather events. Unfortunately, both ability and integrity may well become less useful in a fast-changing environment.

In the future, leaders and the organizations they serve will face a difficult challenge. They will be expected to understand what their values are and know how to communicate their vision and corporate culture to their stakeholders. They will also need to be extremely intentional and consistent in how they communicate with all involved. Promises will need to focus on processes rather than outcomes, such as the steps to be taken to tackle new challenges that arise.

Benevolence is the one trust lever that should remain relatively unscathed by the pace of change. While what's best for people may evolve, it is unlikely that having others' best interests at heart will lose its positive effect or its ability to help build trust. In my experience, for those being led, benevolence is the lever that has the greatest impact. Recent work on positive leadership and strengths-based approaches aligns with this concept. For example, a friend of mine, Craig Dowden, wrote *Do Good to Lead Well*, a book that puts a great deal of emphasis on the importance of benevolence for leadership.

Many of the existing theories on leadership may fall by the wayside in a fast-changing global environment. Leaders will need to understand that having the best interests at heart of those they lead will not be enough if they are not also effectively communicating their benevolent intentions.

Context

As I am prone to saying, context is king. The pandemic, massive advances in technology, and changes in norms, beliefs, and political ideology have affected everyone's context. Context changes the rules. I can't predict the future any better than anyone else, but it is obvious that a variety of trends have been accelerated by responses to COVID-19. One clear example is more people working remotely; another is that the sheer pace of technological advancement in areas such as virtual reality and artificial intelligence is changing the way organizations operate at a fundamental level. Companies and leaders need to be able to adapt, innovate, and manage change like never before.

Vulnerability

You will recall from chapter 5 that the trust decision is driven by a combination of uncertainty and vulnerability. Uncertainty multiplied by vulnerability gives us a level of perceived risk. If our uncertainty goes up and our vulnerability stays constant, then our perception of the risk rises. If either uncertainty or vulnerability becomes too high, the other element needs to be lowered for us to remain beneath our risk threshold and make the decision to trust. While we can take steps to reduce or limit uncertainty, the pace of change we are experiencing will often lead to increased perceptions of uncertainty overall. If you can't consistently maintain low levels of uncertainty, it follows that you will need to address vulnerability. As a leader, you need to understand how to limit the perception of vulnerability for those you work with so that they don't become paralyzed.

A number of well-known authors are working in this area and provide insights into managing vulnerability. Daniel Goleman's work on emotional intelligence speaks to being aware of our own states and those of our social connections. Brené Brown's work on courage talks about making ourselves more vulnerable. Amy Edmondson discusses psychological safety and the impact it has on high-performing teams. And finally, Daniel Kahneman's work on "thinking fast and slow" explores biases in the way we think that might cause us to feel more or less vulnerable. These talented authors' perspectives on how we can approach the topic of vulnerability are valuable.

Emotional Intelligence

Daniel Goleman's work on emotional intelligence focuses on awareness, identification, and management of the emotions we experience ourselves, and of the emotions experienced by those to whom we are connected. This can be applied to how we and others experience feeling vulnerable. Awareness of our own vulnerability can allow us to manage it more effectively and to understand our responses in a more reasoned way. Often, people finding it hard to trust don't immediately attribute this to a sense of vulnerability; rather, the reluctance to trust manifests itself as a sense of discomfort or unease. Even if they do recognize their vulnerability, they often don't know why they feel vulnerable in a given situation. Increasing awareness allows one to actually take steps to make oneself more comfortable. Being able to empathize and recognize how and why others feel vulnerable also prepares us to problem-solve with them. You don't need to be psychic to understand other people's feelings; usually those people are right there in front of you, so you can simply ask them how they're feeling. I find the Socratic coaching approach is often helpful in these settings. Helping people bring their concerns and feelings to the surface and then problem-solving with them about ways they could better handle a situation can be very productive.

Courage

Brené Brown has written and presented extensively on courage, vulnerability, and shame. She rightfully argues that making oneself vulnerable is a sign of strength rather than weakness. However, some cultures believe that showing vulnerability invites others to take advantage. She points to numerous interviews with people in dangerous jobs who argue that there is no such thing as courage without the presence of vulnerability, a sentiment with which I completely agree. Those with real strength are not afraid that others may attempt to take advantage. Instead, they are aware that showing vulnerability is a great way to see who your friends really are or could be.

In some of her earlier work, Dr. Brown suggests that we are often far too cautious and that we should simply make ourselves more vulnerable to others. I never completely agreed with this approach and was pleased to see that recently she began to say that we should only make ourselves "appropriately" vulnerable. In my opinion, it's perfectly rational to not make ourselves excessively vulnerable. However, figuring out what "appropriately vulnerable" means for each of us could be a challenge.

Brown focuses on personal levels of vulnerability: how we show up and make ourselves more vulnerable. This is important when we talk about building trust because one of the best ways to promote trust is to start by making ourselves a little vulnerable to another person. Taking small steps also addresses the notion of "appropriate vulnerability" because we can slowly increase our level of vulnerability and see how others respond. If they respond by making themselves vulnerable in return, then we can slowly increase how vulnerable we are to them.

Psychological Safety

Amy Edmondson popularized the concept of psychological safety during her work on Google's Project Aristotle. The Aristotle team spent years trying to understand what made some teams more effective than others. The one consistent finding was that psychological safety was common in all top-performing teams. Psychological safety has been defined as the belief that one can show and employ one's true self without fear of negative consequences to one's self-image, status, or career.[39]

Psychological safety implies a certain level of trust: people being willing to make themselves vulnerable by speaking up, disagreeing, or risking making mistakes. I make no apology for repeating the fact that the world is changing around us with relentless and increasing speed; we need to evolve and adapt faster than ever to keep pace. To do this we will need everyone to feel comfortable with taking risks and speaking up. We will need to learn new skills and ways of working because the road to success will constantly change underneath us. Psychological safety will be increasingly important because we will need honest and helpful feedback from those we work with and from our stakeholders.

Fostering psychological safety means creating environments where people feel more certain about how they will be received. It will also require that they feel less vulnerable for speaking up and taking risks. Psychologically safe workplaces will be characterized by the celebration of innovative attempts, candor, and even failures that come as a result of honest attempts to make things better. These environments will need to be tempered with reason. Constant dissent does not lead to progress, nor can you be all things to all people.

While psychological safety means that group members are safe from harm, it should not be confused with the notion of safe spaces where people are discouraged from being candid or having frank and honest conversations. The difference may well be the acceptance of criticism and feedback on ideas rather than on people.

You will need to be thoughtful about creating a context and striking the right balance.

SAP: A Case Study in the Future of Leadership

Kelsy Trigg boarded a Vancouver-bound flight in Frankfurt, Germany, after a business trip. She worked for SAP, a large global organization with over 100,000 employees and operations in more than 140 countries around the world. SAP provides enterprise software solutions for organizations and has more than 200 million subscribers to its cloud-based services. The company generated over €27 billion in revenue in 2020 and provides services all over the world through a blend of local, regional, and global teams.

I chose SAP for this case study for two reasons: first, because, as you will see, I met Kelsy on that flight, and second, because the company provides a good example of an organization faced with the challenges of a world shrinking due to fast-paced technological change.

Kelsy was tired after several intense weeks in Europe working with her SAP colleagues; she was looking forward to getting home to Vancouver. She was determined to put her head down and ignore everyone else for the nine-hour flight, but as she entered the cabin she was greeted by a pair of warm brown eyes and the wagging tail of Drake, my guide dog. The connection between Drake and Kelsy was warm, mutual, and immediate.

Kelsy had been missing her own dog, Maggie, a lot over the previous few weeks, so a little doggy therapy was just what she needed. She loved her job, and connecting with colleagues, many of whom she didn't often get to see in person, always led to wonderful exchanges and collaboration; but it had sapped her energy. I soon learned that Kelsy was the global vice president of the HR Project Office at SAP, and her team members and peers were spread all over the world—a situation I found intriguing. They managed to get together only infrequently, so when they did, they had to make the best use of their time.

I was sitting in a window seat in premium economy with Drake at my feet. I suppose this might have raised a few of my fellow travelers' eyebrows—why would a blind guy want a window seat? The reason was actually quite logical: I didn't want Drake's long and vigorous tail flapping about in the aisle where it might get run over by the flight attendants' carts. Kelsy, whose seat was in the row behind mine, asked the person sitting in the aisle seat in my row whether he'd be willing to trade seats. He politely declined; he also wanted to sit next to Drake. His name was Vladimir, a Russian physical fitness trainer who turned out to be great company during the journey. I discovered that Vladimir hated to fly and Drake, sensing this, had crawled up onto his lap, all the while staring back at Kelsy.

During the flight, Kelsy made several visits to spend time with Drake. She also chatted with me and Vladimir about a variety of topics and soaked up some of the positive energy that Drake exudes. Later in the terminal we were standing together by the luggage carousel, and she asked me what I did for a living. I turned and said, "I teach people how to build trust and strengthen relationships." It was the start of a beautiful friendship—Kelsy and I get along really well too.

A Little Background on SAP

SAP's position in the world as a leader in its field means that many people know of them and their products. Some have positive stories and experiences, and others have the opposite. The intent is not to present a positive or negative account of SAP's products or business model but rather to look at them as a possible example of where organizations may be headed and the challenges SAP already faces from a trust perspective.

Before I became involved with the company, SAP's leadership had already determined that trust was a critical element in their potential success. The CEO at the time of my initial work with SAP was Bill McDermott; he has been quoted as saying that trust is the ultimate form of human capital. Bill has often spoken about the importance of trust and of closing the trust deficit. SAP's marketing strategy also includes the message that trust is central to its, and its clients', success. The current SAP CEO, Christian Klein, has pledged that employment at SAP will be flexible and trust-based.

SAP measures trust levels for its leaders, treating this as a key performance indicator. Leaders are told that trust is a critical dimension on which they will be evaluated. Although included in a comprehensive employee satisfaction survey, it features in only one 10-point scale question about how much employees trust their managers. This falls short of being ideal. As mentioned earlier, we often have an overwhelming lack of awareness when it comes to trust. Yet, despite the flaws in the measures used by SAP, it should be applauded that they were incorporating them at all, and it puts SAP firmly in a leadership position.

However, when trust levels are found to be low, limited guidance is provided to managers on how to improve their scores. In essence, leaders are told to fix a problem but are not provided with training in how to do so. Nevertheless, SAP is well ahead of the vast majority of organizations in understanding the importance of trust and taking steps to measure it.

Although trust is a major topic of conversation in corporate life, political life, and just about every area of our existence, few people are talking about, much less focusing on, how to build trust. SAP is enlightened enough to be a corporate pioneer in this area. The company already has a host of virtual teams spanning many regions and cultures of the world. SAP was doing the "virtual team" thing long before the pandemic made it a normal part of working life for so many of us. The company's leaders face significant challenges due to the varied and widespread geographic locations of their team members. Leaders manage a remarkably diverse workforce across different time zones, cultures, and legal environments, and for the most part, they are doing this remotely. Another significant leadership challenge is that SAP naturally (given its product line) hires most of its employees for their technical skills rather than people skills.

SAP's recent strategy appears to be to provide its clients with a one-stop shop for a variety of enterprise software needs. The company is pursuing a cloud-based approach that will consolidate a wide range of functions and hopefully provide efficiency for its customers. While this approach has many positive attributes, it requires clients to have a significant level of trust in the company. Customers are being asked to forgo multiple vendors and trust a single source. It is easy to identify the questions they must be asking themselves: What if something goes wrong with my relationship with SAP? What if SAP raises its prices once we have fully committed and purchased the suite of tools and trained everyone? How do we go back to a previous system if it doesn't work? The level of vulnerability for clients in a setting like this is high.

A Skilled Leader

Kelsy manages a remarkably complex environment with incredible skill. Her team provides support for over six thousand leaders at SAP worldwide.

Unknown to me at the time I met Kelsy on that flight, she had been considering hiring a career and life coach. We kept in touch and began having regular conversations about trust and her role at SAP. Over time, she introduced me to some of her colleagues and presented my thoughts on trust challenges; one of those people was another vice president at SAP, Susan Moran. As a result, Kelsy and Susan decided to attend one of my open enrollment courses at the Luxembourg School of Business. To make a long story short, this led to a contract with SAP to work with some of Kelsy and Susan's team members. With another colleague, Austin Ransom, they sponsored a training program for a global group of leaders within the SAP human resources department. The result was a series of virtual training courses along with coaching for a number of SAP's leaders to help them get a better introduction to my company's material on trust.

Kelsy and her team have done remarkably well. They have thrived despite the significant challenges that leaders face in organizations like SAP and the added challenges posed by the pandemic. While trust levels are in decline throughout the rest of the world, Kelsy and her team have consistently maintained a Leadership Trust Score at or near the top of the scale, which ranges from -100 to 100, and have achieved nearly perfect customer satisfaction scores. Results such as these demonstrate that it is possible to do remarkably well with regard to building trust even in extremely difficult settings.

It's always a challenge to determine what success was caused by my intervention and ideas on building trust and what occurred through people's innate ability. The people I worked with at SAP already had excellent client relationship skills before I became involved, and, as I've said, Kelsy is one of the best leaders I've ever met.

While she's exceptionally technically proficient, these are not the skills generating her success. Rather, it is her ability to listen and understand.

She has, as a core strength, the ability to foster collaboration among her team. Kelsy's focus is consistently on her team members and the needs of her customers and stakeholders. Her conversations with her leadership team about what excellence looks like cover not just her role but also that of the team itself. Kelsy and her team excel by monitoring their clients' and other stakeholders' perceptions of excellence (which are often a moving target) and trying to anticipate their needs.

Kelsy also demonstrates integrity by consistently following through on her commitments and being conscious of exactly what she's committing to. She has frequent discussions about her team's values and how team members are showing up in a way that aligns with those values. She has invested time, effort, and a portion of her budget, not to mention some of her social capital with other leaders, to bring trust training to SAP's leaders.

Benevolence is where Kelsy truly shines. She genuinely has at heart the best interest of those she leads and those she serves; it is transparent and frequently on display in her words and deeds.

Since we met, Kelsy has moved into a new and important role within the company; she is now the global vice president for human resource advisors. She leads a team of thirty-one people in seventeen countries and consults with SAP's approximately six thousand first- and mid-level leaders in nine languages. Kelsy's team's focus is on helping leaders make well-informed, fair, and people-centered decisions and to thrive in the area of people problems. I've had the privilege of presenting to her new team on the topic of building trust, which is a significant part of what they need to successfully serve their clients. When she transitioned roles within the company, she thought actively about the team she was leaving and spent time considering what might be best for them. This involved helping members of her old team transition into new roles if that was what they wanted. It also involved communicating with the team's new leader about the approaches she had been taking to help her team grow and develop. Kelsy worked hard to ensure the success of the people she was transitioning away from, despite their no longer being her direct reports.

There can be different perceptions of HR and its role within an organization. For some, HR exists as a controlling mechanism focused on ensuring decision makers follow the company's rules, whether they originate from within the company or from external legal entities, to prevent potential lawsuits from disgruntled employees. For others, HR is a thought partner to help leaders anticipate issues and excel because they have the right people in place at the right time.

How leaders perceive the human resources department's role drives how those leaders treat HR representatives. Those who view HR as an obstacle to their plans tend to pull HR into the decision-making process at the last possible minute, asking them to review and sign off on things with little opportunity for input. For example, imagine a leader thinking about transferring or removing one of their subordinates who is integral to a project but who is performing poorly. Obviously, they are also going to have to replace the person. If they tell HR in advance, a replacement can be found ahead of time, the correct termination procedures can be adhered to, and everything can happen seamlessly. If, on the other hand, they simply fire the person, they will be left short-staffed and could potentially face a wrongful termination suit. The first scenario is what a collaborative, trust-based approach with an HR department would look like.

Kelsy and I have talked about managing levels of vulnerability for her team and for the leaders they serve. She clearly has a high level of emotional intelligence and tries her best to understand the level of vulnerability she and others are experiencing. She doesn't appear to have a huge ego, which allows her to show some level of vulnerability with her key stakeholders without feeling unduly threatened.

I mentioned the importance of managing levels of vulnerability in settings with significant uncertainty. Kelsy does that by highlighting to the rest of the organization the work done by those she leads. Giving her team members the appropriate credit raises their profile within the organization and increases their perceived value. She also actively promotes ongoing professional development for her team. The result of these approaches is that her team members are more likely to be in demand if and when organizational restructuring occurs or if they choose to seek employment elsewhere. By improving their access to various opportunities, both within and outside the organization, and by making them less dependent, the level of vulnerability Kelsy's team members feel is significantly reduced.

In short, Kelsy does an exceptional job of fostering psychological safety for her team and for the leaders her team serves. She provides opportunities for open dialogue and feedback, responds positively to the feedback she receives, and demonstrates an openness to honest conversations.

Kelsy and her team have created an environment where they clearly demonstrate that they are there to help leaders be successful, which encourages leaders to reach out to her department. It also means the leaders they serve are far more likely to be open and honest about the problems with which they are struggling. This honesty allows the team to be more effective at providing the right types of support in a timely manner.

The Future of Leadership

As it always is, the future is unclear. The pace of change seems relentless, and we appear to be headed for uncharted territory in terms of what it means to be an effective leader. What I can predict is that the traditional command-and-control style of leadership is destined to become increasingly ineffective. Even today, it's virtually impossible for a leader to rely only on technical expertise to dictate the actions of those they lead. Technical expertise becomes obsolete in the blink of an eye as one transitions into a leadership role, simply because everything is evolving at breakneck speed. By the time some commands are given and distributed, they are already out of date and need to be amended.

In the future, more and more successful leaders will look a lot like Kelsy Trigg. They will inspire collaboration and build trust. Leaders will also begin to trust those they lead and empower them to respond to unexpected situations. New world leaders will foster open communication and become more intentional about the relationships in which they are embedded. They will apply the trust model consciously and consistently; they will reduce uncertainty for those they lead and will be aware of their vulnerability and emotional triggers.

Organizations of the Future:
Key Points Review

- The blurring of borders and the shrinking of the world will result in many leaders being forced to consider an increasingly complex array of issues. It will become increasingly challenging to rely on shared backgrounds or history to provide shortcuts to building better relationships.

- In an evolving future, the definition of excellence within an organization may change dramatically over increasingly shorter periods of time.

- A new type of skill will become more valued—knowing how to change and adapt to new situations.

- Having the skills required to build consensus across diverse populations will become incredibly valuable.

- Benevolence is the one trust lever that should remain relatively unscathed by the pace of change.

- The traditional command-and-control style of leadership is destined to become increasingly ineffective in the future.

- Future leaders will inspire collaboration and build trust. They will foster open communication and become more intentional about their relationships, reduce uncertainty for those they lead, and be aware of their vulnerability and emotional triggers.

CHAPTER 10

There Are Many Miles to Go Before We Sleep

My goal for this final chapter is to remind you of the ground we've covered and create a call to action. First, though, let me take a few moments to reflect on how I've tried to walk the walk, not just talk the talk. Writing this book has been, in itself, a model of building trust with you, the reader. I have demonstrated my ability, knowledge, and experience to speak authoritatively about how trust works and how to build it. Along the way, I've described certain situations and used a trust lens to try and make sense of them. I've also given examples of approaches you can take to strengthen your own relationships. Within the confines of this medium, I've attempted to show benevolence by openly sharing as much as I can about the trust model I use. I've shared stories of situations in which I provided support for others free of charge because it was the right thing to do, including the work I've done with families and the Canadian military. Throughout this process I've also made myself vulnerable by sharing information, including the model I use and suggestions for how to apply it. This makes me susceptible to others copying my work; for example, people and organizations who may do a better marketing job in spreading the message to the world. No matter, I believe I've followed through on the promises I've made and that everything I've written aligns with the values I hold around helping people better understand what trust is and how they can build stronger relationships.

In the first chapter, I talked about my personal life, particularly about periods that demonstrated vulnerability, in the hope that this provided you with an insight into the origins of my perspective on the topic of trust.

Next, I discussed the importance of trust both for you as a leader and more broadly within the organizations with which you are involved, your community, and society as a whole. While there is often consensus on the fact that trust matters, people are frequently unclear on why it matters, how it helps us when it's present, or how it hurts us when it's absent. In chapters 5 and 6 I focused on the trust model and its application, and in chapters 7 through 9 I provided case studies demonstrating how the model can be applied. My passionate hope is that I can reach a wider audience who not only understands how the model works but also applies it in their day-to-day life. If I have convinced you of the importance of building trust within your own team, organization, social circle, and beyond, you will need to practice the skills outlined in this book and be motivated to improve the world by building trust one person at a time.

I began writing this book a year ago and began by talking about some of the "big, hairy problems" that exist in the world today: problems such as climate change, race relations, the pandemic, splits along political ideology lines, and the relationship between the police and the communities they serve. During the past year there have been many further developments on these fronts, few of them positive. The Taliban has overrun Afghanistan, seemingly moments after allied forces pulled out. January 6, 2021, saw an attack on the US Capitol building by an angry mob in what could be described as a graphic manifestation of failed trust.

Climate change hit the headlines through a series of extreme weather events, including forest fires in the United States, Canada, Greece, Turkey, and Italy. A wildfire destroyed a whole town in British Columbia, Canada, when temperatures reached a record-breaking 121°F in the town of Lytton. The heat dome, or heat bubble effect as it was called, wasn't just a North American phenomenon; northern

Europe and Russia also felt the effects. Heat waves are killing people in areas unaccustomed to, or ill-prepared for, extreme temperatures. And it's not all about heat; extreme flooding events occurred across western Europe, the United Kingdom, New South Wales, Australia, and New York in the summer of 2021, causing 184 deaths in Germany alone. A record-breaking snowfall in Madrid, Spain, caused billions of dollars of damage. Add tornados, hurricanes and cyclones, and rising sea levels, and this is one big, hairy problem that seems to be getting worse very quickly.

During the COVID-19 pandemic, scientists achieved a remarkable feat by creating effective vaccines in record time, but as I write this, a shocking number of people are unwilling to get vaccinated because they don't trust the vaccines, or more specifically they don't trust their governments. Protesters, including anti-vaxxers, have become violent over COVID-19 precautions, including regulations around mask-wearing, and this ramped up during the fall of 2021 when various authorities introduced a requirement that people had to show a vaccine passport to access nonessential services. These arguments are as deeply emotional as they are divisive.

Tensions have continued to mount along political and racial divides. In the six months prior to finishing this book, media coverage about mistrust of the police quieted down significantly—not because the issue went away but rather because "we" have an inability to remain focused on a problem as significant as this while there are so many other things vying for our attention.

Our collective inability to focus for extended periods and work through the challenges presented by complex problems is an issue in itself. The challenge is that we often fail to get past the initial period of intense disagreement and become entrenched in our respective positions. Barely have we started to make progress before something else snatches our focus away. I am afraid things don't seem to be trending in a positive direction, which is worrying.

Trust acts as a social lubricant. In higher-trust environments people can work toward solutions far quicker. Today the world doesn't seem to grasp the concept that if we can find ways to work together more effectively and efficiently, we might actually make positive strides instead of finding ourselves in nearly constant conflict.

The exceptionally low trust levels we are currently experiencing are not solely due to natural causes. Unfortunately, small segments of society appear to benefit from our inability to get along. Politicians separate us by emphasizing our differences. The media focuses on conflict and division, using their pulpits and often skewed perspective to stoke the fire and foment our outrage. There is ample evidence that various special interest groups and outsiders such as hostile nation-states, religious groups, and hacker collectives thrive on discontent and fear.

To counteract the potential sabotage and cut through the noise made by those who would act against us, we need to be well informed and intentional in our actions. If we are to inspire collective collaborative action, we need to build trust with one another. One of the first steps we can take is to stop vilifying and finger-pointing at those with whom we do not yet agree. The strategy of telling someone they are a jerk or that they are simply wrong hasn't had much success in creating lasting, impactful change. People feel negatively toward someone who tells them they are wrong and are therefore even less likely to trust what the other person is saying. It ends up being a negative emotional spiral. How often do you think someone says, "Oh my goodness, you're right, I am a jerk. Why didn't someone tell me sooner?" It's far more likely that they respond to being called a jerk by digging in their heels and actively seeking out people who agree with them (confirming their existing beliefs rather than feeding into their positive emotional spiral) so that they can feel better about themselves.

If we want to achieve collective collaborative action, we will need to actually be collaborative. This rarely involves claiming the moral high ground, as we see it, and expecting everyone else to think and do things our way. Compromise is required, and we may have to be the first to make concessions to get the ball rolling. If we are, as a society, going to work together to resolve the problems we face, we will need to be more understanding of other people's positions.

Big, Hairy Problems

I have previously outlined the role that trust can play in resolving the big, hairy problems confronting the world. Let us now speculate on what things will look like if nothing is done.

Climate Change

We have seen the number of extreme weather events increase dramatically. While the pandemic reduced the amount of travel and other carbon-emitting activities, it only slowed the damage being done to the environment temporarily—it did not stop or reverse it. If we revert to a business-as-usual scenario after the pandemic, things will get steadily worse. We will experience more wildfires across larger geographic areas. This will not only create smoke and destroy property but also reduce the number of trees that can absorb carbon dioxide, safely store it, and release oxygen into the atmosphere.

If we are not able to make significant change, and soon, we will see irreparable damage done to whole ecosystems. There will be an acceleration in weather pattern changes, and we will struggle to adapt; the human race and many other species will suffer.

Dramatic changes in technology and behavior will be required for us to halt current trends and provide some hope of stabilizing the situation. Developing new technology will not in itself be sufficient; it will need to be successfully deployed if we are to make the changes needed to have a significant impact. This will require us to stand up to various lobby groups and reduce our investments in traditional sources of power generation.

What would this look like in a higher-trust world? We would attempt to understand the vulnerability of all parties—for instance, by helping people who are currently dependent on fossil fuels for their livelihood to find alternative jobs and careers. They would have a seat at the table next to climate migrants and those who require uninterrupted power to survive. All key stakeholders would have a voice and would work together to minimize harm during a period of transition.

The Police

As I write this (September 2021), recent events have distracted us from the troubled relationship between the police and the communities they serve. This won't last. We have seen such lulls occur before, and inevitably the issue returns, often with increased intensity. We don't need to use our imagination to see how this might play out; countries throughout the world provide examples. In some parts of the world, local police serve only in wealthy neighborhoods or tourist areas. Calls to defund the police are often accompanied by the notion that diverted funds will be used for preventative measures or to benefit poorer communities. In my opinion, it's just as likely that any funds taken from the police would find their way into the hands of politicians who would in turn use the money to generate as much political capital as possible. While some of the money might find its way to fund useful programs, tax cuts and unrelated spending seem every bit as likely.

The result of reducing funding for police forces guarantees little more than that they have fewer resources and become less effective. This in turn increases the likelihood of wealthy people banding together to create private security forces, concentrated in the areas they inhabit. The less fortunate, on the other hand, would see their levels of support and protection drop.

Rather than focus on symptoms, a better approach would be to have all parties come together to discuss the underlying problems. Police officers, and the members of the communities they serve, all have a significant level of vulnerability when things go wrong. The key point here is that all parties are vulnerable, all parties are uncertain, and all parties bear some of the responsibility for making things better.

Policing is another remarkably complex problem rooted in economic need, mental health, stereotypes, mismatched norms, and failures in communication and education. The solution lies in identifying the underlying causes and encouraging all parties to work together to create a shared response. Currently a patchwork of programs is in place that is geared toward proactive reduction in crime and confrontation—that is, different groups with a variety of partial solutions. The challenge is that, generally, they don't have the impact they'd like to have because there isn't enough support for them.

Another factor is that we are dealing with the residue of past decisions. Dramatic reductions in spending on mental health, along with a host of other social programs, have steadily expanded the responsibilities of the police. Our expectations of police forces have increased, making their task increasingly complex and dangerous. The training of, and communication with, police officers hasn't kept pace with these increasing demands. Police departments and their officers face such vilification and animosity that it is no wonder they find it difficult to hire the best possible people to police their communities. The actions of those who are frustrated with the current state of affairs may actually be making things worse instead of better.

The Pandemic

In the late summer of 2021, the fourth wave of the pandemic hit the world, fueled by a more highly transmissible variant. The Delta variant was a more virulent form of the disease, far more contagious and dramatically more harmful. Scientific evidence pointed to the fact that those hit hardest were the unvaccinated. In spite of this, vaccine hesitancy was remarkably prevalent in many areas, with a lack of trust in the government being cited as the primary reason.

A divide is growing between those who are vaccinated, wearing masks, frequently washing their hands, and social distancing, and those who are in denial. Scenes of anger and resentment are playing out around the world, with many protests ending in violence. In some cases, even health workers have been threatened. Those in favor of caution use logic, science, and reason to attempt to convince those opposed, but they have little impact because people become less rational the more emotionally attached they are to an issue.

As hostility increases, people's positions become further and more deeply entrenched, and those hypersensitive to the COVID-19 situation may also be alienating those around them. As certain political factions attack the credibility of organizations such as the CDC and the World

Health Organization, some people have become skeptical of science itself. The use of science and logic are aligned with pulling the ability lever. When others don't trust the source of that information, pulling the ability lever has little effect. We would likely be better served focusing on other levers like benevolence, integrity, and emotions. Vaccine skeptics may also wonder about the context and question exactly who is providing the information and their motives.

In a televised interview in August 2021, the surgeon general of the United States stated that vaccine hesitancy was completely a trust problem. The virus will continue to mutate, as will the trust problem. COVID-19 will not magically disappear; it has the potential to mutate and become increasingly aggressive the longer it remains unchecked.

Governments need to find ways to overcome the trust problem so that we can bring people together to fight a common enemy that thrives on distrust.

Viewing Big, Hairy Problems through a Trust Lens

I've talked about trust as a decision that is made in the face of a combination of uncertainty and vulnerability. I've also mentioned the central role our emotions play when we are making the decision to trust others. In each of the big, hairy problems described above, and the vast majority of other problems we encounter, we need to promote collective collaborative action. This means building trust, not only with those that agree with us but also with those who disagree and anyone in between.

Our first step should be to identify the key stakeholders. Who has something at stake in the issue at hand? How do we get them to have an honest conversation? How do we promote collective action that will lead to greater outcomes for all or at least minimize harm?

Next, we need to understand the other parties' position. How are they vulnerable? Why are they resistant to change? What do they stand to lose, and what is driving their sense of uncertainty? Is there an emotional element at play?

Creating an environment where people can be thoughtful and honest will help us move toward a collaborative approach to solutions.

To do this, we need to create an environment in which people don't get punished for having opinions that don't align with someone else's.

I often struggle when people suggest that we "just be authentic." To me, it seems they are saying they want to be accepted when they are "authentic" but are less tolerant when other people are authentic. These are the same people who often decry other people who express themselves in ways they themselves don't find acceptable. There are reasons we are cautious with our words; many of us have been publicly vilified and punished for things we have said. The world needs more leaders who create environments where people can speak honestly and openly about even the most controversial topics.

The Challenge to Leaders

Leaders have an opportunity to amplify messages, provoke conversations, and promote change. I mentioned at one point that I feel like I'm dropping grains of sand in the ocean and creating only small ripples with my work. Leaders have the potential to create larger ripples than other people. By pushing for more trust in those you lead and by acting as a role model, you have the potential to be a significant part of the solution to the challenges the world is facing.

The evolution of social media appears to have made us vulnerable to false signals. A report on the Hidden Tribes of America website suggested that only about 12 percent of the population really cares about politically correct language.[40] This seems like a remarkably small number given all the noise this issue creates. Those that care deeply about anything are remarkably active on social media, which creates a false impression of general consensus. We saw a similar effect at play when it was reported by the Center for Countering Digital Hate (CCDH) that most of the false information about COVID-19 vaccines was coming from just twelve individual anti-vaxxers.[41] As leaders, we can't assume that the noise we hear actually represents reality for all the people we lead. We need to create safe environments where people can be open and honest rather than saying what they think others want to hear. We need to constantly ask questions and promote feedback.

We may well be at a point of potential divergence. The question is: Are we headed toward enlightenment or a new dark age? Peter Diamandis gives an excellent description of this in his book *The Future Is Faster Than You Think*. He provides numerous examples of technological advances that will help certain sectors of the population. The advances that are here, or imminent, will help with some of the significant challenges we face and bring us to the verge of a new age of enlightenment. However, for others we are on the verge of a new dark age with escalating levels of tension, intolerance, and conflict. From this perspective, we fail to address the big, hairy problems we face and end up overwhelmed and in decline as the world burns. It is my belief that how well we can learn to work together will determine which path we end up taking.

We all have a responsibility to talk about trust more frequently. As leaders, we need to take steps to raise awareness of the topic and educate people as to how it works. Sharing the model with others will help you have conversations that are more intentional and productive. You, as a leader, have more influence than most; you can make building trust a priority for the organizations or departments that you lead.

Remember, resistance to change usually comes from fear or a sense of vulnerability. If you are going to successfully promote collaboration and encourage a movement toward change, you will need to understand how other parties are vulnerable. You will also need to become far better at reducing people's perceptions of vulnerability and uncertainty. At the very least, you will need to keep up with the inflated levels of uncertainty and vulnerability we are seeing in the world.

In the future, part of your job as a leader will be to foster environments that feel like safe harbors: environments where uncertainty is low, vulnerabilities are understood and managed, and where people can have open, honest conversations. Creating spaces like this will help you and your organization flourish, so it's in your own best interest. You will also act as a role model to help spread the trust-building skill more broadly through the world.

How Do You Start?

Let's start with a thought exercise. What if there were no villains? What if the bad behaviors we see and experience were primarily driven by their context rather than an underlying malevolence? Can you imagine that world? Currently, we tend to assume that anyone who doesn't agree with us is either evil or stupid. A more generous approach could lead to more collaboration. By changing the formal and informal rules, we could witness a change in behaviors.

Just to be clear, I know there are bad people in the world. I just feel that we are better off assuming the best when trying to work with others. When I taught negotiation some years ago, I suggested that people be nice but provocable, meaning it's okay to start nice, but feel free to respond more forcefully if the other party tries to take advantage of you. Once the other party learns that your kindness is not a sign of weakness, you can return to being nice. It is a strategy that works well in a remarkable number of situations.

I hope this book has given you a working framework for understanding and building trust. What you do with this information is up to you. Applying the model will be the hard part. It's like exercising a new muscle: expect it to feel awkward at first. It may take some time for you to feel comfortable pulling the various levers for building trust, but, I assure you, your adeptness at recognizing and diagnosing trust problems will grow as you practice and become more aware.

Sometimes starting feels like the hardest part. You may well be thinking, *What do I say? How do I begin?* Often when I'm working with people, I'll suggest opening with a blend of benevolence and vulnerability. Perhaps start by saying, "I've been reading this book on trust, and it has me thinking about how I show up in relationships." There are several variations on this opening that you might find fit you better. Other options include, "I'd like to be more intentional in my relationships," "I just want to be better understood," or "I'd like to communicate better." Essentially, you're just trying to get the conversation started. You are making yourself a little vulnerable by admitting that you are trying to work on something and that you're thinking of ways to improve yourself.

I find that it's best to begin with an intentional approach. Conversations should start broad and then narrow to issues specific to the other party. For instance, if I was hoping to talk about benevolence, I might start by talking about the topic in general. Something such as, "I've read that benevolence, having someone's best interest at heart, plays a significant role in getting them to trust us. What do you think?" This should start a conversation. At some point, you can follow up with, "I think I'm acting in people's best interests, but it doesn't always seem to land that way. Have you ever had that experience?" Once again this will hopefully move the conversation forward. Ask the person you're interacting with if they have any examples of situations where they were misunderstood. Now you can begin to focus the conversation by asking the other person what benevolence they've experienced from others. Ask them what matters most to them or what success looks like for them. You can then ask them what it would look like if you were benevolent toward them.

This approach should work for any of the levers you want to try and pull. If you wanted to pull the integrity lever, the conversation might start by you defining integrity as following through on your promises and having your actions align with the values you express. You could then follow this with a comment on how you feel you do, or don't, follow through on all your promises. You might provide examples of situations in the past where you thought you had followed through but others didn't think so. You could then narrow the conversation with whomever you are talking by saying something such as, "Have I made promises in the past where I didn't follow through with you?" Depending on the answer, you might then say, "Could you give me a heads-up if that happens in the future?" You might also ask, "Do my actions seem to line up with the values I espouse?"

Similar conversations could be repeated when you discuss ability, the various elements of context, vulnerability, emotions, and perceptions of outcomes.

I'll leave you with a quote from one of my favorite books, *The Lorax* by Dr. Seuss. In this story the Once-ler is telling the tale of how he destroyed the environment despite the warnings of the Lorax, who spoke for the trees. In his tale he reveals that the Lorax left behind only the word UNLESS on a pile of rocks. This word troubled the Once-ler, who was unsure of its meaning among the devastation he had wrought. The quote seems appropriate to our current situation:

> *"But now," says the Once-ler, "Now that you're*
> *here, the word of the Lorax seems perfectly clear.*
> UNLESS *someone like you cares a whole*
> *awful lot, nothing is going to get better.*
> *It's not."*[42]

Presumably, you're reading this book because you *do* care a whole awful lot about improving yourself and the world. On a positive note, we got here collectively and we can dig ourselves out collectively. I hope I have given you some additional tools to help you do so.

Notes

Chapter 1

1   Roger C. Mayer, James H. Davis, and F. David Schoorman, "An Integrative Model of Organizational Trust," *The Academy of Management Review* 20, no. 3 (July 1995): 709–34, https://doi.org/10.2307/258792.

2   "Game Theory III: Repeated Games," *Policonomics*, accessed February 21, 2022, https://bit.ly/2Y5iO5s.

3   Karl Weick, *The Social Psychology of Organizing* , 2nd ed. (New York: McGraw-Hill, 1979) 194.

Chapter 2

4   "Secretary-General Highlights 'Trust Deficit' amid Rising Global Turbulence, in Remarks to Security Council Debate on 'Upholding United Nations Charter,'" United Nations, January 9, 2020, https://www.un.org/press/en/2020/sgsm19934.doc.htm.

5   "2020 Edelman Trust Barometer," Edelman, January 19, 2020, https://www.edelman.com/trustbarometer.

6   Charles Duhigg, "Seattle's Leaders Let Scientists Take the Lead. New York's Did Not," *The New Yorker*, April 26, 2020, https://www.newyorker.com/magazine/2020/05/04/seattles-leaders-let-scientists-take-the-lead-new-yorks-did-not.

7   Jenny Yang, "Trust Levels Towards Healthcare by Country 2021," Statista, September 14, 2021, https://www.statista.com/statistics/1071027/trust-levels-towards-healthcare-in-select-countries/.

8   Warren Cornwall, "Just 50% of Americans Plan to Get a COVID-19 Vaccine. Here's How to Win Over the Rest," *Science*, June 30, 2020, https://www.sciencemag.org/news/2020/06/just-50-americans-plan-get-covid-19-vaccine-here-s-how-win-over-rest.

9   "United States Coronavirus Cases," Worldometer, accessed November 18, 2021, https://www.worldometers.info/coronavirus/country/us/.

10 Darryl Stickel, "The Fatal Cost of Failed Trust: Rebuilding Trust in the Police," Trust Unlimited, accessed February 22, 2022, https://www.trustunlimited.com/the-fatal-cost-of-failed-trust-rebuilding-trust-in-the-police/.

11 Alex Boutilier, "Many Canadians 'don't feel protected by the police,' Justin Trudeau Says," *Toronto Star*, June 8, 2020, https://www.thestar.com/politics/federal/2020/06/08/trudeau-says-hell-push-provinces-on-body-cameras-for-police.html.

12 "PM Trudeau Discusses Racism in Policing, Provides COVID-19 Update," CPAC, June 8, 2020, https://www.cpac.ca/episode?id=d32743c7-8ab4-4dd4-a30e-7b7b2b-c9b8e2.

13 Baher Kamal, "Climate Migrants Might Reach One Billion by 2050," ReliefWeb, August 21, 2017, https://reliefweb.int/report/world/climate-migrants-might-reach-one-billion-2050.

14 Moira Fagan and Christine Huang, "A Look at How People around the World View Climate Change," Pew Research Center, April 18, 2019, https://www.pewresearch.org/fact-tank/2019/04/18/a-look-at-how-people-around-the-world-view-climate-change/.

Chapter 3

15 "Where We Work," More in Common, accessed February 22, 2022, https://www.moreincommon.com/where-we-work/more-in-common-us/.

16 Jon del Arroz, "Author John Ringo Responds to SJW Assault that Led to Sci-Fi Convention Ban," *Dangerous,* April 17, 2018, https://web.archive.org/web/20190831205807/https://www.dangerous.com/43569/author-john-ringo-responds-sjw-assault-led-sci-fi-convention-ban/.

17 "The sharing of one's point of view on a social or political issue, often on social media, in order to garner praise or acknowledgment of one's righteousness from others who share that point of view, or to passively rebuke those who do not." Dictionary.com, s.v. "virtue signaling," accessed February 22, 2022, https://www.dictionary.com/browse/virtue-signaling.

18 In 2006, the #MeToo movement was founded by survivor and activist Tarana Burke. See www.metoomvmt.org.

19 See "2020 Edelman Trust Barometer," Edelman, January 19, 2020, https://www.edelman.com/trustbarometer.

20 Martin Gilens and Benjamin I. Page, "Testing Theories of American Politics: Elites, Interest Groups, and Average Citizens," *Perspective on Politics* 12, no. 3 (September 2014), 564–81, https://doi.org/10.1017/S1537592714001595.

21 Dylan Matthews, "Remember That Study Saying America Is an Oligarchy? 3 Rebuttals Say It's Wrong," *Vox,* May 9, 2016, https://www.vox.com/2016/5/9/11502464/gilens-page-oligarchy-study.

22 Paul Elie, "Pope Francis Supports Same-Sex Civil Unions, but the Church Must Do

More," *The New Yorker*, October 25, 2020, https://www.newyorker.com/news/daily-comment/pope-francis-supports-same-sex-civil-unions-but-the-church-must-do-more.

23 https://scholar.google.ca/citations?view_op=view_citation&hl=en&user=WwOtw_kAAAAJ&citation_for_view=WwOtw_kAAAAJ:Y0pCki6q_DkC

Chapter 4

24 Kevin Kruse, "What Is Leadership?," *Forbes*, April 9, 2013, https://www.forbes.com/sites/kevinkruse/2013/04/09/what-is-leadership/?sh=1c4258a85b90.

25 Sim B. Sitkin, "Learning through Failure: The Strategy of Small Losses," *Journal of Research in Organizational Behavior* 14, no. 1 (January 1992): 231–66.

26 Albert O. Hirschman, *Exit, Voice, and Loyalty: Responses to Decline in Firms, Organizations, and States* (Cambridge, MA: Harvard University Press, 1970).

27 E. Allan Lind and Tom R. Tyler, *The Social Psychology of Procedural Justice*, Critical Issues in Social Justice (Boston: Springer, 1988).

28 M. Szmigiera, "Countries with the Highest Military Spending 2020," Statista, May 7, 2021, https://www.statista.com/statistics/262742/countries-with-the-highest-military-spending/.

29 Roger Fisher, William L. Ury, and Bruce Patton, *Getting to Yes: Negotiating Agreement Without Giving In* (New York: Penguin Books, 2011).

30 Michigan State University, "'Power Poses' Don't Work, Eleven New Studies Suggest," *Science Daily*, September 11, 2017, https://www.sciencedaily.com/releases/2017/09/170911095932.htm.

31 Richard A. D'Aveni, "Strategic Supremacy through Disruption and Dominance," *MIT Sloan Management Review*, April 15, 1999, https://sloanreview.mit.edu/article/strategic-supremacy-through-disruption-and-dominance/.

32 "Most Trusted Brands 2020," Morning Consult, accessed February 23, 2022,https://morningconsult.com/most-trusted-brands/.

33 Daniel Kahneman, *Thinking, Fast and Slow* (New York: Farrar, Straus and Giroux, 2011).

34 Artur Nilsson, Arvid Erlandsson, Daniel Västfjäll, "Moral Foundations Theory and the Psychology of Charitable Giving," *European Journal of Personality* 34, no. 3 (May/June 2020): 431–47, https://doi.org/10.1002/per.2256.

35 Mike Robinson and the Arctic Institute of North America, "Coping with the Cash," *Arctic Institute of North America* 43, no. 3 (September 1990).

Chapter 5

36 Roger C. Mayer, James H. Davis, and F. Davi Schoorman, "An Integrative Model of Organizational Trust," *The Academy of Management Review* 20, no. 3 (July 1995): 709–34, https://doi.org/10.2307/258792

37 Tony Simons, *The Integrity Dividend: Leading by the Power of Your Word* (San Francisco: Jossey-Bass, 2008).

Chapter 9

38 *Primal Leadership: Unleashing the Power of Emotional Intelligence*, with Richard Boyatzis and Annie McKee, Harvard Business Review Press.
39 William A. Kahn, "Psychological Conditions of Personal Engagement and Disengagement at Work," *Academy of Management Journal* 33, no. 4 (December 1990), 692–724. See also Amy Edmondson, "Psychological Safety and Learning Behavior in Work Teams," *Administrative Science Quarterly* 44, no. 2 (June 1999): 350–83.

Chapter 10

40 Stephen Hawkins, Daniel Yudkin, Míriam Juan-Torres, and Tim Dixon, *Hidden Tribes: A Study of America's Polarized Landscape* (New York: More in Common, 2018), https://hiddentribes.us/media/qfpekz4g/hidden_tribes_report.pdf.
41 "Pandemic Profiteers: The Business of Anti-Vaxx," Center for Countering Digital Hate, June 1, 2021, https://www.counterhate.com/pandemicprofiteers.
42 Dr. Seuss, *The Lorax* (New York: Random House, 1971), 8.

Acknowledgments

T**HIS BOOK WAS A COLLABORATIVE EFFORT, AND** I **WANT TO SINCERELY** thank the people who helped turn it into a reality. While my experiences and studies have given me a deeper understanding of trust, I don't claim to have that same expertise when it comes to writing. Often as we come to understand a topic more deeply, we begin to take for granted some of the things we've learned. Things that seem obvious are often not as apparent to others. My goal was to take what I had learned and make it accessible to a broader audience. I don't have the space here to individually thank the legion of people who have helped me better understand trust over the years—but you know who you are, and I sincerely thank you.

There are three people I would like to single out for their significant involvement and for whose help and support I am eternally grateful. Rather than using any debatable analysis of the value of their contributions, I will mention them based on how long I have known them.

Hannah Carbone has been a close friend since we first met as new hires at a McKinsey training program in 1999. We have worked together not only at McKinsey but also at Trust Unlimited. Hannah has a remarkable eye for detail, is one of the fastest mental processors I've ever met, and is an incredible friend. She has read almost everything I've written over the last twenty years and has an uncanny ability to understand what I'm trying to say rather than what I've said. Hannah has always stood by me, not only during the good times but also during my long journey back into the light after I was seriously injured in an accident. Hannah, I am eternally grateful for your friendship and for being on the receiving end of your astonishing professional talents.

Eric Lott has worked alongside me at Trust Unlimited for several years and helped me move both the company and the thinking behind it forward. He helps me understand and deconstruct some things I do naturally or have learned to do and turns them into lessons for others. Eric plays a significant role in my life as a thought partner and close colleague. He has skills that I lack and has made my company and this book better through his unique involvement. His project management skills have kept me moving forward, and his insight and questions have forced me to think more deeply about the topic of trust, for which I have unlimited passion.

I hired Mike Wicks as a ghostwriter but he ended up being so much more. He became a friend and colleague and guided me through the book publication process. He has become a champion for my book, helping me connect with the right professionals and better understand the publishing industry's expectations of me. Mike also provided added value by representing my readers' perspectives.

After completing a Ph.D. on trust, I have spent the past twenty years helping people solve real-world problems and training others to do the same. My challenge was that I got to a point where things that seemed obvious to me were not as apparent to others. Mike helped smooth the rough edges of my observations and asked direct honest questions. His writing and communication skills have ensured this book is both readable and accessible.